Systemically Treating

Systemically Treating Autism provides a unique resource for family therapists and other mental health professionals who want to increase their understanding of families with children with autism spectrum disorder (ASD). Through a combination of research, practical interventions, and case vignettes, this text covers the diagnosis of ASD, how ASD impacts the family, systemic theories that can be used when treating families with children with ASD, spirituality and cultural dynamics, and collaboration with other professionals. Providing a systemic framework for conceptualizing a diagnosis that is typically discussed from an individual perspective, this book guides mental health clinicians toward a better understanding of how they can help the entire family unit.

Brie Turns, PhD, LMFT-A is an assistant professor at Fuller Theological Seminary–Arizona and provides clinical treatment to families raising a child with autism spectrum disorder at the Family Christian Counseling Center.

Julie Ramisch, PhD, LMFT is the director of Coastal Center for Collaborative Health where she offers counseling, supervises other therapists, and authors publications about working with families with children with autism spectrum disorder.

Jason Whiting, PhD, LMFT is a professor at Brigham Young University where he researches conflict and challenges in families. He is the author of books and blogs to help strengthen couples.

Systemically Treating Autism

A Clinician's Guide for Empowering Families

Edited by Brie Turns, Julie Ramisch, and Jason Whiting

Routledge
Taylor & Francis Group

NEW YORK AND LONDON

First published 2019
by Routledge
52 Vanderbilt Avenue, New York, NY 10017

and by Routledge
2 Park Square, Milton Park, Abingdon, Oxon, OX14 4RN

Routledge is an imprint of the Taylor & Francis Group, an informa business

Library of Congress Cataloging-in-Publication Data
A Names: Turns, Brie, editor. | Ramisch, Julie, editor. | Whiting, Jason
B., editor.
Title: Systemically treating autism : a clinician's guide for empowering
families / edited by Brie Turns, Julie Ramisch, and Jason Whiting.
Description: New York, NY : Routledge, 2019. | Includes bibliographical
references and index.
Identifiers: LCCN 2018051639 (print) | LCCN 2018053045 (ebook) |
ISBN 9781315141831 (E-book) | ISBN 9781138306578 (hardback) |
ISBN 9781138306585 (pbk.) | ISBN 9781315141831 (ebk.)
Subjects: | MESH: Autism Spectrum Disorder–psychology | Autism
Spectrum Disorder–therapy | Family Therapy–methods | Child | Infant
Classification: LCC RC553.A88 (ebook) | LCC RC553.A88 (print) |
NLM WS 350.8.P4 | DDC 616.85/882–dc23
LC record available at https://lccn.loc.gov/2018051639

ISBN: 978-1-138-30657-8 (hbk)
ISBN: 978-1-138-30658-5 (pbk)
ISBN: 978-1-315-14183-1 (ebk)

Typeset in Goudy
by Wearset Ltd, Boldon, Tyne and Wear

Contents

Contributors

Lauren Andersen; Doctoral Candidate, Teachers College, Columbia University.

Lacey Bagley, MS, AMFT; PhD student, Brigham Young University.

Kevin Callahan, PhD; Executive Director, University of North Texas Kristin Farmer Autism Center, Denton, Texas.

Erik W. Carter, PhD; Cornelius Vanderbilt Professor, Department of Special Education, Vanderbilt University.

Hsu-Min Chiang, PhD; Assistant Professor, Faculty of Education, University of Macau, Taipa, Macau.

Morgan Cohen, BA; St. John's University, Queens, New York.

Jason Cohen, MS, BCBA; Positive Behavior Supports Corporation, Eagle Mountain Saginaw Independent School District, Saginaw, Texas.

Christa Clayton, BA; Graduate Assistant, Couple and Family Therapy Program, University of Nevada-Las Vegas.

Rachael A. Dansby Olufowote, PhD, LMFTA; Adjunct Professor, Online Marriage and Family Therapy Program, Abilene Christian University.

Brandon Eddy, PhD; Assistant Professor, Couple and Family Therapy Program, University of Nevada-Las Vegas.

Kimberlee Flatt, MA, LPC, BCBA; Adult Intervention Coordinator, University of North Texas Kristin Farmer Autism Center, Denton, Texas.

Benjamin Finlayson, BA; Doctoral Student, Texas Tech University.

Kami Gallus, PhD, LMFT; Associate Professor, Department of Human Development and Family Science, Oklahoma State University.

Jocelyn Bessette Gorlin, PhD, CPNP; Assistant Professor, Henrietta Schmoll School of Health, Saint Catherine University.

Rebecca Grzadzinski, PhD; Carolina Institute for Developmental Disabilities at The University of North Carolina.

Sigan L. Hartley, PhD; Associate Professor, School of Human Ecology and Waisman Center, University of Wisconsin, Madison, Wisconsin.

Jeffry B. Jackson, PhD, LMFT; Assistant Professor, Marriage and Family Therapy Program, Department of Human Development & Family Science, Virginia Tech.

Jake Johnson, PhD, LMFT; Assistant Professor, School of Psychology, Counseling, and Family Therapy, Wheaton College.

Jennifer Jones, PhD; Assistant Professor, Department of Human Development and Family Science, Oklahoma State University.

Sara Smock Jordan, PhD, LMFT; Associate Professor, Graduate Coordinator and Program Director, University of Nevada-Las Vegas.

Mitzi Lauderdale, JD, CFP®; Associate Professor, Personal Financial Planning, Texas Tech University.

Ashley Lovell, BS; Master's student, Brigham Young University.

Joshua Masse, PhD; Assistant Professor, University of Massachusetts Dartmouth.

Cody Morris, MA, BCBA; Doctoral Student in Behavior Analysis, Department of Psychology, Western Michigan University.

Kathleen Nash, MFT, LMFT, AAMFT-S; Legacy Therapy Services; Harleysville, Pennsylvania.

Susan M. Nichols, PhD, BCBA-D; Associate Executive Director, University of North Texas Kristin Farmer Autism Center, Denton, Texas.

Patricia Steinert-Otto, PhD, BCBA-D; Special Education Supervisor, Southern Service Area of Kalamazoo County, Adjunct Professor, Western Michigan University.

Denice Rios, MA, BCBA; Doctoral Candidate, Western Michigan University.

Carlos Perez, PhD, LPC, LMFT-A; Associate Professor, Department of Psychology and Counseling, Lubbock Christian University.

Mandy Perl, LMSW; Youth and Family Program Supervisor, Kalamazoo Community Mental Health and Substance Abuse Services, Kalamazoo, Michigan.

Stephanie M. Peterson, PhD, BCBA-D; Professor and Chair, Department of Psychology, Western Michigan University.

Von Poll, MS, LAMFT; Siskin Children's Institute; Chattanooga, TN.

Julie Ramisch, PhD, LMFT; Coastal Center for Collaborative Health, Lincoln City, Oregon.

Geovanna Rodriguez, PhD; Postdoctoral Fellow, Waisman Center, Madison, Wisconsin.

Rachita Sharma, PhD, CRC, LPC-S; Senior Lecturer and Clinical Director, Department of Rehabilitation and Health Services, University of North Texas.

Stephanie Shire, PhD; Assistant Professor, Special Education and Clinical Sciences, College of Education, University of Oregon.

Nicole Piland Springer, PhD, LMFT; Associate Professor of Practice, Department of Community, Family, and Addiction Sciences, Texas Tech University.

Alyssa Tan, MS, AMFT; Staff Research Associate, University of California-Los Angeles.

Brie Turns, PhD, LAMFT; Assistant Professor, Department of Marriage and Family Therapy, Fuller Theological Seminary-Arizona.

Jason Whiting, PhD, LMFT-S; Professor, Brigham Young University.

Acknowledgments

Brie Turns

Philippians 4:13: "I can do all things through Christ who strengthens me." I owe my life, career, success, and strength to my Lord and Savior, Jesus Christ. Not only have I been able to accomplish more in this life than I could ever imagine, but I have been able to help others do the same. I would also like to thank my amazing siblings and extended family members for the never-ending love and support. Additionally, I would like to thank all of my colleagues, mentors, and friends who have taught me how to be a better therapist, professor, and researcher; specifically: Sara Smock Jordan, Joe Wetchler, Brandon Eddy, Scott Sibley, Julie Ramisch, Rachael Dansby Olufowote, and Jason Whiting. I would also like to thank each of the authors who graciously agreed to contribute to this book. Finally, I'd like to thank my parents for the amazing life, education, and support they have continuously provided me with over the years. I could not have done this without you. Thank you.

Julie Ramisch

First, I would like to thank Brie and Jason for asking me to join them as an editor and to come with them on this journey. It was a fun ride. I also want to express my gratitude to all of our authors as we could not have put together this book without all of their expertise and hard work. Thank you especially to Rachael Dansby Olufowote, as she was essential to quite a few of these chapters. I adore her helping spirit and her dedication to her research and writing. I hope that I can still convince her to work with me on projects as her own career unfolds and evolves. Additionally, I would like to thank my best friend, Christi, for all of her support and encouragement. I always appreciate her listening ear and guidance when I need it. Finally, I would like to thank all of the families with children with autism who have helped us write this book. Thank you for sharing your lives with us.

Jason Whiting

Thanks to Brie Turns, whose leadership and energy made this book happen, and Julie Ramisch, for her expertise and support. Also, a special thank you to all families affected by ASD who inspire with stories of interesting challenges, hilarious surprises, and consistent courage. And most personally, I am grateful for my son Zachary, who shares his quirky joy with me every day.

Introduction

Brie Turns, Julie Ramisch, and Jason Whiting

ASD Within the Family

Cameron, a dark-haired, energetic ten-year old boy, was talking nonstop about dinosaurs to his new therapist, Lucy. Cameron had recently been diagnosed with autism spectrum disorder (ASD), when he started fifth grade, and his parents were exhausted, worried, and seeking answers. They told Lucy that Cameron could not make friends, concentrate in school, and was consistently placed in the back of his classroom. His sister Tia reported that Cameron was "sometimes hilarious and a spaz," but that other times he "freaked out when things didn't go his way and was really embarrassing." Cameron's father worked at the local airport and struggled to connect with him. Cameron's mother, Nancy, recently quit her job to care for Cameron and Tia at home. This reduction in income was another stress for the family and they were concerned about the costs of possible intervention for Cameron, including speech therapy, occupational therapy, medication, and applied behavioral analysis. Lucy reduced their session fee for family therapy, but she was overwhelmed with how to help them. Lucy was only exposed to ASD when she took a Behavioral Diagnosis class during her master's degree. She knew the general indicators of ASD but not how it was contributing to the family's various challenges, how the diagnosis was impacting the parents, their marriage, or the relationship with Cameron's sister.

Overview

Unfortunately, many therapists find themselves in a position similar to Lucy's. Rarely do mental health clinicians have specific training about ASD and how the diagnosis can impact the family. *Systemically Treating Autism: A Clinician's Guide for Empowering Families* is a resource for mental health clinicians who seek to effectively and efficiently work with families raising a child with an ASD. This book is divided into five parts: *Understanding Autism Spectrum Disorder*; *Autism, The Family, and The Wider Community*; *Applying Systemic Theories*; *ASD Through the Lifespan*; and *Special Topics*.

The first part, *Understanding Autism Spectrum Disorder*, reviews the history of ASD, the DSM-5 criteria, and other disabilities and disorders that may appear to be ASD but are not. The second part, *Autism, The Family, and The Wider Community*, discusses how an ASD diagnosis can impact the parental and sibling subsystem, extended family members, and society. Financial challenges that are commonly faced by families raising a child with ASD are also included. Part III, *Applying Systemic Theories*, provides brief summaries on some of the most common models of marriage and family therapy and how they can be applied to families raising a child with ASD. Part IV, *ASD Through the Lifespan*, discusses various strengths and challenges that families frequently face throughout their child's life. How clinicians can help families successfully transition through early and middle childhood and throughout early adulthood are also reviewed. The final part, *Special Topics*, provides aspects of working with families that all mental health clinicians should consider, such as spirituality, technology, and financial challenges.

Why the Book is Important

Autism is an individual diagnosis, with the majority of treatment and research focusing on the person with ASD. *Systemically Treating Autism* broadens this framework by placing ASD within a family-based, systemic perspective. This text serves as a clinician's guide to understanding the basics of ASD, how it impacts the family, and systemic models that can be used to strengthen and empower the family. This book is intended for clinicians who are newly introduced to the diagnosis of ASD to seasoned clinicians who are looking for a new approach to treating ASD. We hope this text is a useful and informative approach for all mental health clinicians.

Commonly Used Terms

Before you begin reading this text, we found it necessary to discuss and clarify commonly used terms that you will see. First, throughout history, numerous terms have been used to describe the diagnosis of *autism*. For the purpose of this text, *autism spectrum disorder*, *ASD*, and *autism* will all be used interchangeably. Next, the Diagnostic and Statistical Manual (DSM) is currently in its fifth edition, so this text will use *DSM 5*. In addition, the term *neurotypical* (NT) is used to describe individuals who are typically developing, or free from any diagnosis in the DSM 5. Finally, the term *mental health clinician* encompasses any licensed professionals who provide clinical, counseling, casework, or therapeutic services. This can include, but is not limited to: marriage and family therapists, psychologists, counselors, social workers, speech, occupational, or physical therapists, and caseworkers.

The Editors

Dr. Brie Turns is an assistant professor at Fuller Theological Seminary-Arizona. She is also a Licensed Associate Marriage and Family Therapist and provides marital and family therapy at the Family Christian Counseling Center in Phoenix, Arizona. Brie received her MS degree from Purdue University Northwest (formerly Calumet) and completed her PhD. in marriage and family therapy from Texas Tech University. She has been working with families raising children with ASD since 2012. Brie has spoken at state, national, and international conferences and has published numerous journal articles and book chapters regarding autism and the family. Brie has conducted trainings at Yale's Developmental Disability Clinic, Texas Tech University, and Brigham Young University for mental health clinicians wanting to work with families raising children with ASD. Brie's dissertation was a clinical outcome study assessing the effectiveness of Solution-Focused Brief Therapy for couples raising a child with ASD. Her dissertation received the Texas Tech Doctoral Dissertation Fellowship, the Solution-Focused Brief Therapy Student Research Award, and the 2018 AAMFT Foundation Dissertation Award.

Dr. Julie Ramisch studied marriage and family therapy at Purdue University Northwest (formerly Calumet) where she completed her master's degree, and Michigan State University where she completed her PhD. As a PhD student and later as an assistant professor, she worked to learn more about how having a child with ASD affects parents, and specifically couple relationships, through her research. It is important to her to continue to find feasible and effective approaches to helping families with children with ASD in therapy. She now directs a thriving mental health practice in Lincoln City, Oregon where she supervises intern therapists and provides counseling to families in the community.

Dr. Jason Whiting is a professor in the School of Family Life at Brigham Young University and a licensed marriage and family therapist. His research has focused primarily on family conflict and abuse, and he has published over 60 articles and chapters related to couples, families, conflict, and healing. Jason is the author of *Love Me True: Overcoming the Surprising Ways We Deceive in Relationships* and an editor of *The Foster Care Therapist Handbook: Relational Approaches to the Children and Their Families*. As a parent of a son on the autism spectrum, he daily experiences the challenges and joys in a family where not everyone is neurotypical.

Part I

Understanding Autism Spectrum Disorder

1 A Century of Autism

The Story of the Diagnosis

Jason Whiting and Ashley Lovell

Hans Asperger was giving a speech that was a matter of life and death. It was 1938 and Asperger was a pediatrician in Nazi Germany, working with an unusual group of children who didn't fit common diagnoses or disabilities. At the time, Asperger's young patients were under the scrutiny of the Gestapo, who were seeking to eliminate "undesirable" children as part of a new Nazi eugenics program. This program eventually became the broader system of mass murder in concentration camps.

Recently, Asperger has fallen under scrutiny by historians seeking to understand the moral spectrum that he embodied (Czech, 2018; Sheffer, 2018). For years, he was portrayed as a hero of children with ASD, as he identified their strengths and unique characteristics, and also was reported to have protected them from the Nazi regime (Silberman, 2015). However, other information paints a different picture of Asperger – a physician who referred dozens of children to Nazi eugenics programs and worked closely with the Third Reich (Sheffer, 2018; Sparrow & Silberman, 2018).

While Asperger's reputation as a courageous champion of youth has changed, his speech was still the first public lecture on autism (Feinstein, 2010) and was radical in its effort to frame some of these children in terms of potential rather than deficits (Silberman, 2015). His lecture and subsequent writings began to define what would become our current understanding of ASD. He was the first to describe the condition as a continuum, with a broad range of presentations.

This chapter tells the story of autism over roughly the last century. The diagnosis has undergone a journey from: a loosely identified set of conditions, to a narrow and severe syndrome caused by parents, to a biological illness needing a cure, to a spectrum of characteristics that are common once someone knows what to look for. Currently, ASD is experiencing mainstream awareness, with popular culture representing neurodiversity in many forms and professionals encouraging the goal of supporting and living well with ASD rather than pathologizing or curing it. This chapter discusses the evolving meanings of the ASD diagnosis over the decades and considers the role of many who raised awareness of the condition.

The Early Years – Autism Emerges

Although many people think of autism as a relatively new disorder, the roots of the word stretch all the way back to the Greeks. Named after the Greek word "autos," autism means "self," a term that describes the tendency to turn inward or limit social situations (History of Autism). In the 1860s, Dr. John Langdon Down, who was the first to define Down syndrome, was doing research on mental disabilities and outlined a condition he called "developmental retardation," which describes what today would generally fit on the autism spectrum (Down, 1866). However, it wasn't until just over a century ago that Eugen Bleuler, a Swiss psychiatrist and eugenicist, first coined the modern term "autism" in 1910 (Kuhn & Cahn, 2004; Möller & Hell, 2002).

The 1930s and 1940s – The Battle to Define Autism

After Bleuler coined the term autism, little happened to clarify what the condition actually was. In the 1930s and 1940s the clinical definition of autism began to transform, which was brought about by two men – Asperger and Leo Kanner. Although Asperger's ideas were more on target with what ASD would eventually become, it was Kanner's conception of ASD that dominated the following decades (Chown & Hughes, 2016).

Asperger's key contribution was his realization that many children he saw in his medical research and practice were mislabeled. Some who were labeled mentally deficient or schizophrenic shared unique characteristics, particularly in how they related to others. These atypical styles sometimes included less eye contact, odd physical gestures, monotonous speaking tones, or muted facial expressions. In spite of these unusual social styles, many had remarkable talents when it came to specific subjects, such as astronomy, math, and technology. Asperger called some of these offbeat but bright children his "little professors" (Silberman, 2015, p. 6.), and according to him, these children showed an extreme personality type that was detrimental only when their environment and support systems were not a good fit for them. As Asperger looked further, he saw autistic traits scattered throughout family trees, and he suggested that these eccentric traits were found in gifted and nonconforming achievers throughout history.

Leo Kanner also hailed from Austria, but after his medical studies in Berlin, he emigrated to South Dakota in 1924 to pursue a career in child psychiatry. Like Asperger, Kanner identified a group of children that, at the time, were lumped into general categories of "imbecility" or "mental retardation" who were different, with tendencies toward isolation and repetition. Unlike Asperger, Kanner thought that autism was an extreme disability, with only those at the severely impaired end of the spectrum fitting the diagnosis. Kanner also saw autism as a childhood disorder rather than a lifelong condition (Sanua, 1990). His primary paper, "Autistic Disturbances of Affective Contact," was published in 1943 and was very influential in shaping the medical and public understanding of what came to be called autism: a distinct, rare, and very serious disorder. Despite Kanner's advocacy for children and the mentally ill, his restrictive version of the diagnosis meant that few received services. To make matters worse, Kanner also made claims that the cause of autism was due to mothers.

The 1950s and 1960s – Autism Gets Canonized and Mothers Get Blamed

Kanner shared details of children in case studies who fit the criteria for his diagnosis of infantile autism. These children were largely from upper-class, educated families, and Kanner deduced that these children were more likely to come from academically inclined, cold, and emotionally unresponsive parents (Kanner, 1943). Kanner is dubiously credited with the term *refrigerator mothers*, which is a mother so unresponsive and cold that her child is permanently altered into an unfeeling automaton (Kanner, 1949). This view found purchase in the social and medical norms of the 1950s, where rigid expectations for mothers, along with the dire consequences of their deficits, were promoted.

This set the stage for another enterprising academic, Bruno Bettelheim, to promote a more insidious version of the root cause of autism. Bettelheim wrote articles and made TV appearances promoting his view that children with autism experienced horrors at home similar to prisoners in Nazi concentration camps (where Bettelheim had been imprisoned for most of a year) (Shapin, 2016). He compared mothers to Nazi guards and suggested that autism was a trauma-reaction, where children refashion themselves into machines to cope with their abuse (Bettelheim, 1959). Bettelheim claimed to be a child developmental professor but his doctorate was in art history, and eventually his stories began to unravel (see Pollak, 1998).

The extremity of these two views had the effect of raising public awareness of autism, but many lives were damaged in the process. As the 1960s progressed, the evidence for parental injury was called into question, and the evidence for a biological basis for autism began to mount. At the end of the decade, Kanner recanted his earlier views, and in a public lecture to families of autistic children, he said, "Herewith I acquit you as parents" (Harris & Piven, 2016).

Influence of the DSM

In 1952, the American Psychological Association (APA) published a slim volume called the *Diagnostic and statistical manual of mental disorders*, or *DSM*. Used by only a few professionals at first, this DSM did not include autism as a diagnosable disorder; instead, children exhibiting symptoms were diagnosed with schizophrenic reaction, childhood type (APA, 1952). This initial codification mostly reflected symptoms that conformed to Kanner's severe, isolated, and nonverbal type.

The DSM-II kept the schizophrenic reaction diagnosis but added language describing these children as having "autistic, atypical and withdrawn behavior and general unevenness" (APA, 1968). Less useful was the speculation about autism's etiology as a child's "failure to develop separate identity from the mother's." Outside of asylum walls, few used the DSM, and autism largely remained in the shadows as a rare and little-understood disorder. The DSM-III would change that.

The 1970s and 1980s – Autism Re-Defined

Dr. Robert Spitzer, charged with the task of redesigning the DSM, gathered teams of data-oriented people to compile information about all known mental illnesses (Wylie, 2014). After a long process, the DSM-III was published in 1980, weighing in at 500 pages. Included among the newly clarified behaviorally based disorders was Kanner's infantile autism, which was given two primary criteria of (A) pervasive lack of responsiveness to other people and (B) resistance to change. A checklist of six symptoms had to be met in order for a person to qualify for the diagnosis (APA, 1980). These six symptoms were: (1) onset before 30 months of age; (2) pervasive lack of responsiveness to other people; (3) gross deficits in language development; (4) if speech is present, peculiar speech patterns such as immediate and delayed echolalia, metaphorical language, pronominal reversal; (5) bizarre responses to various aspects of the environment; and (6) absence of delusions, hallucinations, loosening of associations, and incoherence as in schizophrenia.

Although the mother blaming was gone, the DSM-III still suggested that autism was more likely to occur in upper socioeconomic classes. This official version of the diagnosis was the start of something new, but continued to neglect those who did not display every symptom, who were not diagnosed until after 30 months, or who were from lower socioeconomic backgrounds.

The DSM-III found its way onto the shelves of government officials, teachers, social workers, lawyers, judges, insurance companies, healthcare workers, and researchers. However, although the DSM-III clarified autism as a distinct condition, practitioners complained that its definition was narrow and difficult to apply to real-life cases. In response, the APA began work on a revised version of the DSM-III, known as the DSM-III-R. For this edition, Spitzer handpicked Lorna Wing, Lynn Waterhouse, and Bryan Siegel to revisit and improve the definition of autism and make the newest version of the DSM easier to use (Silberman, 2015).

Lorna Wing's work on the diagnostic guidelines proved particularly influential. A British psychiatrist and a parent of an autistic child, Wing was curious about the children who met some criteria but not all and therefore went undiagnosed. Wing gave fresh energy to Asperger's idea of autism as a broad continuum, and she began using the term *spectrum* as a way to emphasize this dimension. Her work with the new taskforce led to the APA replacing infantile autism with autistic disorder and expanding the definition to a lifelong condition rather than a rare childhood occurrence in the DSM-III-R. Additionally, the age of onset was no longer limited to before 30 months (Factor, Freeman, & Kardash, 1989). The symptom checklist was also radically changed, with criteria becoming more concrete and observable. Clinicians could now diagnose an autistic disorder when patients exhibited eight of 16 total symptoms and at least two items from section (A) qualitative impairment in reciprocal social interaction; one item from section (B) qualitative impairment in verbal and nonverbal communication and in imaginative activity; and one item from section (C) markedly restricted repertoire of activities and interests (APA, 1987). Finally, adults, high-functioning ASD people, and those who exhibited only some symptoms could receive support and services, and autism began to lose its reputation as severe and rare.

Wing, Waterhouse, and Siegel anticipated inflation in numbers of those diagnosed and were pleased to see this broader inclusion of those who formerly would have been left undiagnosed. They were blindsided, however, by the increasing popularity of an alternative diagnosis related to autistic disorder: Pervasive Developmental Disorder – Not Otherwise Specified (PDD-NOS). This diagnosis quickly became the most popular autism-related diagnosis because it omitted the word autism and was a little easier for parents to accept (Silberman, 2015).

The DSM-III-R overshadowed the DSM-III in popularity. Half a million copies sold, and the DSM-III-R pushed autism further into the public sphere. Growing support accompanied the growing awareness. After the publication of the DSM-III-R in 1987, autism-related legislation increased, and in the United States, the Individuals with Disabilities Education Act (IDEA) incorporated autism into its programs, providing special services and individualized instruction for children on the spectrum. IDEA made it obligatory for schools to report the number of diagnosed children enrolled in school, so a count could be made (Gernsbacher, Dawson, & Goldsmith, 2005). Additionally, state legislatures passed laws so funds would be disbursed to families that chose to embark on early-intervention therapy.

The 1990s – Autism as an Epidemic?

With increasing awareness, better screening tools, and an expansion of diagnostic criteria, autism rates continued to soar. After the publication of the DSM-IV (APA, 1994), numbers spiked again. However, one of the causes for the increase was a typo. In the DSM-IV, there was a small change in the wording for diagnostic criteria. Previously it said that symptoms must be present in communication, social interaction, *and* behavior, but version IV required the identification of symptoms in communication, social interaction, *or* behavior (Grinker, 2008). Additionally, in the DSM-IV, Asperger's Disorder was added as a distinct diagnosis, which was similar to autistic disorder but with higher-functioning verbal and communicative skills.

This increased flexibility and general awareness continued to increase numbers of people with the diagnosis. However, many concerned parents and doctors speculated over what could be causing autism, blaming everything from polluted water to cell phones. The Family Fund database for the UK Department of Education and Skill undertook a study and confirmed that the increase in cases was due to better recognition rather than other external factors, but in spite of this report, rumors and speculation continued to grow. One of the voices of alarm belonged to autism advocate Bernard Rimland.

Rimland's efforts to advocate for children and parents started in the 1960s and by the 1990s he was established as a well-respected leader in the ASD community. In 1995, Rimland wrote a newsletter article that was fueled by the countless stories he had heard of children who began showing symptoms soon after they were vaccinated. Harris Coulter and Barbara Loe Fisher's book *DPT: A Shot in the Dark* argued this as well, and Rimland's article suggested that something environmental was contributing to rising rates of autism (Coulter & Fisher, 1986).

As the anxiety mounted about an autism contagion, gastroenterologist Andrew Wakefield published his now-infamous article in the British medical journal *The Lancet*. Wakefield was not an autism expert but studied the relationship between viruses and diseases, such as Inflammatory Bowel Disease (Silberman, 2015). Wakefield's article suggested that there was a causal relationship between Thermisol, a preservative used in certain vaccines, and autism. Wakefield used a press conference to present these findings to reporters who had been prepped by promotional videos and hype ahead of time. However, other research soon emerged that systematically debunked Wakefield's claims. After further investigation, his medical license was revoked, ten co-authors removed their names from the paper, and eventually the entire paper was retracted and deemed a fraud (Godlee, Smith, & Marcovitch, 2011; Retraction, 2010). Despite evidence of Wakefield's dishonesty and claims of child abuse in his research, Wakefield continued to assert his innocence.

The 2000s and Beyond – A Return to the Spectrum

In recent years, the controversies of an autism epidemic have died down as evidence continues to accumulate that the condition is rooted in genetic and neurological processes. It is now generally argued that research on awareness and support is preferable to seeking dubious causes and cures. The quality of life for families and individuals affected by ASD is much better than it was in past decades. Allowance for quirks in behavior is high, programs to support those with ASD diagnoses are proliferating, and a vision of a broad spectrum has been restored.

This is reflected in the DSM 5, which has a broader and more inclusive definition than previous editions. In 2013, the DSM rechristened the condition as autism spectrum disorder (ASD) and dropped the separate diagnoses of Asperger's and Pervasive Developmental Disorders, which now fit within the range of presentations of ASD. According to the DSM 5, there are only two diagnostic criteria: (A) social communication/interaction and (B) restricted and repetitive behaviors (APA, 2013). See Chapter 2 for a thorough review of the current diagnostic criteria.

Conclusion

There are current questions whether ASD should be categorized as a medical or psychiatric disorder at all. Clearly there are many on the spectrum that require substantial support, or whose life includes serious challenges. However, there are many who, although not neurotypical, enjoy full and productive lives, share joy with those around them, and contribute interesting and important strands to the tapestry of humanity (Shapin, 2016). In this view, ASD is an alternate, but equally legitimate mode of being. Over the next century the spectrum will continue to stretch and accommodate many, as will our understanding and appreciation of those with ASD and their families.

References

American Psychiatric Association. (1952). *Diagnostic and statistical manual of mental disorders* (1st ed.). Washington, DC: Author.

American Psychiatric Association. (1968). *Diagnostic and statistical manual of mental disorders* (2nd ed.). Washington, DC: Author.

American Psychiatric Association. (1980). *Diagnostic and statistical manual of mental disorders* (3rd ed.). Washington, DC: Author.

American Psychiatric Association. (1987). Diagnostic *and statistical manual of mental disorders* (3rd ed., revised). Washington, DC: Author.

American Psychiatric Association. (1994). Diagnostic and statistical manual of mental disorders (4th ed.). Washington, DC: Author.

American Psychiatric Association. (2013). *Diagnostic and statistical manual of mental disorders* (5th ed.). Washington, DC: Author.

Bettelheim, B. (1959). Joey: A "mechanical boy." *Scientific American, 200*(3), 116–127. doi:10.1038/scientificAmerican0359-116.

Chown, N., & Hughes, L. (2016). History and first descriptions of autism: Asperger versus Kanner revisited. *Journal of Autism & Developmental Disorders, 46*(6), 2270–2272.

Coulter, H., & Fisher, B. L. (1986). *DPT: A shot in the dark*. New York: Warner Books.

Czech, H. (2018). Hans Asperger, National Socialism, and "race hygiene" in Nazi-era Vienna. *Molecular Autism, 9*(1), 29.

Down, J. L. (1866). Observations on an ethnic classification of idiots. *The British Journal of Psychiatry, 13*(61), 121–123. doi:10.1192/bjp.13.61.121.

Factor, D. C., Freeman, N. L., & Kardash, A. (1989). Brief report: a comparison of DSM-III and DSM-III-R criteria for autism. *Journal of Autism and Developmental Disorders, 19*(4), 637–640.

Feinstein, A. (2010). A history of autism: Conversations *with the pioneers*. Chichester, West Sussex, UK: Wiley-Blackwell.

Gernsbacher, M. A., Dawson, M., Goldsmith, H. H. (2005). Three reasons not to believe in an autism epidemic. Current Directions in Psychological Science, 14(2), 55–58.

Godlee, F., Smith, J., & Marcovitch, H. (2011, January 8). Wakefield's article linking MMR vaccine and autism was fraudulent. BMJ: *British Medical Journal (Overseas & Retired Doctors Edition)*, 64–66. doi:10.1136/bmj.c7452.

Grinker, R. R. (2008). *Unstrange minds: Remapping the world of autism*. New York: Basic Books.

Harris, J., & Piven, J. (2016, April 26). Correcting the record: Leo Kanner and the broad autism phenotype. Retrieved from https://spectrumnews.org/opinion/viewpoint/correcting-the-record-leo-kanner-and-the-broad-autism-phenotype/.

History of Autism. (n.d.). Retrieved from http://projectautism.org/history-of-autism/.

Kanner, L. (1943). Autistic disturbances of affective contact. *Nervous Child: Journal of Psychopathology, Psychotherapy, Mental Hygiene, and Guidance of the Child, 2*, 217–250.

Kanner, L. (1949). Problems of nosology and psychodynamics of early infantile autism. *American Journal of Orthopsychiatry, 19*(3), 416–426.

Kuhn, R., & Cahn, C. H. (2004). Eugen Bleuler's concepts of psychopathology. *History of Psychiatry, 15*(59:3), 361–366. doi:10.1177/0957154X04044603.

Möller, A., & Hell, D. (2002). Eugen Bleuler and forensic psychiatry. *International Journal of Law and Psychiatry, 25*(4), 351–360. doi:10.1016/S0160-2527(02)00127-9.

Pollak, R. (1998). *The creation of Dr. B: A biography of Bruno Bettelheim.* New York: Simon & Schuster.

Retraction – Ileal-lymphoid-nodular hyperplasia, non-specific colitis, and pervasive developmental disorder in children. (2010). *Lancet* (London, England), *375*(9713), 445.

Sanua, V. D. (1990). Leo Kanner (1894–1981): The man and the scientist. *Child psychiatry and Human Development, 21*(1), 3–23. doi:10.1007/bf00709924.

Shapin, S. (2016, January 25). Seeing the spectrum. *The New Yorker.* Retrieved from www.newyorker.com/magazine/2016/01/25/seeing-the-spectrum.

Sheffer, E. (2018). *Asperger's children the origins of autism in Nazi Vienna.* New York, NY: W. W. Norton & Company.

Silberman, S. (2015). *NeuroTribes.* New York: Avery.

Sparrow, M., & Silberman, S. (2018). On Hans Asperger, the Nazis, and autism: A conversation across neurologies. Retrieved from www.thinkingautismguide.com/2018/04/on-hans-asperger-nazis-and-autism.html.

Wylie, M. S. (2014). The book we love to hate: Why DSM-5 makes nobody happy. *Psychotherapy Networker,* March/April, 28–35.

2   It's a Wide Spectrum

Understanding the Characteristics and Tendencies of ASD

Jason Cohen

The purpose of this chapter is to provide an overview of behaviors of individuals with ASD in order to help clinicians better understand or refresh their knowledge of the disorder. In this way, clinicians will be prepared to answer questions when they inevitably arise. Although there are several specific characteristics of the disorder, they can present in an endless variety of configurations. For a complete description of the diagnostic criteria, the best reference is the current version of the DSM (DSM 5). According to a summary of the current standards, ASD is characterized by clinically and socially significant symptoms present early in a child's life (usually around or before age two) involving persistent deficits in social communication and social interaction across multiple contexts and the presence of restricted, repetitive behavior (APA, 2013).

Why it is Called a Spectrum

ASD is called a spectrum disorder due to the wide variety of skills and deficits that are present in the repertoires of diagnosed individuals. Some people with ASD have severe impairments and will need constant care throughout their lives. Some will have their diagnosis removed after skill deficits have improved. Most of the population fall somewhere in the middle. Between the time a child is first diagnosed until they turn six years old, predicting how severely their life will be affected by ASD is nearly impossible. However, a few factors that seem to have the highest impact on prognosis are comorbid conditions, ability to communicate by age 6, and how early a child is diagnosed and begins receiving treatment.

Comorbid conditions have been found to affect people with ASD at higher rates than the rest of the population (Kohane et al., 2012). These conditions include, but are not limited to, epilepsy, bowel disorders, gastrointestinal problems, and migraines. Comorbid conditions highlight the need for a multidisciplinary approach to treatment. Some of these conditions can be treated and managed early on, such as sleep disorders and asthma, but others, like diabetes and schizophrenia, are more likely to present later in life.

When discussing diagnostic criteria, an important distinction is whether a child's behavioral repertoire is deficient in a certain skill or if the child is able to perform the skill but prefers not to do so. In practice, this is often referred to as "can't do" versus "won't do." Another factor in diagnostic and clinical practices to consider is frequency of behavior. Combined, whether a child can or can't engage in a specific skill and how frequently they emit those behaviors are important. For example, a child who engages in frequent eye contact and social interaction with only one or two people will trigger different concerns from parents and mental health professionals than a child who avoids eye contact and social interaction with everyone.

DSM 5 Criteria

The DSM 5 lists two main criteria of symptoms, which are explained below. When coding using the DSM 5, severity should be recorded first for each of the two psychopathological domains using the three levels provided in the DSM (see Table 2 on page 52 of DSM 5; APA 2013). Following severity, the diagnosing professional needs to specify whether or not there is an accompanying intellectual impairment or language impairment. Additional specifiers or conditions should be noted thereafter. All specifiers should be described at the time of diagnosis.

Criteria A: Deficits in Social Communication and Social Interaction

One of the main diagnostic criteria for ASD is social deficits. These are comprised of the verbal and nonverbal behaviors that are used to interact and communicate with others. It is difficult to separate social behavior from communication since communication is a social behavior. Also, there is no need to think that communication means talking; in fact, many people cannot talk but can communicate just fine. Communication happens through writing or typing, sign language, or augmentative communication devices. These are all types of verbal behavior. However, there is a need to consider communication disorders and deficits in communicative repertoires without referring to social interactions. With improvements in diagnostic criteria and targeted interventions for developing children's communication skills, fewer children with an initial ASD diagnosis will remain on the spectrum for the rest of their lives (Barbaro & Dissanayake, 2017; Turner & Stone, 2007).

Although many parents have no knowledge or training in developmental milestones, deficits in social communication can quickly lead to a family seeking assistance for their child. Early milestones for typically developing babies include making eye contact, looking and smiling at others, babbling, and orienting toward certain noises including their name. It is common for parents of children diagnosed with ASD to report that their children did not develop those skills on time or at all.

Some children with ASD develop typically in infancy, meet the age-appropriate milestones for a period of time, and then halt or regress in their behavioral development (Barger, Campbell, & McDonough, 2013). Other babies do not reach the first milestones within the first few months after being born. Some children will only seek attention and interact with adults but not their peers, although the opposite is rarely the case in children with ASD (Carter, Davis, Klin, & Volkmar, 2005).

If the give-and-take of social interactions is impaired or lacking, if a child prefers solitude, does not frequently engage in and seek social interaction, or uses a parent's hand as a tool instead of other developmentally appropriate forms of seeking assistance, then it is likely that the child is lacking in social reciprocity (Williams, Keonig, & Scahill, 2007). This is one of the defining characteristics of ASD, as well as one of the first noticed by parents.

Criteria B: Restricted, Repetitive Patterns of Behavior, Interests, or Activities

The second main criteria of an ASD diagnosis describes restricted interests. Many individuals with ASD have limited and specific reinforcers, hobbies, or activities in which they choose to engage. Some have described the ways in which people interact with these specific interests as obsessions. Sometimes the topics or objects may be typical for individuals in their respective age groups, but the ways or intensity with which individuals on the spectrum interact with them are typically not age appropriate. For example, many children love playing with and talking about dinosaurs, cars, and trains. It is not uncommon for children with ASD who have age-typical verbal repertoires to know very specific information about each type of dinosaur, makes, models, and histories of cars, and weights and schedules of trains. Also, some adolescents and young adults with ASD may still engage in conversation and play with toys that typically interest younger children. Other children may prefer toys and topics of conversation that are not typical for young children, such as vacuum cleaners and lawn mowers.

Most clinicians understand that, to some extent, there is no clear right or wrong when considering someone's personal interests. It is not wrong for a young child to be interested in anatomy and chemistry, nor for an adult to be interested in cartoons and Legos. Most practitioners won't necessarily try to stop someone with ASD from being interested in a preferred topic as long as it does not pose any risk to themselves or others. Instead, a practitioner may try to increase the variety of interests, decrease the frequency of settings in which they interact with those interests, or use those specific interests as incentives to build new skills.

Insistence on sameness. One of the characteristics of repetitive or restricted interests is what is commonly referred to as "insistence on sameness." It is not unusual for a child with ASD to refuse to engage in certain activities because something is different or missing. For example, a child with ASD may not drink from a cup that is blue instead of the preferable green. They may refuse to sit in a different chair at the dinner table or have a bowel movement if they aren't wearing a diaper and standing in a corner of their bedroom. Changes in parents' hairstyle or furniture arrangement may also be a trigger for challenging behavior. A child may only play with a favorite toy in a specific way, and trying to play with it in a different way may evoke stress or tantrums. Changes in certain patterns of behavior may be difficult, such as putting on clothes in the bedroom instead of the bathroom, grabbing food to eat in the car instead of at the table, or taking a different route to get from home to school. There is a certain amount of comfort that comes with predictability, and changes to that familiarity can be aversive.

Just like many of the other characteristics of ASD, this is not only specific to this population. Many people experience a certain amount of discomfort when they see a peer or significant other prepare a sandwich, make a bed, fold clothes, or surf the internet the "wrong way." However, it is difficult for children with ASD to redirect their behavior or accept changes when they are encountered. Commonly, individuals with ASD will perseverate on a specific topic or action that bothers them rather than move on as others typically do.

Transitions. Closely related to insistence on sameness is difficulty with transitions. Like most children (and adults), leaving a preferred activity or transitioning to a nonpreferred activity can be difficult. No one likes to turn off the TV when their favorite show is on or leave a fun game with friends. Many of us do not like to go to the doctor. What makes this characteristic of ASD important to consider is the frequency of transitions in our lives. For example, changing topics of conversation, going into another room, going to school in the morning, new people entering the room, the air conditioner turning on (transition from a quiet, warm environment to a louder and cooler one), and clouds moving in front of the sun (transition from a bright to a dark environment) are all transitions that can affect behavior. If transitions are defined by a change in environment or activity, then it can be argued that hundreds or thousands of transitions take place each day. Reactions to unwanted transitions by someone with ASD vary, but often include tantrums, disengagement, resistance, or whatever has worked in the past to prolong the onset of the nonpreferred activity or regain access to the preferred activity.

There are many reasons children with ASD have difficulties with transition. Two reasons, exemplified above, have to do with an increased effort of making a change, and the amount of predictability or familiarity with the location or activity. For many individuals with ASD, the more routines in place the better. Conversely, fewer routines and less predictability can result in anxiety and higher rates of challenging behavior. These routines, however, shouldn't necessarily be implemented for long periods of time. Many clinicians will arrange routines to teach new skills, then after the skill is mastered remove the routine so the behavior can occur more naturally.

Sensory differences. Another characteristic is sensory differences. Clinicians attempt to cast a wide net that includes terms such as sensory sensitivity, sensory defensiveness, sensory impairments, sensory processing, etc. This is a controversial topic, partly because of the lack of standard assessment for sensory differences, but also because it is a frequently reported and widely accepted phenomenon (Ben-Sasson et al., 2009; Tomchek & Dunn, 2007) without scientific explanations to target structural or neural differences unique to ASD (Marco, Hinkley, Hill, & Nagarajan, 2011; Rogers & Ozonoff, 2005). Rather than explore the nuances of the research or get caught up in a philosophical debate of perception, the author hopes readers will agree it is a complex topic and take a look at common examples that are observed and reported by those affected by ASD.

Sensory differences refer to the fact that some people's bodies perceive environmental stimuli differently than others. This characteristic is not unique to autism. Many people avoid bright lights, loud music, high pitched noises, and certain types of foods and clothing. For some, it may simply be personal preference. For others, such as individuals with ASD, perceptual differences seem to stem from neurophysiological differences. For these individuals, all forms of stimulus perception can be affected, often in ways that are extremely discomforting.

Because of their sensory differences, many children with ASD have a difficult time making eye contact or being in busy stores. It is common for these children to avoid touching others, certain textures, or wearing particular types of clothing, no matter the type of fabric or how loose or tight the article fits. Many children need to be gradually introduced to touching various things such as sand or objects that are cold, wet, or fuzzy. For some, a headache or hitting their toe on a piece of furniture can evoke extreme challenging behavior, while others are bothered by certain odors and flavors. Furthermore, some individuals experience nausea and vertigo while experiencing certain types of movement.

In addition to visual, tactile, and kinesthetic stimulation, auditory stimulation is another common source of concern for parents and practitioners. Sounds that many children with ASD find aversive are singing, a baby crying, background noises, people talking, and electronic devices such as cash registers and cell phones. An interesting note on the auditory system is that a significantly higher percentage of individuals with ASD have perfect pitch compared to people without ASD.

The examples above illustrate *hyper*sensitivities to stimuli, but individuals with ASD may also be *hypo*sensitive to stimuli. Some argue that hyposensitivity to visual and auditory stimuli make it difficult for people to learn faces and discriminate sounds. For someone who is hyposensitive to tactile or kinesthetic stimuli, they may have a high tolerance for pain. Some may even seek out stimulation and engage in behavior that produces a desired effect. People with ASD often report that this is one of the reasons that they may engage in stereotypic behavior (Bogdashina, 2016).

Stereotypic behavior. Stereotypic behavior, also called self-stimulatory behavior and stimming, refers to repetitive movements of the body and objects. These behaviors are common across all populations, and people engage in them frequently. Tapping your foot, clicking or shaking a pen, rocking back and forth or side to side in a chair are all examples.

One of the main reasons these behaviors happen is because of the proprioceptive feedback that occurs, because "it feels good." Being bored or in a situation where movement is limited might set the occasion for these behaviors, but someone who engages in these behaviors when they are bored is not likely to do so in an enriched environment. Someone on a long plane flight may be more likely to move their arms and torsos in stereotyped movements. Someone who is excited or anxious may pace around the room, rock back and forth, or shake their foot. The examples above are usually socially acceptable, and most people learn to discriminate appropriate times to engage in them.

While there is nothing "wrong" with stereotypic behavior under certain situations, it can be problematic for a few reasons. First, it may occur at high rates across many settings, which may disrupt social interactions or opportunities to learn new skills. People at a social gathering may not want to approach an adult who is jumping up and down and a child who frequently flaps his hands will miss out on handwriting and typing instruction in school.

Additionally, certain topographies of stereotypic behavior are problematic. Grinding one's teeth, vocally scripting dialog from TV shows for minutes at a time, replaying a 10-second clip of video or music hundreds of times, and rubbing one's genitals are examples of behavior that can prevent someone from being successful in certain situations. Sometimes, intensive and intrusive interventions are necessary to address harmful types of stereotypic behavior. However, if there is no danger for harming oneself or others, most clinicians will aim to decrease the probability of behavior in certain situations rather than try to make certain types of stereotypic behavior stop altogether.

Other Common Characteristics

Dietary Needs

Feeding disorders are a common characteristic of individuals with ASD (Ledford & Gast, 2006; Sharp et al., 2013). A high percentage of those with ASD require some type of feeding therapy to get their nutritional needs met compared to neurotypical peers. Several contributing factors result in feeding therapy, including oral motor delays and structural differences that affect chewing and swallowing, allergies, reflux, feeding restricted to certain brands or restaurants, sensitivities to textures, colors, tastes, sounds, and smells, and social anxiety (since meals are often in a social setting). Because of the variety of factors that may influence a child's feeding behavior, it is often necessary to have assistance from specialists in various fields.

It is common for children to be picky eaters, but most typically developing children will simply outgrow it, or their feeding behavior will be easily redirected to more healthy eating habits. On the other hand, it is not uncommon for children with ASD to receive intensive interventions to address feeding and digestion issues. Many young children with ASD require feeding interventions early in life due to the inability to breast or bottle feed, swallow without difficulties, and absorb the essential nutrients that their bodies need. Later, a child with ASD may be sensitive to textures or flavors, develop an aversion to certain foods or eating altogether. Later in life, allergies or gastrointestinal issues may arise or become difficult enough to seek treatment.

Feeding problems can be a major source of stress on families. The source(s) of a child's feeding difficulty can be hard to identify, and parents often feel responsible or guilty about their child's poor eating habits. Many parents become exhausted after seeing multiple specialists without success, and some spend an exorbitant amount of time and money seeking out specific types of food. In addition to the cost of food, feeding interventions can be expensive and require a lot of time and effort from parents. In some cases, these interventions involve feeding tubes or restraining children and removing the restraints after a certain amount of food has been eaten.

Meltdowns

Extreme fits are common in some individuals with ASD. People have described meltdowns as a temporary loss of control, usually as a result of being overwhelmed. This pattern of behavior is not unique to individuals with ASD. Many people lose control of their behavior when they reach a certain point. Meltdowns can be difficult to watch, and can become loud, destructive, and violent. Belongings can get broken, individuals may hurt themselves or others, relationships can be strained, and police and Child Protective Services could get involved. A meltdown may be brief or it can last for hours.

It can be difficult for parents to determine why meltdowns happen; the causes are as unique as each individual who experiences them. The result is that families may avoid many activities both at home and in the community out of concern that a meltdown might take place. It is important for families who are experiencing meltdowns to seek immediate assistance before the behavior gets more complex and the families miss out on opportunities to learn from and enjoy each other's company. Parents are less likely and less able to interact with their children when challenging behaviors occur at high rates, contributing to high levels of stress over time (Baker et al., 2003). Many parents avoid taking their children camping, shopping, or even to restaurants because of the high probability of meltdowns.

Some people will distinguish between meltdowns and tantrums that almost every toddler may engage in from time to time. However, they both happen for similar reasons: getting one's needs met. We have all seen toddlers who have learned that if they scream long enough, they can escape a situation they do not like, get attention from their parents, or score the toy that they really want. It is often the case for individuals with ASD that their meltdowns may not be as voluntary as the meltdowns toddlers commonly express. Neither may be able to describe why their behavior became so extreme; however, the behavior of a typically developing child is usually more flexible and sensitive to social interaction and social rules, which means it can be modified more easily. For individuals with ASD, their behavior is often very rigid, and social interaction and rules, especially during meltdowns, may not matter very much.

Sleep Disorders

Difficulty sleeping is a very common problem reported by families with children with ASD (Krakowiak, Goodlin-Jones, Hertz-Picciotto, Croen, & Hansen, 2008). Poor sleep can contribute to delays in brain and body development, higher rates of challenging behavior, learning difficulties, and weakened immune system. The most commonly reported sleep problems for this population are resisting the bedtime transition, difficulty falling asleep, and inability to sleep for extended periods of time.

Sleeping problems for children with ASD occur for several reasons. Behavioral and medical issues are the most common causes. A few examples of potential causes are unstructured night-time and sleeping routines, poor diet, lack of exercise, incontinence, free access to electronics, and sensitivities to touch, light, and sound. Comorbid conditions such as reflux, chemical and hormone imbalances, epilepsy, and anxiety can also affect a child's ability to sleep (Liu, Hubbard, Fabes, & Adam, 2006). Most people have experienced poor sleep at some point in their lives, so it is not hard to imagine the negative impact of these sleep disorders with children who are already difficult to soothe. This is yet another source of stress for family members, and one that likely affects their everyday ability to function. While some interventions may offer a quick fix, others are conditions that families must accept as part of their lives.

Assessment Help for Professionals

Each family raising a child with ASD is unique and every story contains a mixture of complex challenges and strengths (see Chapter 1). It may take time to understand the complete account of the issues they face. The problems may be a combination of any of the issues discussed in this chapter, and likely include some not mentioned. Aside from common, structured, intake paperwork that could provide valuable information, face-to-face conversations and observations are often necessary.

For many reasons, clinicians may struggle when first meeting a family seeking treatment. A weakness with certain types of structured questionnaires is that situations and behavior can change quickly. It is not uncommon for a family's reason for seeking treatment to change between the time of applying and the beginning of services. Questionnaires can provide a snapshot of symptoms but do not fully describe the variety and extent of the family's challenges and circumstances. Furthermore, while observations are often necessary for clinicians to see the types of problems they are treating, it is rarely the case that specific behaviors will occur during a one-hour visit in an unfamiliar setting. To bridge this gap, sometimes families are asked to create video recordings of instances of the problems for which they are seeking assistance.

It is often best practice to conduct multiple observations across a variety of settings. This can enable clinicians to understand more of what the families are facing. Also, open-ended questionnaires and conversations can allow families more opportunities to discuss their problems. Sometimes, these conversations will lead a parent or clinician to identify potential sources of problems. Another recommended practice is sharing information across service providers. Most families will receive services from multiple specialists, and coordination of care is not widely practiced for service providers who reside in different locations. When clinicians communicate and coordinate their efforts, the benefits to a family can be significant.

Conclusion

This chapter covered the main diagnostic criteria for ASD. It is important that clinicians are familiar with the defining characteristics of ASD such as deficits in social communication and social interaction as well as restricted, repetitive patterns of behavior, interests, or activities. Throughout this chapter, other common characteristics and challenges for individuals with ASD have been described such as dietary needs, meltdowns, and sleep disorders. Hopefully clinicians can work with families to use this information to better help families in the beginning stages who are searching for answers about their child's behaviors.

References

American Psychiatric Association. (2013). *Diagnostic and statistical manual of mental disorders* (5th ed.). Arlington, VA: American Psychiatric Publishing.

Baker, B. L., McIntyre, L. L., Blacher, J., Crnic, K., Edelbrock, C., & Low, C. (2003). Pre-school children with and without developmental delay: Behaviour problems and parenting stress over time. *Journal of Intellectual Disability Research, 47*(4–5), 217–230.

Barbaro, J., & Dissanayake, C. (2017). Diagnostic stability of autism spectrum disorder in toddlers prospectively identified in a community-based setting: Behavioural characteristics and predictors of change over time. *Autism, 21*(7), 830–840.

Barger, B. D., Campbell, J. M., & McDonough, J. D. (2013). Prevalence and onset of regression within autism spectrum disorders: A meta-analytic review. *Journal of autism and developmental disorders, 43*(4), 817–828.

Ben-Sasson, A., Hen, L., Fluss, R. Cermak, S. A., Engel-Yeger, B., & Gal, E. (2009). A meta-analysis of sensory modulation symptoms in individuals with autism spectrum disorders. *Journal of Autism and Developmental Disorders, 39*(1), 1–11.

Bogdashina, O. (2016). *Sensory perceptual issues in autism and asperger syndrome: Different sensory experiences-different perceptual worlds.* Jessica Kingsley Publishers, London, UK, 2003.

Carter, A. S., Davis, N. O., Klin, A., & Volkmar, F. R. (2005). Social development in autism. In F. R. Volkmar, R. Paul, A. Klin, & D. Cohen (Eds.), *Handbook of autism and pervasive developmental disorders: Diagnosis, development, neurobiology, and behavior* (pp. 312–334). Hoboken, NJ: John Wiley & Sons Inc.

Kohane, I. S., McMurry, A., Weber, G., MacFadden, D., Rappaport, L., Kunkel, L., et al. (2012). The co-morbidity burden of children and young adults with autism spectrum disorders. *PLoS ONE 7*(4): e33224.

Krakowiak, P., Goodlin-Jones, B., Hertz-Picciotto, I., Croen, L. A., & Hansen, R. L. (2008). Sleep problems in children with autism spectrum disorders, developmental delays, and typical development: A population-based study. *Journal of Sleep Research, 17*(2), 197–206.

Ledford, J. R., & Gast, D. L. (2006). Feeding problems in children with autism spectrum disorders: A review. *Focus on Autism and Other Developmental Disabilities, 21*(3), 153–166.

Liu, X., Hubbard, J. A., Fabes, R. A., & Adam, J. B. (2006). Sleep disturbances and correlates of children with autism spectrum disorders. *Child Psychiatry and Human Development, 37*(2), 179–191. doi:10.1007/s10578-006-0028-3.

Marco, E. J., Hinkley, L. B. N., Hill, S. S., & Nagarajan, S. S. (2011). Sensory processing in autism: A review of neurophysiologic findings. *Pediatric Research, 69*(5 Pt 2), 48R–54R.

Rogers, S. J., & Ozonoff, S. (2005). Annotation: What do we know about sensory dysfunction in autism? A critical review of the empirical evidence. *Journal of Child Psychology and Psychiatry, 46*(12), 1255–1268.

Sharp, W. G., Berry, R. C., McCracken, C., Nuhu, N. N., Marvel, E., Saulnier, C. A., et al. (2013). Feeding problems and nutrient intake in children with autism spectrum disorders: A meta-analysis and comprehensive review of the literature. *Journal of Autism and Developmental Disorders, 43*(9), 2159–2173. doi:10.1007/s10803-013-1771-5.

Tomchek, S. D., & Dunn, W. (2007). Sensory processing in children with and without autism: A comparative study using the short sensory profile. *American Journal of Occupational Therapy, 61*(2), 190–200. doi:10.5014/ajot.61.2.190.

Turner, L. M., & Stone, W. L. (2007). Variability in outcome for children with an ASD diagnosis at age 2. *Journal of Child Psychology and Psychiatry, 48*, 793–802.

Williams, W. S., Keonig, K., & Scahill, L. (2007). Social skills development in children with autism spectrum disorders: A review of the intervention research. *Journal of Autism and Developmental Disorders, 37*, 1858–1868. doi:10.1007/s10803-006-0320-x.

3 It May Not Be ASD

Distinguishing Autism Spectrum Issues from Other Diagnoses

Rebecca Grzadzinski and Morgan Cohen

"I didn't know what to expect," a parent said about her son's first visit for a diagnostic evaluation. "I didn't know what they would say or whether I was even in the right place." While this parental anxiety is common and can feel daunting, a thorough assessment is often necessary to guide treatment planning and fund interventions such as insurance coverage. Diagnostic labels give treatment providers and families a general sense of the child's strengths as well as challenges. This leads to more informed and supportive environments for the child and family. Throughout the evaluation process, clinicians have the difficult job of balancing the needs, anxieties, and expectations of the family and the child while also providing valuable insights that facilitate effective treatment. So, while the diagnostic process is undoubtedly stressful for families, it is the first step toward treatment planning and ultimately intervening in a helpful way.

During the evaluation process for ASD, clinicians spend time learning about the child by gathering a detailed history of the child's development from the caregivers and conducting several standardized tests to assess specific symptoms and determine the child's developmental level. When determining whether an individual has ASD, the clinician must also consider several other diagnoses in order to determine which diagnosis matches the child's symptoms best. This process is called a "differential diagnosis." The goal and challenge for clinicians is to determine which symptoms are consistent with ASD and which may be better explained by other diagnoses. Distinguishing between ASD and other disorders requires the expertise of a trained professional who integrates information from direct observation and multiple reporters, such as caregivers and teachers. This process can also be particularly difficult since currently there is no biological test (e.g., blood test or brain scan) that can definitively determine the presence or absence of ASD. Clinicians must rely solely on observed and reported behavior when determining a diagnosis (Huerta & Lord, 2012).

This chapter will feature disorders that can be confused with ASD. Specifically, it highlights attention deficit/hyperactivity disorder (ADHD), intellectual disability (ID), and oppositional defiant disorder (ODD). It is important to note that this is not an exhaustive list of all the psychiatric disorders with possible symptom presentations similar to ASD, but rather a few selected disorders that are commonly seen in children presenting for evaluation. This chapter will focus on symptoms that seem similar across disorders as well as ways in which clinicians may distinguish between disorders. It is important to consult the DSM for other differential diagnoses (APA, 2013). The current DSM (DSM 5) lists the following diagnoses that should be ruled out before making an ASD diagnosis: Rhett syndrome, selective mutism, language disorders and social (pragmatic) communication disorders, stereotypic movement disorder, and schizophrenia.

What is Autism Spectrum Disorder?

ASD is a lifelong neurodevelopmental disorder. Research has revealed that ASD is related to atypical development and functioning of the brain (Ha, Sohn, Kim, Sim, & Cheon, 2015), though studies continue to explore what is *consistently* different about the structure and function of the brains of individuals with ASD (Ha et al., 2015). As a result, neuroimaging techniques, such as Magnetic Resonance Imaging (MRI) or other biological tests, cannot currently be used to definitively diagnose ASD. Rather, clinicians look for symptomatic behaviors in two domains: (1) challenges in social communication and (2) the presence of restricted and repetitive behaviors (RRBs) or interests (see Chapters 1 and 2).

For most individuals diagnosed with ASD, symptoms create impairments in daily functioning, such as the ability to complete daily expectations, take care of oneself, complete schoolwork or chores, and interact with peers and parents. While these general definitions of behaviors are useful, they do not highlight the complexity and heterogeneity of symptoms seen in ASD. Diagnosing ASD can be a complex process that needs to be individualized and clinicians need to be savvy about distinguishing social-communication difficulties and RRBs related to ASD from social communication difficulties and RRBs often seen in other disorders.

Disorders Commonly Confused for ASD

Vignette 1. Cameron is a nine-year-old boy who has difficulties staying in his seat, paying attention, and listening to instructions. Cameron's teachers repeat instructions for him several times and provide instructions one step at a time. He often makes comments that are off-topic and his teachers frequently redirect him to appropriate activities. Cameron has difficulty getting along with peers; he often interrupts others while they are speaking and impulsively grabs items from them, such as classwork and pencils. At home, Cameron is constantly moving. His parents describe him as "on the go." His parents have a hard time keeping him in his seat at the dinner table and it is difficult for him to follow all the steps of his bedtime routine. Cameron's mom has signed him up for several after-school sports and activities in order to reduce his activity level; however, he continues to run and jump on furniture at home, even more so than his six-year-old brother. Cameron's behavior is consistent with a diagnosis of ADHD.

What is Attention Deficit/Hyperactivity Disorder (ADHD)?

Children with ADHD demonstrate difficulties with sustaining attention and/or over-activity and impulsivity (APA, 2013). Approximately 5 percent of children are diagnosed annually with ADHD (APA, 2013). Behaviors related to inattention include forgetfulness, disorganization, and frequently losing things. Inattentiveness can lead to children missing instructions, forgetting to turn homework in on time, and getting easily distracted in the classroom.

Hyperactive and impulsive behaviors include an inability to remain seated, talking excessively, and blurting out answers or interrupting others. These behaviors are often difficult to manage and lead to poor school performance. ADHD is separated into three different subtypes: inattentive subtype, hyperactive subtype, and combined subtype. Most children with ADHD experience inattentive, overactive, and impulsive symptoms, leading to a diagnosis of combined subtype. A national US sample of children and adolescents diagnosed with ADHD revealed that approximately 60 percent of children have combined subtype, 30 percent have inattentive subtype, and 10 percent have hyperactive/impulsive subtype (Froehlich et al., 2007).

How to Distinguish ADHD from ASD?

Some children with ADHD may be referred for an ASD evaluation because often there are many overlapping symptoms between the two disorders. For example, both children with ASD or ADHD may exhibit sensory aversions or difficulty making friends (Zablotsky, Bramlett, & Blumberg, 2017). These overlapping symptoms can make it difficult to distinguish children with ADHD from ASD and the discussion on assessment and diagnosis is still ongoing (Mayes, Calhoun, Mayes, & Molitoris, 2012). Although both of these groups can experience social difficulties such as trouble making and maintaining friends, it is diagnostically important to consider the underlying reasons for why these difficulties occur. Children with ADHD often experience peer rejection as a result of symptoms of over-activity (Stenseng, Belsky, Skalicka, & Wichstrøm, 2016). They are also more likely to engage in impulsive behaviors that can be inappropriate for their developmental age (Cordier, Bundy, Hocking, & Einfeld, 2010) and these impulsive behaviors may lead to rejection from peers. Children with ASD also experience social difficulties such as peer rejection, but this often is a result of missing social cues, trouble sustaining conversations, and a lack of understanding of social rules. Children with ASD may interrupt others while they are speaking because they have a limited ability to understand the perspective of another person or knowing that interrupting may be interpreted as rude.

Although children with ADHD experience difficulties with social communication and making friends, unlike children with ASD, children with ADHD often display in-tact nonverbal communicative skills (e.g., eye contact). For example, children with ADHD can direct a range of facial expressions and use a variety of gestures (e.g., waving goodbye or using one's hands to indicate the size or function of something) to communicate with others. Additionally, most RRBs are not present in children with ADHD. Children with ADHD, unlike children with ASD, typically do not line up objects repetitively or demonstrate an intense interest in a particular topic. However, children with ADHD often display sensory aversions, which is also seen in ASD (Mayes et al., 2012). For instance, children with ADHD may have negative reactions to loud or specific noises.

Clinicians distinguishing between ASD and ADHD must gather detailed information about situations in which social difficulties arise to better understand whether the social problems are a result of limited social *understanding* (as a result of ASD symptoms) or limited social *execution* (as a result of ADHD symptoms). In addition, clinicians should explore whether a child has a variety of RRB symptoms consistent with ASD or whether the child displays one or two RRB symptoms, such as sensory aversions, which may be more consistent with ADHD.

Vignette 2. Charlie is a 12-year-old girl who has difficulty remembering her daily routine, requires support from her parents for self-care, and often needs repeated instruction and practice while learning new skills. At school, Charlie is in a special education classroom with eight other children, and during lunch she repeatedly sits with a group of children who tease and bully her. In spite of their bullying, Charlie seems unaware of these negative interactions. Charlie is easily deceived by her peers and has trouble making and maintaining friendships. While she does learn new skills, it takes her a significantly longer time to learn these skills than it takes for other children. For example, Charlie is working on learning safety skills at home, school, and in the community. She needs reminders for skills such as how to safely operate hot appliances like the stove, when it is safe to cross the street, or when it is inappropriate to talk to strangers. Charlie was most recently evaluated through the school district three months ago when she entered middle school. At that time, the school psychologist assessed Charlie using a standard measure of verbal and nonverbal problem-solving and daily living skills. The results of this assessment indicated that Charlie's functioning is consistent with a younger child. Charlie's presentation is consistent with a diagnosis of intellectual disability (ID).

What is Intellectual Disability (ID)?

ID is characterized by deficits in cognitive abilities including the ability to reason, think abstractly, and learn from experience. These deficits lead to impairments in self-care (e.g., grooming), social communication (e.g., making and keeping same-age friends), and community skills (e.g., placing orders at restaurants). This ultimately impacts one's ability to achieve personal independence and participate in age-appropriate social interactions successfully (APA, 2013). Approximately 1 percent of the population has a diagnosis of ID (APA, 2013). Children with ID often require ongoing support and experience challenges across multiple contexts such as home, school, or work (Pedersen et al., 2017).

How to Distinguish ID from ASD?

Sometimes children with ID are referred for a diagnostic evaluation for ASD because symptoms are similar. For example, children with ASD and ID may both have language and social-communication deficits, demonstrate deficits in daily living skills, and display repetitive motor movements or self-injurious behavior. Children with ID display verbal and nonverbal problem-solving skills significantly below other children their age. Though children with ID often demonstrate delayed verbal abilities, they tend to compensate for this delay with nonverbal skills that are consistent with their developmental level, which is unlike ASD. For children with ID, the levels of delay seen in standard measures of intellectual functioning are typically consistent with delays seen in social and daily living skills. For example, a 12-year-old child with ID who has intellectual skills consistent with a six-year-old also has other daily living abilities (e.g., maintaining hygiene or interacting with peers) similar to a six-year-old. In contrast, children with ASD often have social skills that are significantly lower than their intellectual skills. For example, a 12-year-old child with ASD may have intellectual skills consistent with a 12-year-old but daily living and social skills consistent with a six-year-old.

Children with ID develop most of their skills at a consistent rate though this is steadily behind their same-age peers. In contrast, children with ASD sometimes develop certain skills (e.g., reading and visual matching) exceptionally faster than their peers and other skills (e.g., appropriately greeting peers) much slower than what is expected (Pedersen et al., 2017). For parents of children with ASD, this can seem like a "Swiss cheese" development, where a child with ASD has mastered skills in some areas as expected but has "holes" or significant delays in other expected areas. For example, a child with ASD may develop advanced math skills beyond what is expected for his age but still may demonstrate difficulties with bathing independently.

Although RRBs are not characteristic of children with ID, behaviors such as self-injury or motor mannerisms may be seen in children with ID (Hartley & Sikora, 2010). In contrast, children with ASD typically exhibit a variety of RRBs including sensory interests or aversions, repetitive use of objects or interests, and ritualistic behaviors. When distinguishing ID from ASD, gathering information from standard intellectual testing can yield information about what would be expected for the individual's everyday functioning. Consistencies or discrepancies between one's intellectual abilities and everyday functioning can help to determine whether ASD or ID is the most appropriate diagnosis.

Vignette 3. Max is an eight-year-old boy who refuses to follow classroom rules and often blames his classmates when he gets answers wrong on assignments. When his teacher asked him to put his books away, he knocked his chair over and screamed, "No!" This refusal happens frequently and makes it difficult to manage Max's behavior in the classroom. He often intentionally annoys his classmates by taking their school supplies. At home, Max refuses to do chores or comply with house rules like "using an inside voice" and putting his shoes in the closet. He often tells his parents to "go away," and his siblings sometimes avoid playing with him because he will only play "his way." These behaviors are consistent with a diagnosis of oppositional defiant disorder (ODD).

What Is Oppositional Defiant Disorder (ODD)?

ODD is characterized by angry and irritable mood and argumentative or defiant behavior (APA, 2013). Children with ODD, like Max, often have temper tantrums, excessively argue with adults, blame others for their mistakes, and display spiteful behavior. Approximately 3 percent of children receive a diagnosis of ODD (APA, 2013). ODD symptoms can occur in one setting or multiple settings. For example, some children only demonstrate symptoms at home with family members while others may demonstrate symptoms at home and at school with teachers and classmates (APA, 2013).

How to Distinguish ODD from ASD?

Sometimes children with ODD may be referred for a diagnostic evaluation for ASD because both children with ASD and ODD may display significant tantrums, irritability, and difficulty maintaining friendships. However, the factors that underlie these behaviors are different, so it is important to consider the context in which a behavior occurs. For example, a child with ODD may tantrum due to low frustration tolerance, or to try to annoy an adult or "get a rise out of" the adult. In contrast, tantrum behavior in children with ASD is most often related to a desire to maintain a routine, a strong interest, or the result of frustration due to an inability to communicate one's needs or wants (Mandy, Roughan, & Skuse, 2014). Irritability is another characteristic seen in many children with ASD and ODD. Children with ODD can be irritable as a result of not wanting to take responsibility for mistakes or reluctance to follow rules (APA, 2013). Children with ODD are often described as having a "short fuse," such that it does not take much for the child with ODD to become irritated. Irritability in children with ASD is often related to difficulty communicating with others or as a direct result of ASD symptoms. For example, a child with ASD who has sensory aversions to loud sounds may become irritable when the bell rings at the end of classes in school or at a carnival with loud music, a lot of people, or loud machinery.

Similar to children with ASD, children with ODD often have difficulty making and maintaining friendships. However, the reasons why children with ODD have trouble making and maintaining friendships is often the result of specific symptoms of ODD. For example, children with ODD often want things their own way and blame others for their mistakes. Therefore, a child with ODD may blame their peers for losing a soccer game or change the rules of the game to be how they want. These symptoms lead to poor social interactions, which in turn leads to difficulty making and maintaining friendships. Unlike children with ASD, children with ODD typically understand what is appropriate behavior, but often have trouble acting in an appropriate manner (Rowe, Maughan, Costello, & Angold, 2005).

Unlike children with ASD, children with ODD display typical nonverbal communication skills. This means that children with ODD use eye contact, facial expressions, and hand gestures as would be expected for their age. Another important distinction is that children with ASD display RRBs, which are not common in children with ODD. Speaking with the parent and the child, observing the child, and obtaining information from other contexts such as the school helps clinicians determine the motivations for disruptive behaviors, aiding in accurate diagnosis, which is essential for planning effective treatments.

Vignette 5. James, a seven-year-old boy with a previous diagnosis of ADHD presented to the clinic for a diagnostic evaluation to assess for ASD. His parents described him as a child who is often happy when he is allowed to engage in activities he enjoys but often resists activities that he dislikes, particularly most school-related activities and his chores. He will protest these activities and has temper tantrums that include throwing objects, yelling, and crying approximately three times per week. His teachers describe him as energetic and resistant to activities if they do not involve his interests in art and insects. He is often out of his seat during class time and will behave as the "class clown" in order to get attention. During the assessment for ASD, James required regular breaks, which included drawing tiger centipedes. James protested when requested to complete tasks, especially when he was required to write. He stood during several tasks and would fidget while seated. He displayed inconsistent eye gaze and smiled throughout most of the session with subtle variation in his facial expression. He enjoyed sharing facts about insects and asked questions about whether the clinician had seen certain bugs.

Co-Occurring Diagnoses. James demonstrates the true complexity of cases that often present to clinics to determine the presence or absence of ASD. James' current presentation includes a constellation of symptoms consistent with ASD as well as other psychiatric diagnoses, including ADHD and ODD. This is called a "comorbid disorder," which means that more than one psychiatric diagnosis is present. In fact, most children with ASD have at least one co-occurring disorder (Simonoff et al., 2008). Therefore, it is important to note that all of the disorders discussed throughout this chapter can occur in addition to an ASD diagnosis. The most common co-occurring psychiatric disorders seen in children with ASD include ID, which occurs in 50–70 percent of children with ASD (Matson & Shoemaker, 2009) as well as ADHD, ODD, and specific language impairment (see DSM 5), which are present in approximately 30 percent of children with ASD (Simonoff et al., 2008; Tomblin, 2011). Other co-occurring disorders include anxiety, depression, and obsessive-compulsive disorder. The challenge for clinicians is determining which symptoms are and are not explained by ASD and which qualify for additional diagnoses.

It can be particularly challenging for clinicians to determine the presence of comorbid diagnoses. This is because clinicians must rely on behavior as well as a variety of different sources to paint a full picture of how consistent and impairing symptoms are. That said, symptom severity might be worsened depending on the environment, adding to the complexity of diagnosis.

Another crucial consideration for clinicians during the diagnostic process is determining the utility of a comorbid diagnosis. Diagnoses are helpful only if they lead to efficacious treatment options, appropriate school placements, and more holistic understanding of the individual's learning style and needs. Sometimes a comorbid diagnosis can help a child to receive the necessary accommodations to not only address the ASD diagnosis but also the comorbid diagnosis. For a child such as James, treating the symptoms of ADHD within the context of ASD symptoms is important. It is also recommended that children with ASD receive a re-evaluation every few years or when new symptoms emerge in order to determine whether a comorbid disorder is appropriate and how best to implement treatments that align with the individual's current difficulties.

Conclusion

Distinguishing between symptoms of ASD and symptoms of other disorders can be a challenge. Every child has a unique presentation and, given the heterogeneity of all the disorders discussed, it can be difficult to identify the underlying reasons for why certain behaviors occur. Clinicians should keep in mind that the disorders discussed in this chapter are only a few of the psychiatric disorders that have symptoms that can co-occur with ASD.

The goal of this chapter is to help clinicians understand the complexity of the diagnostic process and their vital role in gathering information from caregivers that helps to better understand the unique challenges that the child faces. Seeking out a diagnostic evaluation can be daunting, but a comprehensive evaluation is an important step toward treatment planning and improving the child and family's quality of life.

References

American Psychiatric Association. (2013). *Diagnostic and statistical manual of mental disorders* (5th ed.). Arlington, VA: American Psychiatric Publishing.

Cordier, R., Bundy, A., Hocking, C., & Einfeld, S. (2010). Comparison of the play of children with attention deficit hyperactivity disorder by subtypes. *Australian Occupational Therapy Journal, 57*(2), 137–145.

Froehlich, T. E., Lanphear, B. P., Epstein, J. N., Barbaresi, W. J., Katusic, S. K., & Kahn, R. S. (2007). Prevalence, recognition, and treatment of attention-deficit/hyperactivity disorder in a national sample of US children. *Archives of pediatrics & adolescent medicine, 161*(9), 857–864.

Ha, S., Sohn, I. J., Kim, N., Sim, H. J., & Cheon, K. A. (2015). Characteristics of brains in autism spectrum disorder: Structure, function and connectivity across the lifespan. *Experimental Neurobiology, 24*(4), 273–284.

Hartley, S. L., & Sikora, D. M. (2010). Detecting autism spectrum disorder in children with intellectual disability: Which DSM-IV-TR criteria are most useful? *Focus on Autism and Other Developmental Disabilities, 25*(2), 85–97.

Huerta, M., & Lord, C. (2012). Diagnostic evaluation of autism spectrum disorders. *Pediatric Clinics of North America, 59*(1), 103–111.

Mandy, W., Roughan, L., & Skuse, D. (2014). Three dimensions of oppositionality in autism spectrum disorder. *Journal of Abnormal Child Psychology, 42*(2), 291.

Matson, J. L., & Shoemaker, M. (2009). Intellectual disability and its relationship to autism spectrum disorders. *Research in Developmental Disabilities, 30*(6), 1107–1114.

Mayes, S. D., Calhoun, S. L., Mayes, R. D., & Molitoris, S. (2012). Autism and ADHD: Overlapping and discriminating symptoms. *Research in Autism Spectrum Disorders, 6*(1), 277–285.

Pedersen, A. L., Pettygrove, S., Lu, Z., Andrews, J., Meaney, F. J., Kurzius-Spencer, M., ... & Cunniff, C. (2017). DSM criteria that best differentiate intellectual disability from autism spectrum disorder. *Child Psychiatry & Human Development, 48*(4), 537–545.

Rowe, R., Maughan, B., Costello, E. J., & Angold, A. (2005). Defining oppositional defiant disorder. *Journal of Child Psychology and Psychiatry, 46* (12), 1309–1316.

Simonoff, E., Pickles, A., Charman, T., Chandler, S., Loucas, T., & Baird, G. (2008). Psychiatric disorders in children with autism spectrum disorders: Prevalence, comorbidity, and associated factors in a population-derived sample. *Journal of the American Academy of Child and Adolescent Psychiatry, 47*(8), 921–929.

Stenseng, F., Belsky, J., Skalicka, V., & Wichstrøm, L. (2015). Peer rejection and attention deficit hyperactivity disorder symptoms: Reciprocal relations through ages 4, 6, and 8. *Child Development, 87*(2), 365–373.

Tomblin, B. (2011). Co-morbidity of autism and SLI: Kinds, kin and complexity. *International Journal of Language & Communication Disorders, 46*(2), 127–137.

Zablotsky, B., Bramlett, M. D., & Blumberg, S. J. (2017). The co-occurrence of autism spectrum disorder in children with ADHD. *Journal of Attention Disorders*, June 2017.

Part II

Autism, The Family, and The Wider Community

4　The Parental Subsystem

The Effects of Raising a Child with ASD

Jake Johnson

Research on ASD and the family has confirmed that ASD affects not only those individuals who have been diagnosed with ASD, but their parents and primary caregivers as well. These ASD-related effects have shown to be both individual (affecting each parent independent of the other) and relational (affecting the parents' couple relationship if parents are coupled) in nature. That said, not all parents raising children with ASD are equally affected. Some experience more of the unique stressors related to ASD than others, and some fair better in dealing with ASD-related stressors than others. In terms of relational outcomes, some couples report feeling closer and more connected to one another because they have a child with ASD, while others do not survive the crucible that is caring for the child.

This chapter will thus explore the childrearing challenges and common parental stressors related to caring for children with ASD that lead to differing individual and relational outcomes for parents. In addition, ways of coping with ASD-related stressors will also be discussed, with particular attention paid to parental strength and resiliency in managing all that comes with caring for a child on the autism spectrum. However, research findings related to the individual and relational impact of ASD on parents will first be delineated.

Individual and Relational Impact of ASD on Parents

In general, raising children with ASD can negatively impact the physical and psychological well-being of both mothers and fathers (Karst & Van Hecke, 2012). Mothers, who are often the primary caregivers for their children with ASD, are more negatively affected than fathers (Hastings, 2003). As compared to parents of neurotypical children, parents of children with ASD have been found to experience more physical and mental health problems, more parenting-related stress, and lower levels of social support (Brobst, Clopton, & Hendrick, 2009; Karst & Van Hecke, 2012). Moreover, as compared to parents of children with other types of developmental disabilities, parents of children with ASD experience greater parenting and psychological stress (Dabrowska & Pisula, 2010; Estes et al., 2009; Hartley, Seltzer, Head, & Abbeduto, 2012). Research on parents as couples has also determined that parents raising children with erience less overall relationship satisfaction, more frequent and severe conflict, and less ability to resolve conflict than parents of neurotypical ren (Brobst et al., 2009; Hartley et al., 2017).

Conversely, other researchers found parents of children with ASD experience more positive outcomes. For example, several studies found raising a child with ASD to have given parents a deeper sense of purpose in life, enriching (among other things) their experiences of compassion, endurance, patience, and joy (Marciano, Drasgow, & Carlson, 2015; Myers, Mackintosh, Goin-Kochel, 2009). Furthermore, parents of children with ASD had higher levels of positive affect, as well as greater sensitivity, in their spousal interactions as compared to parents of neurotypical children (Hartley et al., 2017). Yet other studies have maintained that couples may experience more closeness and connection despite the stress of having a child with ASD (Hock, Timm, & Ramisch, 2012), and that parents may even feel they have a stronger relationship because they have a child with ASD (Marciano et al., 2015; Myers et al., 2009).

Common ASD-Related Parental Stressors

Given these varied experiences and outcomes for parents, it follows that the ASD-related stressors they face may also vary. There are several unique ways in which ASD places stress on parents. Although not every parent and couple will experience these stressors equally, or at all, the following ASD-related challenges should be considered common to the experience.

Ambiguous Loss

Ambiguous loss (Boss, 2006) is a type of loss that is not easily explained or understood. It often involves experiencing a loved one as both absent and present. Parents of children with ASD may experience ambiguous loss in relation to their child in several ways. First, their child may look "normal" (i.e., neurotypical) while not developing in a neurotypical fashion. Having a child with a neurotypical appearance who exhibits social and emotional delays can be hard for parents to reconcile. Furthermore, as the etiology of ASD is yet unknown, parents may struggle to make sense of how their child came by the disorder in the first place and feel uncertain of their role in their child's acquisition of ASD. Finally, for a number of parents, their child may have been developing neurotypically for the first year or two of life before beginning to experience developmental delays. In these situations, parents experience the ambiguous loss of their child in that the child is no longer socially and emotionally who they understood him/her to be before the onset of delayed development. Learning to live with this ambiguity, discerning what losses to grieve, and how to do so, can be a stressful experience for parents. This is especially true for parents in situations where one spouse is feeling unclear about how to make sense of ASD and its effects on the family compared to the other.

Lack of Resources

Caring for children with ASD may also place strain on parents' available financial and temporal resources. Raising a child with ASD can be an extraordinarily expensive undertaking with the real cost of childrearing for children with ASD estimated to be $1.4 million over the course of the child's lifetime (Buescher, Cidav, Knapp, & Mandell, 2014) and the costs of various ASD-related therapies alone ranging between $40,000 to $60,000 annually (Amendah, Grosse, Peacock, & Mandell, 2011). As such, many parents have to make difficult decisions (about which they do not always agree) regarding where to appropriate financial resources, including what therapies to pursue and what non-essential activities to drop.

Parents raising children with ASD also experience restrictions on their time (Karst & Van Hecke, 2012). They often have to provide round-the-clock supervision for their children, shuttle them from therapy to therapy and doctor to doctor, and spend time advocating on behalf of their children in a variety of settings (e.g., school, social service, healthcare). These time constraints limit the amount of time parents are able to spend with each other, any other children they may have, and themselves. It may also inhibit parents' (especially mothers') participation in the work force or in other social activities (e.g., time with friends, participation in religious services/practices; Myers et al., 2009). This lack of free time can be particularly stressful for couples in situations where one partner is perceived to have much more of it than the other, such as in situations where the husband works full-time and the wife only works part-time or not at all in order to serve as primary caregiver for the couple's child with ASD.

Behavioral Concerns

Many parents find dealing with ASD-related behavioral issues to be the most stressful part of caring for children on the autism spectrum. Ranging from temper-tantrums to self-stimulation to difficulties with activities of daily living, ASD-related behaviors, in particular those that occur in public, are often difficult for parents to control (Marciano et al., 2015; Myers et al., 2009). The presentation of aggressive behaviors such as self-injury (e.g., head banging) or sexual inappropriateness (e.g., touching oneself in public) or causing harm to others may leave parents at loggerheads, or just simply lost, regarding how to address such concerns. Generally speaking, parents who deal with more of these types of aggressive behaviors will experience higher levels of stress than parents who deal with little to no ASD-related aggressive behaviors in their children. With self-stimulatory behaviors (e.g., echolalia, hand flapping), parents may disagree on when and where such activities can take place, if they should be allowed at all. Regarding activities of daily living (e.g., going to the bathroom, managing personal hygiene, getting dressed, feeding oneself), children with ASD may present with a wide range of abilities. Some children may be able to manage all of their own activities of daily living while others lack the ability to do so. As such, parents whose children are more able to care for themselves may experience less stress and have more free time than parents who must daily supervise or help their children with these activities. Getting on a consistent sleep schedule and ensuring one's child does not elope in the middle of the night may also be an area of concern for parents (Myers et al., 2009). Parents charged with handling these behaviors often report feeling exhausted and stressed out due to a chronic lack of adequate sleep. Finally, because many children with ASD also have comorbid diagnoses, such as an intellectual disability, oppositional defiant disorder, or social anxiety disorder (See Chapter 3; Simonoff et al., 2008), it could be the case that parents are not only dealing with specific ASD-related behavioral concerns but also with other behavioral issues stemming from these comorbid diagnoses (e.g., impulsivity, irritable mood).

Social Stigma

For many parents, closely related to child behavioral concerns is the experience of social stigma (Marciano et al., 2015; Myers et al., 2009). Social stigma may come in many forms, ranging from aggressive (e.g., someone telling a parent to "get control of your child!") to passive aggressive (e.g., someone saying, "I understand you've got your hands full, but you should really think about other people before you bring your child out again"), and almost always occurs in relation to the public presentation of ASD-related behaviors by one's child. Being on the receiving end of such stigma can cause parents a great deal of humiliation and shame, leading them to reduce the amount of time they spend with their child in public and making them feel on edge when they do have to take their child out. In response to feeling stigmatized, parents may also limit their use of social supports such as community centers and places of worship, cutting themselves off from potential resources due to their concerns over how they will be received.

Parents may not only choose to isolate themselves in response to social stigma, but they may also feel excluded from social activities and gatherings (Myers et al., 2009). They may not feel welcome in the homes of extended family and friends because of their child's potential for inappropriate behaviors, or they may feel that at the very least their child is not welcome. In some instances, frustration may arise for couples in which one partner's family is not supportive of their situation. In other instances, both partners may feel misunderstood by extended family and excluded (either explicitly or implicitly) from much-needed family support.

Coping with ASD-Related Stressors

Making sense of the variance in how ASD affects parents individually and relationally does not only relate to the type and amount of ASD-related stressors with which they are confronted; rather, ways in which parents cope with these challenges – both individually and relationally – must also be considered. Parents who engage in maladaptive forms of individual and relational coping will be more susceptible to caregiver burnout and other negative outcomes than parents who use more adaptive ways to cope with the unique stressors associated with their child's disorder.

Individual Ways of Coping

Meaning making is a fundamental way in which parents are able to adaptively cope with having a child with ASD. To this point, multiple studies have pointed out the importance of parents being able to make some sense of having been charged with the care of a child with ASD (Hock, Timm, & Ramisch, 2012; Marciano et al., 2015; Myers et al., 2009). In particular, these studies maintain that parents who believe their lives have been enriched because they have a child with ASD, who connect the diagnosis to a larger religious/spiritual worldview, and who find the positive impact of ASD on their sense of self and their relationships with others will fare better than parents who cannot. See Chapter 14 for further explanation and discussion about meaning making and how it applies to families with children with ASD.

Relatedly, in their study of coping styles among parents of children with ASD, Pottie and Ingram (2008) found certain parental coping styles to be associated with parental well-being and others to be related to negative parental mood. Those coping styles predicting positive parental mood included: problem solving (e.g., taking concrete action in response to ASD-related stressors), seeking support (e.g., reaching out to others for help), focusing on the positive or accepting (e.g., seeing ASD-related problems in a more tolerable light), expressing or controlling emotions (e.g., managing one's distress in ways that are appropriate given the context), and compromising or negotiating (e.g., finding a balance between one's individual needs and one's contextual demands/limitations). Conversely, coping styles associated with decreased positive mood for parents involved escaping or avoiding (e.g., disengaging or refusing to accept the reality of all that comes with caring for a child with ASD), blaming or directing anger at someone (e.g., making ASD someone else's fault), withdrawing socially (e.g., keeping others from knowing about one's ASD-related stressors), and feeling helpless (e.g., giving up on trying to manage ASD-related stressors). Furthermore, expressing or controlling emotions and seeking distraction (e.g., engaging in pleasurable activities) helped to decrease parents' negative moods while problem solving, blaming others, withdrawing socially, and feeling helpless were coping styles that only served to exacerbate one's negative mood.

Relational Ways of Coping

Research on how parents as a couple dyad cope with the ASD-related stressors they face is just beginning to emerge. This emerging research is beginning to shed light on why it is the case that some couples feel stronger together because they have a child with ASD while others fall apart in the autism crucible. For example, Hock and colleagues (2012) found teamwork to be a key aspect of maintaining a couple relationship while caring for a child with ASD. More specifically, the researchers found that being able to reorganize professional and family roles, coordinating parenting tasks, and maintaining unity as a parental team were variables that led couples to find deeper intimacy and commitment despite the stressors they faced. Ramisch, Onaga, and Oh (2014) examined variables that contribute to marital success for couples and noted that communication between partners and shared foundational expectations for one's marital relationship (e.g., marriage as a lifelong commitment) were vital to a couple's ability to effectively cope with ASD-related stress.

Johnson and Piercy (2017) offer the most comprehensive analysis of how couples raising children with ASD relationally cope with the unique stressors associated with ASD and maintain their couple relationships. Their qualitative investigation found that couples needed to make several key shifts in order to mitigate the effects of ASD-related stressors and promote intimacy in their relationships. Namely, couples needed first to adjust their expectations of the amount of couple time they would realistically have together as well as their perceptions of how caring for a child with ASD impacted their relationship, especially with regard to the unique childcare challenges parents of children on the autism spectrum are regularly called on to address. The researchers labeled these changes in expectation and perception as "cognitive shifts."

In addition to making cognitive shifts, Johnson and Piercy also found that couples needed to engage in four types of relational practices, which they called "relational shifts," in order to remain close and connected to one another. Similar to Hock et al.'s (2012) findings, the first of these shifts related to couples working as a team by sharing the childcare workload, giving each partner the opportunity to take "me time" when needed, and learning about ASD-related issues together. In line with the results from Ramisch et al. (2014), the second shift dealt with couples practicing enhanced communication skills, particularly with regard to active and receptive communication of emotional content and conflict resolution.

The final two shifts were unique to Johnson and Piercy's research. The third had to do with overcoming the unique barriers to couple time faced by couples raising children with ASD. In particular, overcoming these barriers involved being highly creative in carving out time together (e.g., having a stay-at-home date night after all the kids were in bed, including one's child with ASD when going out on a date) and finding good, trustworthy childcare. The final relational shift pertained to partners showing one another that they are both sensitive and emotionally responsive to each other's contributions to family life. This was demonstrated by empathizing with one another's experiences of caring for a child with ASD as well as through appreciating each other's contributions toward the well-being of the family.

Johnson and Piercy (2017) also found that several contextual and environmental factors came to bear on the degree to which couples were free to or constrained from making the cognitive and relational shifts mentioned above. For example, a couple's access to outside supports, both personal (e.g., family and friends) and professional (e.g., social services, various therapies) as well as their beliefs about the parameters of commitment in one's marriage (or committed partnership) were factors that either inhibited or facilitated closeness and connection to one's partner. In addition, partner physical and mental health, the level of behavioral issues displayed by their children, and school- and work-related difficulties also influenced a couple's ability to cope with ASD. Lastly, the authors found that coping with the stressors associated with ASD would be an ongoing process that required the continual practice of the previously mentioned cognitive and relational shifts. That said, it was also true that the longer couples had been able to cope with ASD-related stressors and maintain a sense of marital intimacy, the easier they would be able to do so in the future. For couples in the early years of raising a child on the autism spectrum, it was particularly important to simply survive these first years however they could. Surviving the early years was seen to give couples both a sense of accomplishment and a belief that their relationships could thrive in the context of raising children with ASD.

Conclusion

As demonstrated in this chapter, parents of children with ASD are impacted in a variety of ways and to varying degrees by the unique challenges of raising a child on the autism spectrum. Due to (a) the multifarious ways in which ASD presents in children, (b) the degree to which parents experience individual and relational stress in the face of ASD, and (c) parents' ability to individually and relationally cope with such stressors, parents will require varying levels of assistance in managing all that comes with their child's disorder. Chapter 5 of this book will present a number of ways to clinically assess and treat the diverse effects of ASD on parents.

References

Amendah, D., Grosse, S. D., Peacock, G., & Mandell, D. S. (2011). The economic costs of autism: A review. In D. Amaral, D. Geschwind, & G. Dawson (Eds.), *Autism spectrum disorders* (pp. 1347–1360). Oxford, UK: Oxford University Press.

Boss, P. (2006). *Loss, trauma, and resilience: therapeutic work with ambiguous loss.* New York, NY: Norton.

Brobst, J. B., Clopton, J. R., & Hendrick, S. S. (2009). Parenting children with autism spectrum disorders: The couple's relationship. *Focus on Autism and Other Developmental Disabilities, 24,* 38–49. doi:10.1177/1088357608323699.

Buescher, A. V. S., Cidav, Z., Knapp, M., & Mandell, D. S. (2014). Costs of autism spectrum disorders in the United Kingdom and the United States. *Journal of the American Medical Association Pediatrics, 168,* 721–728. doi:10.1001/jamapediatrics.2014.210.

Dabrowska, A., & Pisula, E. (2010). Parenting stress and coping styles in mothers and fathers of pre-school children with autism and Down syndrome. *Journal of Intellectual Disability Research, 54,* 266–280. doi:10.1111/j.1365-2788.2010.01258.x.

Estes, A., Munson, J., Dawson, G., Koehler, E., Zhou, X., & Abbott, R. (2009). Parenting stress and psychological functioning among mothers of preschool children with autism and developmental delay. *Autism, 13,* 375–387. doi:10.1177/1362361 309105658.

Hartley, S. L., Papp, L. M., Mihaila, I., Bussanich, P. N., Goetz, G., & Hickey, E. J. (2017). Couple conflict in parents of children with versus without autism: Self-reported and observed findings. *Journal of Child and Family Studies, 26,* 2152–2165.

Hartley, S. L., Seltzer, M. M., Head, L., & Abbeduto, L. (2012). Psychological well-being in fathers of adolescents and young adults with Down syndrome, Fragile X syndrome, and autism. *Family Relations, 61,* 327–342. doi:10.1111/j.1741-3729.2011.00693.x.

Hastings, R. P. (2003). Child behavior problems and partner mental health as correlates of stress in mothers and fathers of children with autism. *Journal of Intellectual Disability Research, 47,* 231–237. doi:10.1046/j.1365-2788.2003.00485.x.

Hock, R. M., Timm, T. M., & Ramisch, J. L. (2012). Parenting children with autism spectrum disorders: A crucible for couple relationships. *Child & Family Social Work, 17,* 406–415.

Johnson, J., & Piercy, F. P. (2017). Exploring partner intimacy among couples raising children on the autism spectrum: A grounded theory investigation. *Journal of Marital and Family Therapy, 43,* 644–661. doi:10.1111/jmft.12247.

Karst, J. S., & Van Hecke, A. V. (2012). Parent and family impact of autism spectrum disorders: A review and proposed model for intervention evaluation. *Clinical Child and Family Psychology Review, 15,* 247–277. doi:10.1007/s10567-012-0119-6.

Marciano, S. T., Drasgow, E., & Carlson, R. G. (2015). The marital experiences of couples who include a child with autism. *The Family Journal: Counseling and Therapy for Couples and Families, 23,* 132–140. doi:10.1177/1066480714564315.

Myers, B. J., Mackintosh, V. H., & Goin-Kochel, R. P. (2009). "My greatest joy and my greatest heart ache:" Parents' own words on how having a child in the autism spectrum has affected their lives and their families' lives. *Research in Autism Spectrum Disorders, 3,* 670–684.

Pottie, C. G., & Ingram, K. M. (2008). Daily stress, coping, and well-being in parents of children with autism: A multilevel modeling approach. *Journal of Family Psychology, 22,* 855–864.

Ramisch, J. L., Onaga, E., & Oh, S. M. (2014). Keeping a sound marriage: How couples with children with autism spectrum disorders maintain their marriages. *Journal of Child and Family Studies, 23,* 975–988. doi:10.1007/s10826-013-9753-y.

Simonoff, E., Pickles, A., Charman, T., Chandler, S., Loucas, T., & Baird, G. (2008). Psychiatric disorders in children with autism spectrum disorders: Prevalence, comorbidity, and associated factors in a population-derived sample. *Journal of the American Academy of Child & Adolescent Psychiatry, 47,* 921–929. doi:10.1097/chi.0b013e318179964f.

5 How to Assist and Empower Parents Raising a Child with ASD

Jake Johnson

As mentioned in Chapter 4, raising a child with ASD affects parents in different ways depending on the type and amount of ASD-related stressors they face, in combination with how they are individually and relationally coping with these challenges. Therefore, clinicians working with parents of children on the autism spectrum will need to be aware of how to assess for and intervene with common ASD-related stressors and the ways in which parents are coping with such stressors. In this chapter, a brief overview of how to assess for specific ASD-related challenges and parental coping will be offered before entering into a larger discussion of what clinical interventions may best serve parents raising children with ASD who seek out psychotherapeutic services. Strategies for how to work individually with parents of children with ASD as well as other contextual considerations will also be provided.

Assessing for ASD-Related Parental Stressors

ASD is not a one-size-fits-all type of developmental disability; accordingly, parents raising children on the autism spectrum will present in therapy with a variety of individual and relational concerns. Although it is beyond the scope of this chapter to offer a model for how to clinically evaluate and diagnose the most relevant ASD-related concerns for parents as individuals and as couples, clinicians serving this population should carefully assess each parent's particular areas of risk and resiliency. Such assessment could potentially be done through use of instruments such as the Autism Parenting Stress Index (to assess for overall parental stress as well as what particular ASD-related challenges are most salient for parents; Silva & Schalock, 2012), the Coping Inventory for Stressful Situations (to assess parents' coping strategies for dealing with the challenges of caring for a child with ASD; Endler & Parker, 1999), and/or the Dyadic Adjustment Scale (to assess the overall quality of a couple's relationship; Spanier, 1976). In addition to the use of these assessment tools, clinicians should exercise judgment in discerning which, if any, of the interventions suggested in this chapter will best help particular individuals/couples to cope with their unique ASD-related challenges. It is also recommended that clinicians make use of their own theoretical/clinical orientations in determining if and when to implement any of the interventions outlined herein.

Recommendations for Systemic Intervention with Parents of Children with ASD

A qualitative content analysis (Denzin & Lincoln, 2005) of literature published in the past decade related to parents raising children with ASD revealed several areas for systemic intervention for clinicians to consider when working with this population. Borrowing upon Johnson and Piercy's (2017) model for how couples manage their partner relationships when raising children with ASD, the various interventions noted in the literature have been organized into two broad categories. The first category comprises interventions centered around "cognitive shifts," or fundamental changes in the ways in which parents conceptualize what it means to have a child with ASD, while the second contains interventions dealing with "relational shifts," or interpersonal practices that can help to keep parents close and connected despite the ASD-related stressors they face. The following discussion further details the findings from this content analysis, with specific suggestions for clinical intervention included.

Cognitive Shifts

In general, clinicians can help parents make cognitive shifts by (a) promoting parental insight into ASD and how it affects family members and (b) assisting parents in adjusting their expectations for what life and couple hood will look like in the context of raising a child on the autism spectrum. Relevant literature has pointed out several ways in which clinicians can help parents to deepen their understandings of and expectations for couple hood when caring for a child with ASD. Most notably, many authors have cited psychoeducational practices as playing an important role in helping parents to develop more insight related to their situations. For example, Hock, Timm, and Ramisch (2012) suggest helping parents to acknowledge the hardships of raising children with ASD while Marciano, Drasgow, and Carlson (2015) mention the importance of normalizing parents' seemingly unique experiences. Ramisch, Onaga, and Oh (2014) also highlighted the need to help parents understand that not all of their relational issues have to do with caring for children with ASD while Neely, Amatea, Echevarria-Doan, and Tannen (2012) reported that parents needed to hear that they were not destined to lives of "battles and negativities" but that they could also experience caring for a child with ASD as something positive (p. 223). Yet other studies have noted that working with parents around how they made sense of their situations could play a significant role in instilling hope and providing reasonable expectations for the future of their couple relationships (Neely et al., 2012; Solomon & Chung, 2012).

Taken together, these findings suggest that clinicians should be prepared to offer parents, especially those in the early years of caring for children with ASD, psychoeducational resources to orient them to what particular joys and sorrows accompany raising children with ASD as well as to give some baseline data for how unique (or relatively typical) their situation really is as compared to other parents of children with ASD. One very helpful psychoeducational resource is Abbott's (2013) therapeutically-oriented article entitled "Love in the time of autism," which focuses on the unique effects raising children with ASD can have on couple relationships. Clinicians should also assess for the degree to which parents feel ill- or well-informed about ASDs in general and, if necessary, offer user-friendly resources such as the Autism Speaks website (www.autism-speaks.org), which provides both basic and in-depth information related to ASD diagnosis and treatment.

Clinicians may also consider employing the guided discovery technique from cognitive-behavioral couple therapy (Baucom, Epstein, LaTaillade, & Kirby, 2008) to help parents modify their expectations for life and couple hood in light of having a child with ASD. In this technique, clinicians help parents to identify their schemas, or mental frameworks, for what they believe parenting, marriage, and family life should look like. Having done so, clinicians next discuss with parents what they perceive to be the various advantages and disadvantages of each of their schemas. Lastly, clinicians address with parents the possibility of having to develop new or adapt previously existing schemas based on the reality of their situations. For example, in dealing with a couple in which one partner has identified and expressed a belief that come hell or high-water couples in intimate relationships should go out on a date at least once a week, the clinician may ask about the benefits and drawbacks of holding this belief within the context of raising a child with ASD. If the partner describes the benefits of going out once a week as making sure that quality couple time occurs on a regular basis and the drawbacks as experiencing a great deal of frustration when parenting a child with ASD gets in the way of the couple's weekly date, the clinician could then ask the partner about the possibility of developing a different standard that did not lead to so much frustration but still ensured that couple time was prioritized as taking place regularly. The clinician could also encourage the couple to work together to consider alternative standards for what quality time could look like for them, honoring their desire to spend time together while also helping them be more realistic about the frequency with which such time together could occur.

Relational Shifts

While cognitive shifts focus on issues related to parental insight and expectations, relational shifts involve helping parents to make certain behavioral changes and to become more emotionally responsive with their partners. As such, the relational shifts category has been divided into two subcategories of clinical intervention for parents dealing with the unique stressors of raising children with ASD: action-oriented shifts and emotion-focused shifts.

Action-oriented shifts. In analyzing the literature, three domains of action-oriented shifts stood out. These domains related to helping parents build their communication skills, renegotiate divisions of labor, and establish sustainable individual and couple boundaries. In particular, training parents in effective communication techniques, especially regarding matters of conflict resolution, was the most prominent action-oriented intervention recommendation found, in part because parents of children with ASD rarely have time to communicate and are often dealing with a great deal of stress (Ramisch, 2012; Saini et al., 2015). As such, clinicians should consider helping parents find ways to engage in healthy conflict. To this end, Gottman (1999) offers several rules for promoting productive couple conflict that clinicians could share with parents who are struggling to communicate successfully with their partners. These rules involve: being concise with one's concerns, complaining to one's partner without blaming one's partner, starting the conversation with something positive to say, making statements that start with the pronoun "I" instead of the pronoun "you," describing the problem without judging one's partner's actions, clearly stating one's needs, showing appreciation for one's partner, and conveying a sense of vulnerability to one's partner by sharing one's primary emotions (e.g., fear, sadness) as opposed to secondary emotions (e.g., anger, annoyance). For times when conversations become too heated, clinicians can also help parents to practice various self-soothing techniques such as taking a 20-minute timeout (including helping parents to set rules for giving and receiving time-outs as well as when they will resume the difficult topic of discussion), deep breathing, self-talk, and finding ways to empathize with their partner's point of view.

The second domain of action-oriented shifts addresses the division of labor between parents. Because role specialization has been found to occur with frequency among these couples (i.e., mothers stay home to caretake their children on the spectrum and fathers are sole breadwinners for the family; Hartley, Mihaila, Otalora-Fadner, & Bussanich, 2014), several studies emphasized that clinicians assess for the degree of role specialization in a couple's relationship and the level of contentment each partner has with his/her specialized role (Hartley et al., 2014; Solomon & Chung, 2012). If one or both partners report being discontented with or stressed out by the division of labor, then clinicians can discuss with couples the perceived problem areas and help them work together to come up with a different division of labor (Hartley et al., 2014; Saini et al., 2015; Solomon & Chung, 2012). Specific areas for clinicians to address with parents regarding their divisions of labor include: housework, childcare responsibilities, and time allotted for rest and relaxation.

A third recommendation for action-oriented intervention with parents caring for children with ASD has to do with individual and relational boundary making. Such boundary making activities relate to helping parents to engage in both self-care and "couple care" (Hock et al., 2012; Ramisch, 2012; Solomon & Chung, 2012). To help foster self-care, clinicians can encourage parents who are married or in committed relationships to take turns taking "me time." This time may come in small or large portions and may occur daily, weekly, or monthly, depending on the family's resources. Examples of "me time" include: a walk alone around the block, a dinner out with friends, or a spa day. When negotiating when and how to take "me time," clinicians should also help couples to take into account each parent's amount of caregiving. Thus, in situations where one parent is the primary caregiver for a child with ASD, the other parent should ensure that the primary caregiver's "me time" takes precedent over his/her own.

To help foster "couple care," clinicians can help parents to think past the restrictions on their time, their finances, and the availability of quality childcare, so that they can get creative in carving out time together. For instance, clinicians may help parents to see that their couple relationship may always include their child with ASD, or that their date nights may look different than other couples' date nights, or that "quality" couple time can come in five-minute increments. Once parents have been able to overcome these barriers, clinicians can help them brainstorm ways to sneak some couple time into their lives. A few ways for parents to still maintain a sense of couplehood when raising a child with ASD include: a couple watching a movie together at home while their child sleeps in the next room (or right next to them), a couple agreeing that they are "out on a date" even if they have their child with them, or a couple being on the lookout for snippets of time they can find together when they are not actively caring for their child with ASD (e.g., engaging in a long embrace while one's child is on the potty).

Emotion-focused shifts. In addition to the action-oriented shifts mentioned above, a number of articles reviewed also suggested interventions for parents targeting their emotional lives. Several of these focused on the need for partners to work together through the various difficult and multifaceted emotions they experienced as a result of caring for children with ASD, such as grief, embarrassment, and shame (Neely et al., 2012; Solomon & Chung, 2012). Specifically, two different studies proffered that emotionally focused therapy (EFT) could be particularly helpful to parents in couple relationships, both in working through their emotional experiences of raising children with ASD and in turning toward (instead of away from) each other during times of stress (Hock et al., 2012; Ramisch, Timm, Hock, & Topor, 2013). Furthermore, Brobst, Clopton, and Hendrick, (2009) noted the importance of partners finding ways to demonstrate respect and gratitude for the work each other is doing on behalf of the family, while Ramisch (2012) highlighted the need to help parents come to accept that their significant others may deal quite differently with the stressors and emotional turmoil that can accompany caring for children on the autism spectrum.

Given these findings, clinicians should consider using various EFT techniques when working with parents of children with ASD. In particular, Johnson (2008) offers several thoughts on how to help foster emotional connection between partners. First, clinicians can help parents to share with one another their more vulnerable feelings (e.g., grief, fear, shame) as related to caring for a child with ASD and how having a child with ASD has impacted their couple relationship (e.g., feeling like ASD has driven a wedge between the couple). In light of these feelings, a clinician may then help the couple to make sense of times they felt disconnected from and hurt by one another, interpreting these attachment injuries through the lens of each partner's ASD-related grief, fear, and shame. After noting how these feelings kept the couple from being able to connect (as each was afraid of being rejected by the other in their bids for support), the clinician may then work with the couple to restructure how they interact when such vulnerable feelings are present (e.g., helping partners to remain present with one another, to be emotionally attuned, to not become reactive). In helping the couple to restructure their interactions, the clinician is specifically looking to help each partner to "soften" with the other. Such softening may be done by helping one or both partners to make a vulnerable request of the other for some level of reassurance or comfort (e.g., "When you come home from work after I have had a hard day with our child, I need you to sit down with me for five minutes to hear me out"). When the partner positively responds to such a request, a more secure attachment is fostered between the partners and each feels more able to make the same or similarly vulnerable requests moving forward.

Recommendations for Individual Intervention

Not all parents raising children with ASD are married, in committed relationships, or have partners who are willing to join them in therapy. Therefore, clinicians must also be cognizant of ways to intervene with parents coming to therapy individually. One key way in which clinicians could help parents presenting individually in therapy would be to assist them in developing their social support networks in order to ease their caregiving burden. To this end, many studies on parents raising children with ASD have pointed out the need for parents to make use of a variety of supports, including groups for parents of children with ASD (Brobst et al., 2009; Neely et al., 2012), personal relationships with other parents raising children on the autism spectrum (Ramisch, 2012), extended family (Saini et al., 2015), respite care (Hock et al., 2012; Ramisch, 2012), and other social services (e.g., case managers and schools social workers; Marciano et al., 2015), to name just a few. As such, clinicians working individually with parents of children with ASD should assess for the level of outside supports parents have and, as needed, help them to consider how they might expand their access to and utilization of both formal (e.g., childcare, support groups, social services) and informal (e.g., extended family, friends, church- and other spiritually-based communities) supports.

In addition, a number of the systemic interventions highlighted in this chapter may also be employed with parents in individual therapy. For example, the recommendations for helping parents make cognitive shifts – psychoeducation and guided discovery – could be utilized in individual therapy without having to make any adaptations. Furthermore, some of the relational shifts mentioned above could also be adapted for individual therapy. For instance, although boundary making related to couple care would not be possible in individual therapy, boundary making as related to self-care and finding "me time" would be. Also, despite the fact that some of the EFT practices noted in the preceding section would require two partners working together in therapy, in individual therapy clinicians could still use principles from EFT to help parents identify their vulnerable feelings, give themselves more grace, and, ultimately, find more adaptive ways to respond to the ASD-related stressors they face.

Other Contextual Considerations

On top of the recommendations for systemic and individual intervention mentioned in this chapter, clinicians can also help parents by offering them other, more environmental, intervention ideas. Namely, as schedule, structure, and routine tend to be very helpful for children with ASD (Solomon & Chung, 2012), clinicians should also help parents to consider how they could provide more of these to their children at home. In this vein, some ideas to offer parents may include: having their children engage in certain activities (e.g., eating, dressing, bathing, resting) at certain pre-determined times of the day, creating a large monthly calendar on which upcoming events, especially those that deviate from the normal flow of family life, are noted for the whole family to see and anticipate, making sure to prep their children well in advance of any upcoming changes to their schedules and routines, and keeping an organized and austere home (so as to not provide too much stimuli for their children). Clinicians should also encourage parents to investigate on their own how other parents of children with ASD have managed issues of schedule, structure, and routine to see if the parents discover any ideas that they would like to use in their own home. Lastly, clinicians could help parents to consider how to mitigate safety concerns with their children by keeping potentially dangerous objects in the home out of reach or by having their children, especially those who frequently elope, wear ID bracelets at all times.

Conclusion

Parents can be some of the most important family members to consult and work with when treating a child living with ASD. Clinicians are advised to thoroughly assess for specific ASD-related challenges and parental coping. Mental health clinicians should also consider the strengths and challenges faced by parents in order to provide treatment that is specific to each family and individual's needs. Regardless of whether the child's parents are married, or separated, clinicians should help them identify support systems and adaptive coping mechanisms.

References

Abbott, A. (2013, September). Love in the time of autism. Retrieved from www.psychologytoday.com/collections/201306/the-truth-about-couples-autistic-children/love-in-the-time-autism.

Baucom, D. H., Epstein, N., LaTaillade, J. J., & Kirby, J. S. (2008). Cognitive behavioral couple therapy. In A. S. Gurman & N. S. Jacobson (Eds.), *Clinical handbook of couple therapy* (4th ed., pp. 31–72). New York, NY: Guilford Press.

Brobst, J. B., Clopton, J. R., & Hendrick, S. S. (2009). Parenting children with autism spectrum disorders: The couple's relationship. *Focus on Autism and Other Developmental Disabilities, 24*, 38–49.

Denzin, N. K., & Lincoln, Y. S. (2005). *Handbook of qualitative research* (3rd ed.). Thousand Oaks, CA: Sage.

Endler, N. S., & Parker, J. D. (1999). *Coping inventory for stressful situations (CISS): Manual.* Toronto, ON, Canada: Multi-Health Systems.

Gottman, J. M. (1999). *The marriage clinic: A scientifically based marital therapy.* New York, NY: W. W. Norton & Company.

Hartley, S. L., Mihaila, I., Otalora-Fadner, H. S., & Bussanich, P. M. (2014). Division of labor in families of children and adolescents with autism spectrum disorder. *Family Relations, 63*, 627–638. doi:10.1111/fare.12093.

Hock, R. M., Timm, T. M., & Ramisch, J. L. (2012). Parenting children with autism spectrum disorders: A crucible for couple relationships. *Child & Family Social Work, 17*, 406–415. doi:10.1111/j.1365-2206.2011.00794.x.

Johnson, J., & Piercy, F. P. (2017). Exploring partner intimacy among couples raising children on the autism spectrum: A grounded theory investigation. *Journal of Marital and Family Therapy, 43*, 644–661. doi:10.1111/jmft.12247.

Johnson, S. M. (2008). Emotionally focused couple therapy. In A. S. Gurman & N. S. Jacobson (Eds.), *Clinical handbook of couple therapy* (4th ed., pp. 107–137). New York, NY: Guilford Press.

Marciano, S. T., Drasgow, E., & Carlson, R. G. (2015). The marital experiences of couples who include a child with autism. *The Family Journal: Counseling and Therapy for Couples and Families, 23*, 132–140. doi:10.1177/1066480714564315.

Neely, J., Amatea, E. S., Echevarria-Doan, S., & Tannen, T. (2012). Working with families living with autism: Potential contributions of marriage and family therapists. *Journal of Marital and Family Therapy, 38*, 211–226. doi:10.1111/j.1752-0606.2011.00265.x.

Ramisch, J. (2012). Marriage and family therapists working with couples who have children with autism. *Journal of Marital and Family Therapy, 38*, 305–316. doi:10.1111/j.1752-0606.2010.00210.x.

Ramisch, J. L., Onaga, E., & Oh, S. M. (2014). Keeping a sound marriage: How couples with children with autism spectrum disorders maintain their marriages. *Journal of Child and Family Studies, 23*, 975–988. doi:10.1007/s10826-013-9753-y.

Ramisch, J. L., Timm, T. M., Hock, R. M., & Topor, J. A. (2013). Experiences delivering a marital intervention for couples with children with autism spectrum disorder. *The American Journal of Family Therapy, 41*, 376–388. doi:10.1080/01926187.2012.713816.

Saini, M., Stoddart, K. P., Gibson, M., Morris, R., Barrett, D., Muskat, B., … Zwaigenbaum, L. (2015). Couple relationships among parents of children and adolescents with Autism Spectrum Disorder: Findings from a scoping review of the literature. *Research in Autism Spectrum Disorders, 17*, 142–157. doi:10.1016/j.rasd.2015.06.014.

Silva, L. M. T., & Schalock, M. (2012). Autism parenting stress index: Initial psychometric evidence. *Journal of Autism and Developmental Disorders, 42*, 566–574. doi:10.1007/s10803-011-1274-1.

Solomon, A. H., & Chung, B. (2012). Understanding autism: How family therapists can support parents of children with autism spectrum disorders. *Family Process, 51*, 250–264. doi:10.1111/j.1545-5300.2012.01399.x.

Spanier, G. B. (1976). Measuring dyadic adjustment: New scales for assessing the quality of marriage and similar dyads. *Journal of Marriage and the Family, 38*, 15–28. doi:10.2307/350547.

6 The Sibling Subsystem

The Effects of Being Raised with an Individual with ASD

Rachael A. Dansby Olufowote, Brie Turns, and Brandon Eddy

Sibling relationships are both one-of-a-kind and formative on children as they grow, and the presence of ASD in a family influences and shapes sibling interactions. The purpose of this chapter is two-fold: first, to explore the literature on sibling relationships and the influence ASD has on them, and second, to highlight the unique experiences of neurotypical siblings being raised with a sibling with ASD. Neurotypical (NT) is a term used to refer to people who are not diagnosed with a developmental disorder, in this case ASD, or one who displays typical neurological development.

The Importance of Sibling Relationships

The sibling relationship is often one of life's enduring relationships (Orsmond & Seltzer, 2007). Most sibling relationships begin during childhood and usually influence each person's development in a variety of ways. For example, siblings influence one another as companions while providing support and nurturance (McHale, Updegraff, & Whiteman, 2012). Siblings can also develop social skills when engaging in disagreements and perspective taking (Dunn, 2007). Additionally, siblings spend a vast majority of their time together. For example, researchers found that typically developing, school-aged children spent more of their non-school time with siblings than with any other playmate or peer (McHale et al., 2012). Sibling relationships are important, also, because they have the potential to affect quality of life in both the here and now and in the future for typically developing siblings and siblings with ASD, especially if parents become unable to be primary caretakers (Beyer, 2009).

Factors That Affect All Sibling Relationships

Research suggests that gender is one factor that influences the development, course, and quality of sibling relationships in families with and without ASD. For example, in one study, neurotypical (NT) girls were more affectionate toward their siblings (Kim, McHale, Osgood, & Crouter, 2006), and in another, older NT brothers were found to be the least involved with their younger siblings (Trevino, 1979). Additionally, positive parent-child relationships are another factor that have been associated with pro-social behavior and positive emotions of NT siblings (Brody, 1998). Outside the local context of one-on-one relationships within the family, the culture, the broader environment, personal interests, and traditions all influence the sibling relationship as well (Beyer, 2009).

Sibling Relationships Throughout the Lifespan

When NT siblings are younger, they may benefit from regular one-on-one time with their parent(s) so they can feel seen, understood, and build a positive bond with their parents (Harris, 2007). In the transition from adolescence to early adulthood, sibling relationships in general often go through noticeable changes (Conger & Little, 2010). For example, general sibling relationships are often affected by life transitions such as graduation from high school, leaving for college, getting married, and having children (Conger & Little, 2010). However, sibling relationships affected by ASD experience life transitions differently (Dansby, Turns, Whiting, & Crane, 2017). For example, in a recent qualitative study, one sibling expressed concern that they would not be able to move away for college because their parents expected they remain close by to help with caretaking. Another individual remarked they chose a career in applied behavioral analysis to work with other kids with ASD because of their own life experience (Dansby et al., 2017). This latter example is one that shows how the sibling subsystem may change from a purely peer level to one of caregiver and child, much like a parent-child relationship would be. In such cases, adult siblings of people with ASD may develop respite needs and require particular help in coping with the challenges of being a sibling caregiver.

Although it is beyond the scope of this chapter to review every type of family structure, we will review the two most common types of sibling dynamics, neurotypical siblings being raised with a single individual with ASD and families raising multiple children with ASD.

Families Raising One Child with ASD

According to previous researchers, there is not one specific experience that encompasses what it is like to be raised with a sibling with ASD; rather, NT siblings report a variety of positive and negative effects of being raised with a sibling with ASD (see Myers & Holl, 2014). Due to the severity levels and various characteristics that may be displayed by an individual with ASD, it has been difficult for researchers to identify one specific "theory" that encompasses all experiences. The general positive effects include close sibling interactions, including NT siblings enjoying their ASD sibling's humor, feeling pride, admiration, and a sense of fulfillment in helping their parents care for their sibling. Negative effects include the impact ASD has on NT siblings' peer relationships, strained relationships with their parents, and the burden of present and future caregiving.

Positive Effects

Close sibling interactions. Research has shown that NT siblings frame their relationships with their ASD siblings in several positive ways. First, some have enjoyed their siblings' humor. For example, in a recent study by Dansby et al. (2017) of siblings of children with ASD, one 22-year-old female sibling framed her ASD brother's behavior positively, saying, "I have come to really enjoy his little quirks and inventive ideas." Furthermore, NT siblings who have a sibling with ASD often experience a relationship that is filled with greater warmth and compassion, and less characterized by conflict when compared with children who only have NT siblings (Kaminsky & Dewey, 2001). Others report experiencing pride in and appreciation for their diagnosed sibling (Angell, Meadan, & Stoner, 2012; Petalas, Hastings, Nash, Reilly, & Dowey, 2012), as well as thinking of their sibling as a close friend (Angell et al., 2012). Finally, some siblings experience enjoyment and a sense of fulfillment in helping their parents with educating and caring for their sibling with ASD.

Personality traits. Having a sibling with ASD has also been related to several positive personality traits found in NT siblings. Examples include empathy and increased patience (Angell et al., 2012; Stalker & Connors, 2004), higher self-concepts (Macks & Reeve, 2007), and an appreciation for the memories they have with their sibling with ASD (Petalas et al., 2012). Interestingly, children who have a sibling with ASD seem to have increased emotional intelligence when it comes to recognizing the emotions of their sibling (Benderix & Sivberg, 2007). Being able to recognize their siblings' emotions can be helpful in calming meltdowns and in providing comfort for their sibling. The ability to recognize emotions in others is a trait that may help the NT sibling throughout his or her life.

Negative Effects

Impact on peer relationships. Unfortunately, the literature on the sibling relationship for those raised with someone with ASD is also fraught with negative experiences. Several studies have documented siblings' challenges with friends and peers (Angell et al., 2012; Dansby, et al., 2017; Hastings, 2003; Ross & Cuskelly, 2006). For example, NT siblings may fear bringing friends over to their house due to their sibling's intense meltdowns or the fear of witnessing frightening or embarrassing behaviors (Dansby et al., 2017). This often limits the NT sibling's social circle and number of close friends they have (Benderix & Sivberg, 2007). As one NT sibling remarked on a Reddit blog post:

> I haven't really been able to spend time with other people my age, because my parents don't want me to leave them with my brothers … I feel like I will just drift away from my friends, because I am not able to keep in contact with them.

Additionally, some NT siblings may experience their peers and friends as lacking understanding of ASD and, subsequently, what their day-to-day life is like, and may be hesitant to introduce outsiders to their families (Dansby et al., 2017).

Strained relationships with parents. Further, it seems many NT siblings may also have more negative than positive experiences when it comes to their relationships with their parents (Dansby et al., 2017). For example, some NT siblings describe feeling forgotten and unloved by their parents. One sibling said in an online forum, "I feel forgotten and unloved. [My parents] are so busy paying attention to him and trying to get him under control that they forget about me ... I am alone" (Dansby et al., 2017). I (R.D.O.) work from an attachment perspective with my clients, and such statements as above are indicative of deep wounds of human connection. Research has shown that unhealed wounds (such as disconnection from parents) can lead to later distress in adult romantic relationships (Hazan & Shaver, 1987). When NT siblings may feel disconnected from the outside world due to the influence of ASD on their peer relationships, the parent-child relationship becomes all the more important. Unfortunately, research suggests many NT siblings are growing up without secure attachment relationships with their parents.

Burden of present and future caregiving choices. Studies demonstrate that NT siblings are also affected by the mountainous task of caring for the child with ASD, and they report often feeling an obligation to help take care of their diagnosed sibling (Angell et al., 2012; Dansby et al., 2017; Hastings, 2003; Ross & Cuskelly, 2006). Sometimes this obligation is overt, as with one sibling from a study who recalled his parents having a conversation with him at age 13 regarding him becoming his sibling's power of attorney in the event something happened to them (Dansby et al., 2017). However, sometimes perceived expectations that NT siblings would be caregivers are unvoiced and assumed (Bagenholm & Gillberg, 1991; Dansby et al., 2017).

Additionally, some children diagnosed with ASD engage in injurious behaviors (Edelson, 2017), and NT siblings may feel obligated to protect others and/ or their sibling from themselves or from potentially dangerous situations. This increased responsibility often leads the NT sibling feeling like their sibling with ASD has become a burden to them (Dansby et al., 2017; Randall & Parker, 1999). Additionally, NT siblings may worry about how their sibling will be cared for in the future, adding complexity to the burden they may feel about whether or not to take part in caregiving (Dansby et al., 2017). For example, in one study, an NT sibling remarked, "I too worry about how difficult it is on my parents and the responsibilities that have been placed on me" (Dansby et al., 2017). Still another wrote about the inner struggle related to moving away or staying close, citing mixed feelings:

> I want to leave here and go far across the country for college, but [I] feel so awful for doing that because it's not [my sibling's] fault and it's not my parents' fault that he was born like this. I feel like I am abandoning my family and my parents, like I will be leaving them all alone.
>
> (Female, age 17)

The sibling relationship produces complex emotions alongside the complex experiences of life, and at times, siblings' complex emotional experiences extend beyond the sibling relationship into broader relationships. One of the most prominent themes we have seen across the literature is that NT siblings often feel alone and isolated, like there are very few people in their world who understand what they're going through (Dansby et al., 2017; Meyer & Holl, 2014).

Families Raising Multiple Children with ASD

The number of families raising multiple children with ASD was previously believed to occur at low rates, ranging between 3 percent to 14 percent (Constantino, Zhang, Frazier, Abbacchi, & Law, 2010; Lauritsen, Pedersen, & Mortensen, 2005). A more recent study found that 18.7 percent of infants with at least one older sibling with ASD also developed ASD later in life (Ozonoff et al., 2011). Because the specific "causes" of ASD are still greatly unknown at this point, many families struggle with the possibility of raising multiple children with ASD. For example, one couple in a recent study stated they were worried about having another child due to their first-born receiving an ASD diagnosis and requiring a great deal of care (Turns, 2017).

Siblings dynamics will likely alter when more than one child is diagnosed with ASD. Unfortunately, there is limited research or resources that have investigated the sibling dynamics between two individuals with ASD diagnoses. Because of the high percentage of infants who develop ASD when one sibling is already diagnosed, we strongly recommend that researchers begin looking at these sibling relationships. It is likely that experiences will change between siblings when both children have ASD. Identifying and understanding these relationships can help therapists assist families during the children's development.

Conclusion

Individuals being raised with siblings with ASD have reported a variety of positive and negative experiences, emotions, and facets of their relationships with siblings with ASD. Because individuals with ASD will not present the same characteristics or severity, it is not surprising that some NT siblings have an easier time than others. Therapists should be mindful of the various experiences, perceptions, and attitudes when working with NT siblings and not assume that everyone's experiences will be the same. In practice, clinicians can work to increase the positive effects and decrease the negative effects of being raised with a person with ASD. For example, the sibling bond can be assessed with a genogram, and if it needs strengthening, the therapist can elicit hobbies or activities that each sibling enjoys and that the family can do together. More practical suggestions for increasing positive effects and decreasing negative effects are discussed in detail in Chapter 7.

58   *Rachael A. Dansby Olufowote et al.*

References

Angell, M. E., Meadan, H., & Stoner, J. B. (2012). Experiences of siblings of individuals with autism spectrum disorders. *Autism Research and Treatment*, 1–11.

Bagenholm, A., & Gillberg, C. (1991). Psychosocial effects on siblings of children with autism and mental retardation: A population-based study. *Journal of Intellectual Disability Research*, 35(4), 291–307.

Benderix, Y., & Sivberg, B. (2007). Siblings' experiences of having a brother or sister with autism and mental retardation: A case study of 14 siblings from five families. *Journal of Pediatric Nursing*, 22(5), 410–418.

Beyer, J. F. (2009). Autism spectrum disorders and sibling relationships: Research and strategies. *Education and Training in Developmental Disabilities*, 44, 444–452.

Brody, G. H. (1998). Sibling relationships' quality, its causes and consequences. *Annual Review Psychology*, 49, 1–24.

Conger, K. J., & Little, W. M. (2010). Sibling relationships during the transition to adulthood. *Child development perspectives*, 4(2), 87–94. doi:10.1111/j.1750-8606.2010.00123.x.

Constantino, J. N., Zhang, Y., Frazier, T., Abbacchi, A. M., & Law, P. (2010). Sibling recurrence and the genetic epidemiology of autism. *American Journal of Psychiatry*, 167(11), 1347–1356.

Dansby, R. A., Turns, B., Whiting, J. B., & Crane, J. (2017). A phenomenological content analysis of online support seeking by siblings of people with autism. *Journal of Family Psychotherapy*. Published online November 28, 2017, 1–20.

Dunn, J. (2007). Siblings and socialization. In J. E. Grusec & P. D. Hastings (Eds.), *Handbook of socialization: Theory and research* (pp. 309–327). New York: Guilford Press.

Edelson, S. M. (2017). Self-injury. *Autism Research Institute*. Retrieved from www.autism.com/symptoms_self-injury.

Harris, S. (2007). Sibling issues. *Autism Society of America*. Retrieved from www.autism-society.org/living-with-autism/family-issues/siblings/.

Hastings, R. P. (2003). Brief report: Behavioral adjustment of siblings of children with autism. *Journal of Autism and Developmental Disorders*, 33(1), 99–104.

Hazan, C., & Shaver, P. (1987). Romantic love conceptualized as an attachment process. *Journal of Personality and Social Psychology*, 52, 511–524. doi:10.1037/0022-3514.52.3.511.

Kaminsky, L., & Dewey, D. (2001). Siblings relationships of children with autism. *Journal of Autism and Developmental Disorders*, 31(4), 399–410.

Kim, J., McHale, S. M., Osgood, D. W., & Crouter, A. C. (2006). Longitudinal course and family correlates of sibling relationships from childhood through adolescence. *Child Development*, 77(6), 1746–61.

Lauritsen, M. B., Pedersen, C. B., & Mortensen, P. B. (2005). Effects of familial risk factors and place of birth on the risk of autism: A nationwide register-based study. *Journal of Child Psychology and Psychiatry*, 46, 963–971.

Macks, R. J., & Reeve, R. E. (2007). The adjustment of non-disabled siblings of children with autism. *Journal of Autism and Developmental Disorders*, 37, 1060–1067.

McHale, S. M., Updegraff, K. A., & Whiteman, S. D. (2012). Sibling relationships and influences in childhood and adolescence. *Journal of Marriage and Family*, 74(5), 913–930.

Myer, D., & Holl, E. (2014). *The sibling survival guide: Indispensable information for brothers and sisters of adults with disabilities*, Bethesda, MD: Woodbine House.

Orsmond, I., & Seltzer, M. (2007). Siblings of individuals with autism spectrum disorders across the life course. *Mental Retardation and Developmental Disabilities Research Reviews*, 13, 315–320.

Ozonoff, S., Young, G. S., Carter, A., Messinger, D., Yirmiya, N., Zwaigenbaum, L. … Stone, W. L. (2011). Recurrence risk for autism spectrum disorders: A baby siblings research consortium study. *Pediatrics, 128*, e1-e8.

Petalas, M. A., Hastings, R. P., Nash, S., Reilly, D., & Dowey, A. (2012). The perceptions and experiences of adolescent siblings who have a brother with autism spectrum disorder. *Journal of Intellectual and Developmental Disability, 37*(4), 303–314.

Randall, P., & Parker, J. (1999). *Supporting the families of children with autism.* New York, NY: John Wiley & Sons Ltd.

Ross, P., & Cuskelly, M. (2006). Adjustment, siblings problems and coping strategies of brothers and sisters of children with autistic spectrum disorder. *Journal of Intellectual and Developmental Disability, 31*(2), 77–86.

Stalker, K., & Connors, C. (2004). Children's perceptions of their disabled siblings: 'She's different but it's normal for us.' *Children and Society, 18*(3), 218–230.

Trevino, F. (1979). Siblings of handicapped children: Identifying those at risk. *Social Casework, 60*(8), 488–493.

Turns, B. A. (2017). *Assessing the effectiveness and experiences of solution-focused brief therapy for couples raising a child with an autism spectrum disorder* (Unpublished doctoral dissertation). Texas Tech University, Lubbock, TX.

7 Providing Resources for Neurotypical Siblings of Children with ASD

Brandon Eddy, Brie Turns, and Rachael A. Dansby Olufowote

As explained in Chapter 6, there are many experiences associated with having a sibling with ASD. This chapter has condensed each of the areas of research presented in Chapter 6 and developed six broad categories that can assist clinicians in their work with siblings. The categories that will be discussed in this chapter include: (a) The importance of sibling relationships; (b) Burden of present and future caregiving choices; (c) Impact on peer relationships; (d) Strained relationship with parents; (e) Increased emotional awareness, and (f) Sense of fulfillment. Each topic discussed will also include suggestions on how to effectively engage NT siblings in therapeutic settings and provides practical tools that families can use at home.

The Importance of Sibling Relationships

The sibling relationship is one of the longest lasting relationships a person will have during his or her lifetime (Orsmond & Seltzer, 2007). Siblings can obtain a great deal of joy from one another, specifically in sharing successes together (Angell, Meadan, & Stoner, 2012). Although some NT siblings often report feelings of satisfaction and pride when their sibling achieves something (Dansby, Turns, Whiting, & Crane, 2017), some siblings may lack this connection. It is important for clinicians to assess the level of closeness that siblings experience with one another and discuss if and how the siblings would like to strengthen that bond.

Suggestions for Clinicians and Families

One suggestion for assessing the level of closeness siblings experience with one another is to have each sibling complete a socially constructed genogram (Milewski-Hertlein, 2001). This activity will allow each child to tangibly lay out individuals in their lives that he or she feels the closest to. Identifying the level of closeness will provide the clinician with an overall idea of how connected the siblings feel to each other. If the connection is distant, the clinician can discuss how the relationship can be enhanced. If the siblings report a level of closeness that is satisfactory, the clinician can discuss how the siblings can maintain their relationship.

During the session, the clinician can also help elicit activities or hobbies that each sibling enjoys participating in. There are a variety of children's toys, such as Legos, that are appropriate for both play and building fine motor skills. Dance and yoga are two alternate activities that can be enjoyable for siblings and have also been used in physical therapy for children with ASD (Hildebrandt, Koch, & Fuchs, 2016; Rosenblatt et al., 2011). These activities may enhance the sibling bond, while providing physical benefits as well. Older siblings may enjoy going on outings together, such as coffee or tea dates.

Children with ASD often participate in a token system or behavioral chart (Fiske et al., 2015), which reward children for engaging in positive behaviors. This is an experience that NT siblings can participate in with their sibling with ASD. Siblings can work together, encourage each other, and bond over successes in completing a behavioral chart (see Turns, Eddy, & Smock Jordan, 2016 for example). Behaviors may include personal hygiene or social skills, team related tasks, or any age-appropriate tasks or behaviors.

Other activities that may help siblings bond are aquatic activities, including swimming. Swimming or aquatic therapy has been shown to improve motor skills, confidence, and athletic ability for children with ASD (Pan, 2011). In addition, children with ASD who participated in aquatic activities had better relationships with their NT sibling (Pan, 2011). Aquatic activities have the potential to help children physically, as well as increasing sibling bonds.

Burden of Present and Future Caregiving Choices

As shown in Chapter 6, the burden of present and future caregiving choices is a prominent theme found among NT siblings. Within this theme are two main concepts, namely fear and responsibility. Children who have a sibling with ASD often experience fear or distress due to behaviors exhibited by their sibling (Benderix & Sivberg, 2007). These fears can cause them to isolate, fear for their sibling's future, or fear for their own goals and dreams (Benderix & Sivberg, 2007). In addition to fear, NT siblings also feel the extra burden of responsibility in helping their sibling with everyday activities in order to remove stress from their parents. The following are suggestions for clinicians to help calm the fears of NT siblings and to ease the burden of responsibility many NT siblings may experience.

Suggestions for Clinicians and Families

One task we recommend clinicians to engage in is providing psychoeducation to the NT sibling and other family members in order to help them understand the behaviors of their sibling. Researchers have found that numerous siblings have not been educated about their sibling's diagnosis, including the name of it and the presenting behaviors (Glasberg, 2000). Many children may not understand why their sibling is engaging in certain behaviors and providing an understanding of why these behaviors or characteristics occur can help the sibling feel safer. Explaining to the NT sibling that although the behaviors, such as self-stimulation, may seem scary or unknown, they are often common for children with ASD. Normalizing the behaviors may also help NT siblings feel less fear and unease over the behaviors.

Some children with ASD may also engage in physical violence with other family members. As children age and grow physically larger than their parents, NT siblings may also fear for their and their family members' physical safety. A mental health clinician should assess the intensity of physical violence in the home and help family members develop a safety plan if situations become violent. For example, one child that I (B.T.) worked with would throw coffee cups at other family members during meltdowns. The family discussed ways to keep breakable items away from the child and slowly learned how to recognize when the child would reach this "point-of-no-return" in order to prevent future violent situations.

It is also important to discuss specific fears NT siblings may have about their future or their sibling's future. Many NT siblings fear that they will be responsible for caring for their siblings throughout the remainder of their lives or that their siblings have a bleak future. It is vital that clinicians provide space for NT siblings to discuss their fears and that these fears be validated by the clinician and the parents. Depending on the age and personality of the NT sibling, clinicians may need to engage in experiential or play activities to help the NT sibling feel comfortable in expressing his or her fears and other feelings. For example, using sand tray activities to have NT siblings "create their future world" can help clinicians identify themes and fears that children have regarding their and their siblings' futures. It can also be powerful for parents to view their NT child's sand tray activity to understand the needs of their child.

Similar to how clinicians can engage siblings in discussions about their fears and responsibilities, parents can do the same at home. Parents should attempt to create an open and empathetic dialog between themselves and their NT children. NT siblings have the tendency to feel obligated to take on extra responsibilities at home, including caring for their siblings. Parents should be aware of the amount of work and responsibility they place on the NT sibling. Parents can learn to ask about the amount of contribution the NT sibling would like to engage in with their sibling. Then, the family can discuss what those contributions would look like in the home. This activity will not only allow NT siblings to have a voice in the responsibility of their sibling, but also allow the family to engage in a dialog about helping the child with ASD.

Impact on Peer Relationships

Another prominent theme clinicians should be aware of is the social life of NT siblings. Children with ASD often rely on their siblings to meet their social needs more than children without ASD (Patalas, Hastings, Nash, & Duff, 2015). This increased reliance for social support can be emotionally taxing for

NT siblings and may leave them with minimal time to satisfy their own social needs. Since peer relationships can be one of the most important relationships in a child's development, clinicians should assess the quality of time NT siblings are spending with peers.

Suggestions for Clinicians and Families

When working with NT siblings, a clinician should assess the child's level of satisfaction with his or her social life, including the activities they participate in and how much time is spent with peers. Some NT siblings may be hesitant to invite friends into their home due to their siblings' behaviors or developmental delays. This may embarrass NT siblings or leave their friends with a general unease about spending time in the home. If NT siblings would like to have friends come over, clinicians should have a conversation with the sibling and parents to discuss how the children can enjoy time without being interrupted by the child with ASD. Clinicians can also encourage parents to connect with the parents of their children's' friends to discuss any particular situations regarding their child with special needs.

Clinicians should help guide parents in assessing their current situation and what can be done to aid the enhancement of their NT children's social life. For example, NT siblings might complain that their brother or sister does not "leave them alone" when they are playing with friends. The intrusion can cause siblings to become frustrated and avoid inviting friends over to their home. Depending on the age of the sibling, parents can have the NT siblings create a physical sign to place on their doors to indicate to the child with ASD that the sibling would like to be left alone.

Although some NT children may have little trouble bringing friends to their home, others may prefer to spend time at their friends' homes instead. Parents are advised to empathize with their children's preferences and provide them with options for spending quality time with friends without possible interruption from their sibling with ASD.

Strained Relationship with Parents

One of the most commonly reported challenges that can strain the parent-child relationship for NT siblings is a lack of quality time with their parents. Parents often spend a disproportionate amount of time providing for the needs of their child with ASD (Myers, Mackintosh, & Goin-Kochel, 2009). As a result, NT children often feel neglected and unimportant when compared to their sibling with ASD (Chan & Goh, 2014). Clinicians should understand the massive amount of time and resources it can take to raise a child with ASD. It may be helpful to adopt the worldview that most parents are good parents who are trying their best. While empathizing the potential constraints that these families may face, clinicians can offer suggestions for how to increase the connection between NT children and their parents.

Suggestions for Clinicians and Families

The first suggestion for mental health clinicians is to invite NT siblings to session, regardless of whether the presenting problem includes the NT child. Oftentimes, only the child with ASD and/or parents are included in treatment. This can unintentionally reinforce the idea that the needs of NT children are secondary. Including NT siblings will send the message that their needs are important and that they have something valuable to contribute to therapy. It is important for clinicians to not focus solely on the needs of the child with ASD, but the needs of each family member. During sessions, clinicians can attempt to structure sessions in which the NT child and parents have separate time together to discuss their thoughts and feelings.

Although parents must meet the demands of their child with ASD, they must also find occasions to engage in quality time with their NT children. Parents may need to take turns in order to spend one-on-one time with each of their children. Clinicians can encourage parents to create a list of "small dates" that they can take each of their children on. For example, grabbing ice cream, a walk around the park, or a quick trip to run errands can all be turned into quality dates with each of the children. It is not necessarily the activity that is of importance; it is the time spent one-on-one that will enhance the parent-child relationship. Even 5–10 minutes of alone time between parent and NT children can make a big difference.

Another option is for parents to investigate activities in which childcare is available for the child with ASD. For example, churches often hold events and activities that include childcare. Local autism organizations may also hold events for the child with ASD, which can provide time for the parent and NT child to engage in an activity while the other child attends an event. Additionally, depending upon the age of the child, a unique bedtime routine for the NT child can enhance their relationship with their parents. For example, being read a bedtime story or engaging in a ten-minute conversation about the child's day, after the child with ASD has gone to bed, can increase the time spent with parents.

Increased Emotional Awareness

NT children are particularly attuned to their sibling's feelings (Benderix & Sivberg, 2007). Meaning, they are acutely aware of how and what their sibling is feeling and experiencing. This can be useful in recognizing the emotions of others and potentially useful in recognizing one's own emotions. Additionally, emotional intelligence has been linked to several positive outcomes for children, both personally and interpersonally (Gottman, 2011). For example, children with higher emotional intelligence tend to get along with others and can more easily adjust to change. Negatively, enhanced emotional attunement of NT siblings toward their siblings with ASD might become an issue if parents over-rely on NT children to function emotionally for the child with ASD.

Suggestions for Clinicians and Families

During treatment, the clinicians and family can work together in recognizing the emotions of each member of the family system. A clinician may use a variety of experiential activities to help family members recognize and name their emotions and then address how to properly express them. If parents are over-relying on their NT children to understand or work with their child with ASD, clinicians should gently reflect this behavior back to parents and collaborate with them on ways to avoid asking their NT children to emotionally over function.

Parents can help NT children express themselves by setting aside time to talk with their child each day. Dinnertime may be an ideal time for this as many families eat the dinnertime meal together. Parents may ask each child about different emotions they felt throughout the day and then process those with their child. Parents may then share a time in which they felt that emotion and how they responded. This dialog could promote emotional closeness within the family while teaching each family member to recognize and validate each other's emotions.

Sense of Fulfillment

Research shows that many NT siblings feel a sense of fulfillment in working alongside their parents to help their sibling(s) with ASD. It can feel rewarding and give NT siblings a sense of purpose and accomplishment when they see their siblings with ASD do well in life. In fact, some siblings feel so passionate about helping those with ASD that they enter the helping professions via psychotherapy, applied behavioral analysis, or other similar roles in healthcare.

Suggestions for Clinicians and Families

Our suggestion for treatment is if NT siblings feel a sense of fulfillment in helping their sibling with ASD, clinicians should encourage NT siblings to continue cultivating and investing in their sibling relationship. On the other hand, if the NT sibling is feeling burdened by the responsibilities for caregiving that may have been placed on them, clinicians can explore these feelings with siblings and find ways to help make the sibling relationship one that is purposeful and fulfilling.

At home, parents should encourage sibling bonding especially as the siblings age. If NT siblings have an interest in working with ASD, in a professional capacity, parents can support these goals by encouraging their children to attend colleges or professional degree programs that will equip the individual for their desired profession. Even if the NT sibling does not wish to work professionally in a career related to ASD or special needs, they still need the support of their parents. The most important thing to remember is that parents need to have open and honest discussions with NT children about the role they wish or do not wish to have with their siblings. It is important that NT siblings do not miss out on their hopes and dreams due to parents being overly involved with their sibling.

Conclusion

While considering the vast amount of research investigating the sibling relationship, this chapter identified six main areas that clinicians will likely observe during treatment. Each of these areas should be assessed by the clinician. Although this chapter provided a few recommendations for clinicians to adhere to in and out of session, clinicians should continue to think of additional resources and suggestions that could be helpful for the family. Because the presentation of ASD will alter across all individuals, no two families present exactly the same. The suggestions provided should not be used as a cookie-cutter treatment process, but rather a starting point for helping clinicians create a unique treatment plan for families.

References

Angell, M. E., Meadan, H., & Stoner, J. B. (2012). Experiences of siblings of individuals with autism spectrum disorders. *Autism Research and Treatment, 2012*, 1–11.

Benderix, Y., & Sivberg, B. (2007). Siblings' experiences of having a brother or sister with autism and mental retardation: A case study of 14 siblings from five families. *Journal of Pediatric Nursing, 22*(5), 410–418.

Chan, G. W. L., & Goh, C. L. G. (2014). "My parents told us that they will always treat my brother differently because he is autistic" – Are siblings of autistic children the forgotten ones? *Journal of Social Work Practice: Psychotherapeutic Approaches in Health, Welfare and the Community, 28*(2), 155–171.

Dansby, R. A., Turns, B., Whiting, J. B., & Crane, J. (2017). A phenomenological content analysis of online support seeking by siblings of people with autism. *Journal of Family Psychotherapy.* Published online November 28, 2017, 1–20.

Fiske, K. E., Isenhower, R. W., Bamond, M. J., Delmolino, L., Sloman, K. N., & LaRue, R. H. (2015). Assessing the value of token reinforcement for individuals with autism. *Journal of Applied Behavioral Analysis, 48*(2), 448–453.

Glasberg, B. (2000). The development of siblings' understanding of autism spectrum disorders. *Journal of Autism and Developmental Disorders, 30*(2), 143–156.

Gottman, J. (2011). *Raising an emotionally intelligent child.* Simon and Schuster.

Hildebrandt, M. K., Koch, S. C., & Fuchs, T. (2016). "We dance and find each other": Effects of dance/movement therapy on negative symptoms in autism spectrum disorder. *Behavioral Sciences, 6*(24), 1–17.

Milewski-Hertlein, K. A. (2001). The use of a socially constructed genogram in clinical practice. *The American Journal of Family Therapy, 29*, 23–38.

Myers, B. J., Mackintosh, V. H., & Goin-Kochel, R. P. (2009). "My greatest joy and my greatest heartache": Parents' own words on how having a child in the autism spectrum has affected their lives and their families' lives. *Research in Autism Spectrum Disorders, 3*(3), 670–684.

Orsmond, I., & Seltzer, M. (2007). Siblings of individuals with autism spectrum disorders across the life course. *Mental Retardation and Developmental Disabilities Research Reviews, 13*, 315–320.

Pan, C. Y. (2011). The efficacy of an aquatic program on physical fitness and aquatic skills in children with and without autism spectrum disorders. *Research in Autism Spectrum Disorders, 5*(1), 657–665.

Patalas, M. A., Hastings, R. P., Nash, S., & Duff, S. (2015). Typicality and subtle difference in sibling relationships: Experiences of adolescents with autism. *Journal of Child and Family Studies*, 24(1), 38-49. doi:10.1007/210826-013-9811-5.

Rosenblatt, L. E., Gorantla, S., Torres, J. A., Yarmush, R. S., Rao, S., Park, E. R., ... Levine, J. B. (2011). Relaxation response-based yoga improves functioning in young children with autism: A pilot study. *The Journal of Alternative and Complementary Medicine*, 17(11), 1029–1035.

Turns, B., Eddy, B. P., & Smock Jordan, S. (2016). Working with siblings of children with autism: A solution-focused approach. *Australian and New Zealand Journal of Family Therapy*, 37(4), 558–571.

8 Autism and Society

How ASD Influences the Extended Family and Society

Jocelyn Bessette Gorlin

Because families are nestled within extended families and society, when children are diagnosed with ASD it affects much more than the nuclear family. This is keeping within an ecological family framework that conceptualizes a child like a Russian doll, which is nested within the family and society in a reciprocal relationship (Bronfenbrenner, 1979; Hook & Paolucci, 1970). This chapter reviews the relationship between the child diagnosed with ASD and those outside the immediate family. Specific questions include (a) How does autism impact extended family members? and (b) How does autism affect society including the general public, friends, and school personnel?

Extended Family Members of a Child with ASD

Few research studies directly assess the experience of extended family members of a child with ASD. In fact, literature reviews that focus on families of children with ASD reveal that those outside the nuclear family, such as grandparents, aunts/uncles, and friends, are rarely included in the research (Davis & Gavidia-Payne, 2009; Gardiner & Iarocci, 2015; Gorlin, 2015). In most studies, the mother is usually the primary participant of the study (Bultas & Pohlman, 2014; Lutz, Patterson, & Klein, 2012). Though some fathers participate in studies, they often represent a small fraction of the participants (Hoogsteen & Woodgate, 2013; Schaaf, Toth-Cohen, Johnson, Outten, & Benevides, 2011).

There is some information about the extended family of a child with ASD that can be highlighted from the existing studies. First, there are overall conflicting accounts about the supportive roles of the extended family when a child has ASD. Among many families of children with ASD, there are reports of a high level of satisfaction of relationships within the immediate family (Brown, Hong, Shearer, Wang, & Wang, 2010; Rillotta, Kirby, Shearer & Nettelbeck, 2012), but low satisfaction with the support from individuals outside the nuclear family, such as extended family and friends.

Unsurprisingly, some parents of children with ASD have reported that the support from extended family members has been more important than the support from friends (Davis & Gavidia-Payne, 2009). In a study that specifically included those outside the nuclear family, the extended family was seen as an important lifeline for those raising a child with more severe ASD (Gorlin, Peden McAlpine, Garwick, & Wieling, 2016). Unfortunately, some families express feeling isolated from their extended families (Bilgin & Kucuk, 2010; Bultas & Pohlman, 2014; Safe, Joosten, & Molineux, 2012). For example, extended family members occasionally help the family of a child with ASD financially, but are not emotionally supportive (Bilgin & Kucuk, 2010). Many parents describe feeling marginalized from extended family members who do not appear to fully understand ASD and its challenges (Bultas and Pohlman, 2014; Safe et al., 2012).

Several nuclear families formed "hybrid families" that included extended family and friends (Gorlin et al., 2016). They often identified extended family members such as grandparents and aunts as "family" and depended on them a great deal, not only for direct care but emotional support. This occurred not only in one-parent households, but also when there were two parents caring for the child with autism. In addition, usually grandparents – specifically grandmothers – have been identified as the extended family member that most often helps the parents raise a child with ASD, but others such as aunts and grandfathers also have been identified. The elder's role appears to not only give physical assistance, but also provide emotional support for the parents (Gorlin et al., 2016).

Parents have identified the variety of ways the extended family help such as cooking, cleaning, and especially with caring for the child so that the parents can run errands. Extended family members sometimes take care of the child for short periods of time, so the parent can participate in exercise or take a mental health break. Some grandparents describe recognizing that they need to support the parents so the mother and father can have the strength to care for their child. Some grandparents take on the responsibility of planning for the future of the child with ASD when the grandparents will no longer be living (Gorlin, 2015; Gorlin et al., 2016).

Extended family members are often adamant that the care extended family provides for the child is qualitatively different than the care that is provided by someone outside the family. For example, an aunt stated that her role is to teach the child to love and this is a skill only she possesses as an aunt. She said: "They [the children with ASD] learn to love … but you don't know how to tell somebody else [outside the family] how to do it" (Gorlin, 2015, p. 99). This perception of having a unique role in caring for the child is also evident in a comment by a grandmother who said:

I won't say I get 100% response, but for the most part I can do it. We'll be sitting here, and if he's eating lunch or something, I'll sing to him [the child with ASD] a little bit. I always try to talk to him because I just think that it's got to be important for him to hear me, and I do believe that that's one of the things I am. I am Grandma!

(Gorlin, 2015, p. 99)

Part of the extended relative's unique role seems to be based on the concept that if a relative is older, that individual is wiser and can accept people unconditionally. This includes accepting the child with ASD wholly, a refreshing concept that is often appreciated by the parents. As one grandmother remarked in describing her relationship to her grandson:

> So her [the mom's] goals for him and frustration, I share them, but I have learned in the frustration. He's my darling. There's no shame in my game. I always say I only got one little egg and it's cracked … I love it!
>
> (Gorlin et al., 2016, p. 593)

In addition, extended family members often work tirelessly with the nuclear family instituting positive behavior therapy to try to teach the child forms of social interaction such as shaking hands or hugging when appropriate. For example, one grandmother wept as she explained that her grandson with autism, who was now 13, had not yet significantly communicated with her daughter. She said: "No, he doesn't say 'Mom.' It breaks my heart. If he would only say 'Mom,' I would be so happy for [her daughter], but he doesn't" (Gorlin et al., 2016, p. 588).

Society and the Child with ASD

The General Public

Similar to research on extended family members, there is limited research that directly assesses the experience of those outside the immediate family when a child has ASD. Many families report that the general public holds a belief or stereotype that ASD is a mild and somewhat magical condition. This may be due to the fact that the ASD diagnosis became familiar to the public due to popular movies such as *The Rain Man*. In this movie, the protagonist has an ASD diagnosis and is extremely intelligent. These types of images can be unhelpful due to the stereotypes that is portrayed about individuals with ASD. One mother states:

> TV has created this unrealistic, weird expectation of kids that are autistic … I'm like, "He has autism; he's not magic." … I get this question all the time: "What's his special thing?" And I'm like, "What do you mean?" Because they saw *Rain Man*, and they think everybody's a savant.… Or they saw *Touch* … and that was worse, because that kid was like super, super low-function on some things, but then was so smart and mystical on all these other things. I'm like, "He's a 7-year-old. All he does is bug me for popsicles and cookies."
>
> (Gorlin, 2015, p. 64)

The public also generally holds beliefs or stereotypes that disabilities are physical, such as a person needing a wheelchair. Autism, however, is often "invisible," and not readily apparent until the child demonstrates atypical behavior, which is often misinterpreted as undisciplined, poor behavior. One mother notes the difference in public opinion when her child with ASD sometimes appears in a department store in a wheelchair. The mother sometimes uses a wheelchair to maneuver him through the store safely when they shop and finds, "People seem to be nicer to him when he's in a wheelchair, because it's like the wheelchair carries the connotation of disability" (Gorlin, 2015, p. 65).

In general, the public is more likely to accept poor behavior from a child who has a visible disability versus one that is invisible (Bristol, 1984; Farrugia, 2009; Hoogsteen & Woodgate; Lutz et al., 2012; Safe et al., 2012). To this end, some families discuss that the public cannot understand that their child's behavior could be related to a severe disability and so the child's behaviors such as meltdowns or crying are interpreted as lack of parental control and "bad parenting." One family member stated:

> The frustrating thing about autism is that it's invisible, so I've heard more than once, "Well, he doesn't look like he's disabled." Would you like me to show you his certificate of disability? Or what can I do to prove it to you?
> (Gorlin, 2015, pp. 64–65)

Families raising a child with ASD often experience stigma and feel like a "bad parent" because of the child's behavior in public (Lutz et al., 2012; Safe et al., 2012). Educating the public about their child's diagnosis often helps the family reduce stigma and negative responses from extended family members and the general public (Farrugia, 2009; Hoogsteen & Woodgate, 2013). The need to constantly give excuses for a child's behavior, however, can be tiring for the family and they may feel uncomfortable making excuses for their child, highlighting the child's shortcomings which they would rather their child not hear (Gorlin, 2015).

Families raising a child with autism can recount the numerous times they encounter sneers and stares from others who assume that the child's behavior is a reflection of bad parenting practices. Many parents recall being publicly rebuked by department store staff because their child was having a meltdown. An example is a mother who describes her experience in a department store when her daughter with severe autism had a meltdown. Note that the grocery store employee calls the young girl "him" and "that."

> [They say] "What the hell is wrong with [the child]?" Things like that, or, "Get it under control; get him out of here! Why do you bring that in public?".... The loud speaker [is turned on at the store and they say] "What's going on?" and "Maybe if you can't get this under control you should leave!" We have left. Sometimes we haven't when you have a whole cart of groceries, and you're like okay, I know what's happened in the past, I just need to leave now.
> (Gorlin et al., 2016, p. 591)

Some families verbalize that they want assistance from the public, but some want to be left to deal with the situation alone. Most say they wish that the public would give them positive reinforcement and ask how they could help rather than give suggestions about how parenting should be done.

In addition, families discuss the challenges of having a child with ASD who sometimes manifests aggression to people in public. This results in the family being watchful of the child and fearful that the child might hurt someone in public. The result of these interactions with the public is socially isolating for many families as they raise a child with ASD. Many families describe isolation from those outside the home who do not understand the child's behaviors (Gorlin et al., 2016; Phelps, Hodgson, McCammon, & Lamson, 2009; Luong, Yoder, & Canham, 2009). Some families describe specifically avoiding public situations that are uncomfortable for the child and family (Gorlin et al., 2016; Larson, 2010; Schaaf et al., 2011).

Family Friends

As families raise a child with ASD some parents embrace friends as family. An example is one mother who formed a national "underground phone network" to help other mothers raising a child with autism. She also welcomes some friends who helped with her child with autism as "sisters." She said, "There's not a blood tie, but there's something that's just as strong, if not stronger, here" (Gorlin et al., 2016, p. 592). The friendships may be stronger if the friends are also raising a child with autism. There is ease with these particular families because parents do not need to explain their child's "bad behavior."

On the other hand, there is often a feeling of isolation from friends. Families discuss the simple logistical challenge of meeting with friends because their schedules were so busy, leaving little free time. It is also often difficult to bring their children to other peoples' homes because of the child's behaviors and the need to be vigilant about the child's safety in an unfamiliar space. Here is an example of one mother who discusses the challenges she and her husband encounter when trying to meet with family friends. She said:

> We've tried to go eat with other people for dinner. They invite us for dinner; we don't get a whole lot of repeat come back…. Just having friends over, it's difficult, sometimes. We have to wait until the kids are asleep and then we can invite friends over, but then their kids are tired and so then they can't come over…. Some people do that [have friends over] for double dates and stuff, but we're not doing it to have fun; we're doing it because we can't come over and play cards. We'd love to come over and play cards….
>
> (Gorlin, 2015, p. 91)

School

School is another area in the societal realm that can result in feelings of isolation for families raising a child with ASD. Though there are several examples of positive experiences at school, specifically in the early-intervention programs that often lead to diagnosis, there is also the overwhelming theme of isolation at school experienced by families.

A child with ASD may be separated from other neurotypical children, and there are often low academic expectations of families' children with ASD at school. Several families report that their child is often not included in the class-room like other children. For example, not having an orientation to the school like other students, not being included in special holiday activities like parades, and let out to wander the halls so they do not disrupt classmates. This may result in the family feeling ostracized from the school community in general. The irony is that separating the child with autism from the other school chil-dren robs not only the child with ASD of a class experience, but it robs other classmates of the opportunity to learn about disabilities and compassion (Gorlin, 2015).

Families often report frequent confrontations with school personnel, which may lead to the child being "kicked out" of school. One mother describes an experience when her child was "kicked out" of her public elementary school. She recounts:

> That's when the principal came down that day and told me, and I quote, "Get the hell out of my school! I'm going to go get [your child]." I said, "Don't you dare go get [my child], I will get [my child]!" And then we never went back.
>
> (Gorlin et al., 2016, p. 591)

Whatever the reason for these confrontations with the school, the families ulti-mately often feel alienated and isolated from the school community, which is typically the hub of a child and family's life.

Advice for Clinicians Assisting Families to Deal with Extended Family and Society

While considering the research above, mental health clinicians should consider the following suggestions. First, clinicians should acknowledge that families raising children with ASD often do not live under one roof. Ask the parents of the child who they consider to be part of the family and who helps care for the child. In exploring who helps to care for the child with ASD, help the parents identify the unique elements of each relationship and how these relationships can be fostered. It might additionally be nice to have those who help care for the child identify and write about what makes their roles and contribution unique. Because some extended family members do not understand ASD it might be wise to encourage parents to explain the nature of their child and the physical, emotional, and financial challenges inherent in raising their child. It is often helpful to take a positive approach and explain why their child is unique and special.

Clinicians should also support families as they deal with public misconceptions, not only concerning ASD severity, but the invisible nature of ASD. Clinicians can prepare parents for reactions they may encounter from the public in the event of a meltdown in a grocery store and have a plan in place. Explore with parents how they usually deal with adversity, such as do they want to stay and explain the situation or would they rather leave?

Parents raising a child with ASD often feel isolation from extended family, the public, friends, and school. Explore these feelings and confirm that it is a common emotion, one that may unfortunately foster more isolation, but encourage connections as a better choice. Clinicians can discuss the role of friends in the lives of families raising a child with ASD. It may also be beneficial to review the potential challenges of building friendships in light of time constraints and the child's potential behaviors, yet discuss how these relationships can be beneficial particularly with friends who are also raising a child with ASD. Technology affords world-wide virtual connections that may lessen the feelings of isolation.

Finally, school and work life is an integral part of a family's life. Explore the child's school and parents' work experiences with the family and provide anticipatory guidance concerning what challenges the family may encounter. Clinicians can work closely with the school healthcare professionals and family in providing the best education possible, which supports the individual needs of the child.

Conclusion

Research on the families of children with ASD rarely includes those outside the immediate family, yet they are often considered integral family members. Within the research, some families experience isolation from extended family members who misunderstand ASD and the subsequent daily challenges. On the other hand, some find extended family a lifeline in caring for the child with ASD. When working with families, mental health clinicians are encouraged to gather information about the family's support system and how the family is affected by the general public and their child's school.

References

Bilgin, H., & Kucuk, L. (2010). Raising an autistic child: Perspectives from Turkish mothers. *Journal of Child and Adolescent Psychiatric Nursing, 23*(2), 92–99.

Bristol, M. (1984). Family resources and successful adaptation to autistic children. In E. Schopler & G. B. Mesibov (Eds.), *The effects of autism on the family* (pp. 289–310). New York, NY: Plenum Press.

Bronfenbrenner, U. (1979). *The ecology of human development: Experiments by nature and design.* Cambridge Massachusetts: Harvard University Press.

Brown, R. I., Hong, K., Shearer, J., Wang, M., & Wang, S. (2010). Family quality of life in several countries: Results and discussion of satisfaction in families where there is a child with a disability. In R. Kober (Ed.), *Enhancing the quality of life of people with intellectual disabilities: From theory to practice* (pp. 377–398). Dordrecht, The Netherlands: Springer.

Bultas, M., & Pohlman, S. (2014). Silver linings. *Journal of Pediatric Nursing, 29*(6), 596–605.

Davis, K., & Gavidia-Payne, S. (2009). The impact of child, family, and professional support characteristics on the quality of life in families of young children with disabilities. *Journal of Intellectual and Developmental Disabilities, 34*(2), 153–162.

Farrugia, D. (2009). Exploring stigma: Medical knowledge and the stigmatization of parents of children diagnosed with autism spectrum disorder. *Sociology of Health and Illness, 31*(7), 1011–1027. doi:10.1111/j.1467-9566.2009.01174.x.

Gardiner, E., & Iarocci, G. (2015). Family quality of life and ASD: The role of child adaptive functioning and behavior problems. *Autism Research, 8*(2), 199–213.

Gorlin, J. B. (2015). Severe childhood autism: The family lived experience (unpublished dissertation). University of Minnesota School of Nursing, Minneapolis, MN.

Gorlin, J. B., Peden McAlpine, C., Garwick, A., & Wieling, E. (2016). Severe childhood autism: The family lived experience. *Journal of Pediatric Nursing, 31*(6), 580–597. (December 2016).

Hoogsteen, L., & Woodgate, R. (2013). The lived experience of parenting a child with autism in a rural area: Making the invisible, visible. *Pediatric Nursing, 39*(5), 233–237.

Hook, N., & Paolucci, B. (1970). The family as an ecosystem. *Journal of Home Economics, 62,* 315–318.

Larson, E. (2010). Ever vigilant: Maternal support of participation in daily life for boys with autism. *Physical and Occupational Therapy in Pediatrics, 30*(1), 16–27.

Luong, J., Yoder, M., & Canham, D. (2009). Southeast Asian parents raising a child with autism: A qualitative investigation of coping styles. *The Journal of School Nursing, 25*(3), 222–229. doi:10.1177/1059840509334365.

Lutz, H. R., Patterson, B. J., & Klein, J. (2012). Coping with autism: A journey toward adaptation. *Journal of Pediatric Nursing, 27*(3), 206–213.

Phelps, K., Hodgson, J., McCammon, S., & Lamson, A. (2009). Caring for an individual with autism disorder: A qualitative analysis. *Journal of Intellectual and Developmental Disability, 34*(10), 27–35. doi:10.1080/13668250802690930.

Rillotta, F., Kirby, N., Shearer, J., & Nettelbeck, T. (2012). Family quality of life of Australian families with a member with an intellectual/developmental disability. *Journal of Intellectual Disability Research, 56*(1), 71–86.

Safe, A., Joosten, A., & Molineux, M. (2012). The experiences of mothers of children with autism: Managing multiple roles. *Journal of Intellectual and Developmental Disabilities, 37*(4), 294–302. doi:10.3109/13668250.2012.736644.

Schaaf, R., C., Toth-Cohen, S., Johnson, S. L., Outten, G., & Benevides, T. (2011). The everyday routines of families of children with autism: Examining the impact of sensory processing difficulties on the family. *Autism, 15*(3), 373–389.

Part III
Applying Systemic Theories

9 The Use of Solution-Focused Brief Therapy with Families

Benjamin Finlayson, Brie Turns, and Sara Smock Jordan

Solution-focused brief therapy (SFBT; de Shazer, 1985, 1988; de Shazer, Dolan, & Korman, 2007) is a systemic approach to treating individuals, couples, and families. SFBT focuses on the co-constructive process between therapists and clients and emphasizes solution building, client resources, exceptions to problems, and strengths. Solution-focused therapy then concentrates on how all of these elements can lead to a desired future (de Shazer et al., 2007). SFBT views therapy as an egalitarian relationship in which the therapist is the expert on asking questions and the client is the expert on how those questions relate to his or her life experiences (De Jong & Berg, 2013). This chapter describes how SFBT is well-suited to helping families affected by ASD.

Assumptions of SFBT

As the name indicates, SFBT therapists guide clients to focus on solutions rather than problems. Since the meaning of a problem can never fully be understood, SFBT therapists assume it is more beneficial to discuss the solution, or preferred future (De Jong & Berg, 2013). For example, rather than discuss the details of when a child with ASD struggles with engaging with peers, a solution-focused therapist would be more curious about times the child uses preferred social skills. The role of the therapist is to create opportunities through dialog in which clients are able to find their own solutions (de Shazer et al., 2007).

Solution-focused therapists believe people have knowledge and resources that will help them achieve a preferred future. Therapists take a non-expert stance and *lead from one step behind* to help clients engage these strengths (De Jong & Berg, 2013; de Shazer et al., 2007). There are three main mechanisms used in assisting clients to become the experts in the therapy room: (a) asking them what they would like to see changed in their lives; (b) asking what would be different; (c) asking clients about their perceptions of exceptions to the problems, which become the solutions (De Jong & Berg, 2013; de Shazer, 1991).

Key Tenets of SFBT

If it isn't broken, don't fix it. Solution-focused therapists let their clients define what needs to be "fixed." Just as solutions vary from client to client, so do problems. What is a problem for one person is not necessarily a problem for someone else. Clients, not their therapists, describe what needs to be fixed.

If something is working, do more of it. This tenet sounds like common sense and it is part of SFBT's focus on using existing resources. If a client is doing something that is helpful, encourage them to do more of that behavior. This can be discovered by asking, "What's working?" or exception questions/ statements such as, "Tell me about a time when the problem was not as severe in your life."

If it's not working, do something different. A reality of human nature is the tendency to try to solve problems by repeating the same behaviors that have not worked before (de Shazer et al., 2007). When a client states that they have done a specific behavior, do not assume that it was helpful. Always ask clients "was that helpful?" to determine if their efforts made a difference.

The solution is not directly related to the problem. The fourth tenet of SFBT is that the solution is not necessarily directly related to the problem. For example, a mother who struggles with anxiety related to raising her child with ASD may come up with the solution to spend more quality time playing with her child to reach her preferred future. Spending time with her child is not directly related to reducing her general anxiety about the diagnosis, but it is helpful for this mother in reducing her day-to-day stress.

No problem happens all of the time. It is common for clients to say "we *always* fight" or "it is *never* better." The reality is that things fluctuate. Even patients suffering from chronic pain report variance in their pain. Solution-focused therapists ask clients about times when the problem is not present or is not as bad. These are called exceptions to the problem (de Shazer et al., 2007). Identifying exceptions helps to increase hope and motivation in families and opens space for new discussion about solutions. Essentially, exceptions are evidence that the family has already found a solution at one time that eliminated or reduced the symptoms of the problem. Because of their ability to instill hope and motivation while identifying forgotten resources, finding exceptions is a crucial part of SFBT.

Small steps can lead to big changes. Most changes in life begin with small decisions that lead to bigger changes. In SFBT, the therapist uses scaling to help clients track these small changes. For example, a therapist might ask, "On a scale of 1–10, how satisfied are you on your ability to work together as a couple for your daughter's social development?" This helps families see their progress and identify small steps toward their eventual goals (de Shazer et al., 2007).

Rationale for Using SFBT

Since many families raising a child with ASD face financial and time constraints, a brief approach to therapy is preferred. Additionally, due to the complex nature of ASD, parents are the experts in their family's functioning and should be placed in such an expert role when receiving psychotherapy. Finally, it is helpful to use an approach that focuses on coping as a key intervention (Smock Jordan & Turns, 2016). This chapter will discuss these and other reasons why SFBT can be beneficial for families with an ASD diagnosis.

Solution-Focused Language

SFBT engages in therapeutic conversations that focus on the client's preferred future, rather than discussing origins or reasons for the problem. Parents raising a child with ASD are often inundated with professionals discussing their child's problems, deficits, and prognosis. By altering the *language* used within therapeutic conversations, families can focus on times when the problem is not occurring, their preferred future, and their small successes that help them reach that future. Society often labels developmental disabilities, including autism, as "problems" that need to be cured. Solution-focused therapists would challenge this notion and not aim to fix the diagnosis, but would instead identify the unique strengths and joys found in the family and the child with the diagnosis.

Compliments

One of the most common interventions in SFBT is the use of compliments (De Jong & Berg, 2013). Parents raising a child with ASD often report a decreased sense of hope regarding their child's potential outcomes (Woodgate, Ateah, & Secco, 2008). Compliments affirm successes and help create hope for the future. Complimenting parents' past and current successes in working with their child, and succeeding despite the challenges of the diagnosis, also tell parents that they are making progress.

One of SFBT's main assumptions is that every client brings skills and resources with them to therapy (De Jong & Berg, 2013). Compliments highlight these resources during therapy sessions. For example, if a mother discusses her ability to calm her child down during a meltdown, a solution-focused therapist will likely ask questions regarding how she was able to do that and the characteristics and resources she used during the situation. Parents raising a child with ASD are likely receiving services from a variety of professionals (e.g., behavior analysts, physical and occupational therapists) and may lose sight of the skills and resources they use themselves on a daily basis.

Altering and Enhancing Interventions for Individuals and Families

Families raising a child with ASD are a unique population that may benefit from slight alterations of traditional SFBT questions and interventions. No single model will be perfect for all populations, and modifications should be made to demonstrate sensitivity to each family's unique needs and circumstances. While discussing these adjustments, it is our intention to keep the underlying principles and framework of SFBT and stay true to the model and epistemological framework.

Goals

Although there are many characteristics of well-formed goals with SFBT, families raising a child with ASD would particularly benefit from goals that had three characteristics: (1) begin with small steps rather than the end result, (2) the goal should be the presence of a desirable behavior rather than the absence of a negative behavior, and (3) the goal should be realistic with achievable terms and timelines. First, most clients think about how they would like to see their life once therapy is completely over. If big, lofty goals are set in place in the beginning, families raising a child with ASD are likely to become discouraged, lose hope, and miss the small changes that are being made. For example, a therapist might ask a couple raising a child with ASD, "When you leave here today, what could be one small change that you could make at home that would indicate to you that you are becoming more patient with your son?" Establishing goals that are small also helps clients receive a few "big wins" closely after beginning therapy. These "big wins" can help motivate clients to make further changes and can show clients that they are competent and capable of achieving their preferred outcomes.

Next, a goal should incorporate the presence of a desirable behavior rather than the absence of a negative behavior. For example, parents raising a child with ASD may ask that the child "stop punching walls." A therapist should ask, "What behavior would you rather see instead." This clarification will be able to help families more quickly identify when the goal has been achieved and allow them to think about a wide variety of behaviors that their child could demonstrate instead. Providing children with a list of behaviors to start or do more of is typically more conducive than giving a list of behaviors not to do.

Another aspect of goal formation is ensuring that goals are realistic and are able to be achieved within an adequate timeline (De Jong & Berg, 2013). This presents an additional opportunity to discuss with families what is achievable for their children noting their unique abilities. For example, a child who struggles with making eye contact when being spoken to by a parent may not benefit from a goal of "always making eye contact during conversations." A good question to ask parents may be: "What is good enough?" This question allows parents and families to think about setting realistic, behavioral goals for the child and themselves. Is it possible that making five seconds of eye contact during a conversation is *good enough* for the parents? In addition, making sure that goals can be achieved within a realistic time frame is crucial to helping clients avoid feeling discouraged if goals are not obtained immediately. Parents may state that after their daughter takes off running down the street, they would immediately like to be able to talk calmly to her. However, the drastic change of their behavior may not be reached immediately. Instead, it may take the parents a couple of weeks to alter their communication style with their child, and being prepared for a realistic timeframe will help them from being discouraged when initially the change seems too small to notice.

Miracle Question

The miracle question (de Shazer, 1988; de Shazer et al., 2007; De Jong & Berg, 2013) is one of the most well-known interventions within SFBT. One of the primary goals of the miracle question is to help clients think about small changes that would occur throughout their day if their presenting problem no longer existed. Although the question can be worded in a variety of ways, the most traditional format includes:

> Suppose that while you are sleeping tonight and the entire house is quiet, a miracle happens. The *miracle* is that *the problem which brought you here is solved.* However, because you are sleeping, you don't know that *the miracle has happened.* So, when you wake up tomorrow morning, *what will be different* that will tell you that a miracle has happened and the problem which brought you here is solved?
>
> (De Jong & Berg, 2013, p. 91)

One study, which investigated experiences of SFBT for families raising a child with severe intellectual disabilities, found that mothers believed the miracle question was irrelevant, confusing, and unhelpful (Lloyd & Dallos, 2008). The term "miracle" was also reported to make mothers think about their child miraculously being cured. A more recent study (Turns, 2017) found three out of four mothers who were raising a child with ASD also perceived the miracle question as non-beneficial and unrealistic. When using the term "miracle" while working with a family or individual facing a lifelong illness, disorder, or disability, the therapist may be perceived as insensitive or ignorant of the client's situation. The first recommendation is to change the word from miracle to "shift" or "jolt." A therapist can also discuss a "flip in the universe." These terms may not immediately make a client think about an unachievable or unrealistic expectation.

Coping Questions

Parents of children with ASD use a range of coping strategies and resources to help adapt to their parenting and caregiving stress (Lai, Goh, Oei, & Sung, 2015; Luong, Yoder, & Canham, 2009). Previous researchers found that parents use a variety of adaptive (e.g., social support, problem solving) and maladaptive (e.g., avoidance, disengagement, substance use) coping mechanisms (Lai & Oei, 2014). Adaptive coping techniques (e.g., acceptance, planning, information seeking) improve parents' mental health (Smith, Seltzer, Tager-Flusberg, Greenberg, & Carter, 2008). Solution-focused therapists are encouraged to first assess for parents' use of adaptive, rather than maladaptive, coping mechanisms. Coping questions are commonly used among clients who are facing long-term situations (De Jong & Berg, 2013). For example, therapists can ask parents, "How do you usually cope when these challenging situations occur?" If more maladaptive mechanisms are currently in place, providing suggestions for more useful coping may be beneficial. A solution-focused therapist would typically provide such suggestions during the end-of-session feedback.

Additional Thoughts

It is important to mention a few added thoughts when working with families and individuals with ASD. First, we caution clinicians to not automatically assume that the family or individual is seeking therapeutic services specifically due to the diagnosis. An ASD diagnosis does not automatically qualify a person(s) to need therapy. In addition, from a solution-focused viewpoint it may not be useful to ask about the origin of the diagnosis or symptoms that the individual with ASD displays if the client does not first discuss it. Rather, a solution-focused therapist would spend more time asking clients about their preferred future.

Effectiveness of SFBT

The effectiveness of SFBT with families raising a child with ASD has only recently been studied. Kenney (2010) assessed the effectiveness of solution-focused interventions on mothers' cognitive distortions and parental stress. One of the mothers demonstrated a reduction in symptoms across all domains of cognitive distortions and stress while two of the mothers reported a decrease in self-blame and preoccupation with danger but not stress.

More recently, Turns, Smock Jordan, Callahan, Whiting, & Piland Springer (under review) conducted a clinical outcome study for couples raising a child with ASD. The study assessed the effectiveness of SFBT on marital satisfaction and overall well-being. Six of the ten participants reported an increase in marital satisfaction as well as overall parental functioning. The results of this study would indicate that SFBT is an effective form of treatment for couples.

Conclusion

The implementation of SFBT can have numerous benefits for families raising children with ASD. In addition to highlighting families' strengths, resources, coping mechanisms, and previous exceptions, SFBT can also help families identify concrete, realistic, measurable goals while in treatment. Similar to working with other populations, various questions and interventions may need to be altered for families of children with ASD in order to meet each family's unique and sensitive needs.

References

De Jong, P., & Berg, I. K. (2013). *Interviewing for solutions* (4th ed). Belmont, CA: Brooks/Cole, Cengage Learning.

de Shazer, S. (1985). *Keys to solution in brief therapy.* New York, NY: W. W. Norton.

de Shazer, S. (1988). *Clues: Investigating solutions in brief therapy.* New York, NY: W. W. Norton.

de Shazer, S. (1991). *Putting differences to work.* New York, NY: W. W. Norton.

de Shazer, S., Dolan, Y. M., & Korman, H. (2007). *More than miracles: the state of the art of solution-focused brief therapy.* New York: Haworth Press.

Kenney, J. (2010). *Solution focused brief intervention for caregivers of children with autism spectrum disorder: A single-subject design.* Minneapolis, MN: Walden University.

Lai, W. W., Goh, T. J., Oei, T. P. S., & Sung, M. (2015). Coping and well-being in parents of children with autism spectrum disorders (ASD). *Journals of Autism and Developmental Disorders, 45,* 2582–2593.

Lai, W. W., & Oei, T. P. S. (2014). Coping in parents of children with autism spectrum disorders: A review. *Review Journal of Autism and Developmental Disorders, 1*(3), 207–224.

Lloyd, H., & Dallos, R. (2008). First session solution-focused brief therapy with families who have a child with severe intellectual disabilities: Mothers' experiences and views. *Journal of Family Therapy, 30,* 5–28.

Luong, J., Yoder, M. K., & Canham, D. (2009). Southeast Asian parents raising a child with autism: A qualitative investigation of coping styles. *The Journal of School Nursing, 25*(3), 222–229.

Smith, L., Seltzer, M., Tager-Flusberg, H., Greenberg, J., & Carter, A. (2008). A comparative analysis of well-being and coping among mothers of toddlers and mothers of adolescents with ASD. *Journal of Autism and Developmental Disorders, 38,* 876–889.

Smock Jordan, S. S., & Turns, B. (2016). Utilizing solution-focused brief therapy with families living with autism spectrum disorders. *Journal of Family Psychotherapy, 27*(3), 155–170.

Turns, B. A., Smock Jordan, S., Callahan, K., Whiting, J., & Piland Springer, N. (under review). Assessing the effectiveness of solution-focused brief therapy for couples raising a child with autism: A clinical outcome study.

Turns, B. A. (2017). *Assessing the effectiveness and experiences of solution-focused brief therapy for couples raising a child with an autism spectrum disorder.* (Unpublished doctoral dissertation). Texas Tech University, Lubbock, TX.

Woodgate, R. L., Ateah, C., & Secco, L. (2008). Living in a world of our own: The experience of parents who have a child with autism. *Qualitative Health Research, 18*(8), 1075–1083.

10 Focusing on Emotions of Couples

Tailoring Emotionally Focused Therapy to Couples with Children with ASD

Julie Ramisch and Rachael A. Dansby Olufowote

Emotionally Focused Therapy (EFT), with its focus on strengthening emotional bonds, has the potential to help strengthen the relationships of couples with children with ASD by addressing some of the specific communication and attachment needs of couples. EFT can help couples to turn toward each other in times of stress and work together as a team, and it can help partners learn to have empathy and patience with each other. Couples can communicate more effectively as the therapist distills emotional messages and helps partners do the same for each other.

Researchers who study couples with children with ASD help us better understand the individual as well as relational struggles that couples may pass through during their relationship. In a study using EFT for couples with children with ASD, Lee, Furrow, and Bradley (2017) discussed that during the first three sessions, wives primarily expressed loneliness in being the primary caregiver and being solely responsible for medical treatment, while husbands were reported to be emotionally distant. Hock, Timm, and Ramisch (2012) added to our understanding of such couples when they described three phases that couples with children with ASD might pass through: ASD crucible, tag-team, and deeper intimacy and commitment.

The ASD crucible phase was described as a time of extraordinary pressure on the relationship with an increase in contextual, emotional, and cognitive demands. After emerging from the crucible, parents often exhibit a tag-team approach and display more efficiency around family structure and routine. Hock et al. (2012) discussed that in this second phase, couples still struggled with emotional distance, criticizing, blaming, and resentment.

If able to emerge through tag-team, Hock et al. (2012) described some couples as being able to arrive at a level of deeper intimacy and commitment. This phase can be characterized by an increase in commitment to the relationship as well as closeness and intimacy between the couple. Researchers report clear communication and the ability to empathize with each other's experiences and show appreciation for each other's contributions to the family as important factors in maintaining these strong couple relationships (Hock et al., 2012; Johnson & Piercy, 2017; Ramisch, Onaga, & Oh, 2014).

The Model of EFT: The Steps and Stages

Overview of Attachment Theory

EFT is a model based on several theories related to systems and connection. However, its primary theoretical base is attachment theory, developed by Dr. John Bowlby, an English psychiatrist who studied the development of children (Bowlby, 1956; Bowlby, Ainsworth, Boston, & Rosenbluth, 1956). Attachment theory is one of the remaining grand theories of human development, and it describes how children and their primary caregivers bond in infancy, early childhood, and beyond. It has been expanded into a theory of adult love, providing a map for navigating distressed intimate relationships (Greenberg & Johnson, 1988; Johnson, 2004).

In EFT, the source of dysfunction is understood in terms of a vicious, negative interactional cycle brought on by wounds to the attachment relationship and fears associated with the bond partners have with one another (Johnson, 2004; Johnson, Hunsley, Greenberg, & Schindler, 1999). Therapists address these problematic cycles through a series of stages. In this chapter, we will use the case of Sasha and Marc, who are raising four children, one of whom has ASD, to illustrate the application of EFT with couples raising a child with ASD. When Sasha and Marc presented to therapy, Marc wanted a closer relationship with Sasha and to learn how to communicate more clearly with her. He reported that she seemed increasingly closed off to him. Sasha, who stays at home full-time with their seven-year-old son with ASD, complains that Marc is selfish and always puts his needs before her own.

Stage 1: The De-Escalation of Negative Cycles of Interaction

Stage 1 combines assessment and beginning of treatment. Some of the general goals of stage 1 are to connect with the couple so they feel safe and accepted, assess their goals and agendas, and create a general consensus about the goals for therapy (Johnson, 2004). By the end of stage 1, the aim is that the couple will have a meta-perspective on their interactions and no longer see one another as the enemy, but rather see the cycle as causing disconnection (Johnson, 2004; Greenberg & Johnson 1988).

Steps 1 and 2. Steps 1 and 2 address the general goals of creating an alliance, identifying conflict issues, and ascertaining the negative interaction cycle (Johnson, 2004; Greenberg & Johnson, 1988). Interaction patterns may present in the common critical pursuit-avoidant withdrawal pattern, or they may present in what looks like pursue-pursue or withdraw-withdraw. In cases of withdraw-withdraw, it is common that one of the withdrawers is actually a burned-out pursuer, and the therapist can ascertain this by doing a complete history with the couple and finding out what their cycle was like in earlier years. In the first two steps of stage 1, it is vital that the therapist stays with and validates the personal landmark incidents of each partner that maintain the cycle

(Johnson, 2004). Some helpful interventions include empathic reflection, validation, use of evocative reflections and questions (evoking emotion), tracking and reflecting interactions, and reframing interactions in terms of the cycle (Johnson, 2004; Greenberg & Johnson, 1988).

With Sasha and Marc, the EFT therapist tracks the emotional dance of the relationship and takes time to hear both spouses' complaints, goals, and histories, while making safety in the therapeutic relationship a top priority. Tracking their negative cycle reveals that Marc often comes across as demanding to Sasha, especially when conversations involve how to respond to their children. Sasha often responds defensively, saying, "I'm here with the kids all the time, why can't you handle this?" The therapist reframes these moves in terms of their cycle. Tracking the cycle also reveals that Marc tends to be the demanding pursuer, and Sasha the avoidant withdrawer. Part of building a therapeutic bond with Sasha may involve talking with her and Marc about ways Sasha can have times of respite from caregiving to engage in self-care.

Steps 3 and 4. Steps 3 and 4 address the accessing of feelings underlying partners' interactions and reframing the negative interactions in terms of the cycle, underlying feelings, and attachment needs (Johnson, 2004; Greenberg & Johnson, 1988). Common secondary (i.e., surface) emotions include frustration, hurt, worry, and anger. The primary emotions underlying secondary responses are typically fear of rejection and/or abandonment, fear of losing one's partner, fear of not being good enough or "cutting it" in the relationship, along with shame/disgust, and sadness. In steps 3 and 4, the therapist must engage the withdrawer around his or her primary emotions before the pursuer will be able to soften toward his or her partner (Johnson, 2004; Greenberg & Johnson, 1988).

One of the most crucial interventions at steps 3 and 4 is validation of the couple's individual emotions as legitimate and understandable human responses (Johnson, 2004). A common phrase used in training EFT therapists is the reminder to have "relentless empathy" fueling validations, reflections, and questions. To open up and expand the couple's emotional experience of their relationship, the therapist tentatively gives evocative reflections and questions (Johnson, 2004). The therapist should also employ heightening (repeating the primary emotions to build up the felt sense of those emotions in the room) to intensify and distill (make clearer) emotional experiences and encourage enactment of key problematic and new emotional responses. The therapist will probably also use empathic conjecture, tracking and reflecting the cycle of interaction, and more reframing of the problem in terms of the cycle.

By the end of step 4, both partners should be able to see a coherent and meaningful picture of their cycle of interaction and understand their roles in creating it (Johnson, 2004; Greenberg & Johnson, 1988). Also, the withdrawn partner should now be talking more in session about how she reacts in the face of the pursuer's demands for engagement, and the pursuer, even if still angry, should not be openly hostile anymore. This new way of being in session constitutes a cycle de-escalation (Johnson, 2004). De-escalation must occur before the couple can proceed to stage 2 (Johnson, 2004; Millikin, 2000).

In the case of Sasha and Marc, the therapist accesses Sasha's feeling of loneliness beneath the secondary response of defensiveness when Marc makes demands for closeness. She reveals that when Marc tries to connect, she feels like he does not understand or care about her feelings and therefore feels alone. Marc, hearing that Sasha still cares about connection and is feeling as lonely as he is, expresses surprise and begins to soften toward her. At this point, they are both able to identify how they get stuck in their cycle at home and how the cycle makes them feel, coming together around the knowledge that the cycle makes them both feel alone and misunderstood.

Stage 2: Changing Interactional Positions

Steps 5 and 6. Steps 5 and 6 constitute a deepening of engagement between partners (Greenberg & Johnson, 1988). Each partner engages intensely with his or her own emotions, marking stage 5 as the most intrapsychically focused part of EFT (Johnson, 2004). In step 5, the therapist engages both partners with their individual emotional experiences and attachment needs, and each one expresses these to the other with the therapist's help. Here the therapeutic tasks are to validate the emotion and the actions tied to it and help both differentiate from their experiences and own them (Johnson, 2004).

As each engage in this emotional exploration, one partner might interrupt the other, or one partner might try to exit the emotional process, as staying in primary emotion is often anxiety provoking. Exit attempts by Marc might look like trying to refocus attention on Sasha's retreating behaviors or changing the subject, and Sasha's exit attempts might be a retreat back into silence or blocking the process by saying phrases such as, "I don't know what I feel." The task of the therapist is to block out interruption and keep the speaking partner engaged in the process (Johnson, 2004; Makinen & Johnson, 2006).

Step 6 involves helping each partner accept the other's experiences by hearing, processing, and, ultimately, responding in new ways to establish a new dance (Johnson, 2004; Greenberg & Johnson, 1988). For example, as Sasha begins speaking to Marc in new and different ways, with more hope and tenderness, Marc is encouraged to accept this new version of who Sasha really is and re-engage in new dialog. Conversely, as Marc explores his fears of Sasha abandoning him and his own sense of inadequacy, Sasha is encouraged to listen and respond in ways she was unable to before, understanding Marc's demands in a different light, instead of freezing and avoiding deeper conversations.

Step 7. Step 7 is about emotional engagement and bonding in a new pattern of interaction (Greenberg & Johnson 1988). By the completion of this step, the goal is to have two key change events occur: the withdrawn partner is re-engaged and owns the hurt she caused by withdrawing, and the pursuer has softened and can ask for his attachment needs to be met in a state of vulnerability, not criticism or blaming (Johnson, 2003, 2004). Once these have occurred, second-order change has happened, and the couple is ready to progress to stage 3, where they consolidate their new interaction cycle.

With Sasha and Marc, for example, Sasha owns the hurt she caused Marc by cutting herself off emotionally from him and is confidently present with him in the moment, eager to hear him share his softer feelings. Marc then turns to Sasha and tells her how afraid he feels that when she "goes away" he will never be able to reach her. He then is able to tell her that he needs connection with her and wants to meet her needs as well. Marc also demonstrates an ability to listen to Sasha as she expresses her needs and makes his best effort to meet those needs.

Stage 3: Consolidation and Termination

Steps 8 and 9. Steps 8 and 9 constitute the termination phase, where emphasis is placed on facilitating new solutions to old issues and then consolidating those positions that the partners take (Johnson, 2004; Greenberg & Johnson, 1988). In step 8, with a more secure bond now in place between the partners, the issues of what to do when faced with old fears are simpler. Here, for example, the therapist's task is to support Sasha, the reengaging spouse, and facilitate acceptance by Marc (Johnson, 2004).

In step 9, the couple consolidates a new, healthier dance and incorporates that cycle into everyday life (Greenberg & Johnson, 1988). Within sessions, the therapist points out these attempts of enacting the new cycle so that the partners are encouraged to continue outside the session (Johnson, 2004). Further, step 9 is where the couple constructs a new story, built on a foundation of secure attachment (Johnson, 2004; Greenberg & Johnson, 1988). The new solutions from step 8 are employed here and play an important role in their new story's construction. According to Johnson (2004), it is the very creation of this new story that elicits a sense of closure to the therapeutic process and readies the couple for life without the aid of the therapist. The therapist's task is to highlight both partners' accomplishments and their courage in taking risks in the process; the therapist's role is also more consistent with a follower than leader at this point (Johnson, 2004).

Sasha and Marc present at the final session with visible increased comfort with one another and easily describe to the therapist how they have been navigating potential moments of distance or distress in new ways. Marc now asks Sasha how she is doing and what she needs from him before expressing his own needs. Additionally, when he expresses his needs, he does so with vulnerability and softness instead of demanding. Sasha describes being more intentional with self-disclosure of her emotions with Marc when he asks. She also expresses renewed hope and confidence that these changes will last, which helps her remain emotionally engaged with Marc.

Effectiveness of EFT with Couples with Children with ASD

Gordon-Walker, Johnson, Manion, and Cloutier (1996) conducted the first study to involve the use of EFT with couples who had a child with special needs. After the intervention, marital adjustment of the treatment group showed to be significantly higher compared to the control group. These effects were also maintained at the five-month follow-up. Seven years later, Cloutier, Manion, Gordon-Walker, and Johnson (2002) published a follow-up study to Gordon-Walker et al.'s 1996 study. Cloutier et al. (2002) found that treatment effects regarding improved marital adjustment were maintained over two years. Additionally, they also found support to suggest that several couples continued to improve after the intervention ended.

In the first study to specifically apply EFT to couples with children with ASD, Ramisch, Timm, Hock, and Topor (2013) conducted in-home therapy with three couples. At the end of treatment, couples reported to have a better understanding of their conflict patterns, improved communication, renewed trust, and a greater understanding of each other's emotions. More recently, Lee, Furrow, and Bradley (2017) published their results from working with couples with children with ASD. At the end of their study, they found dyadic adjustment significantly improved over time, and gains were sustained at the six-month follow-up. They also analyzed content from the sessions and found that couples primarily reported and discussed persistent stress that challenged their relationships, feelings of isolation from others, and struggles to remain emotionally connected when caring for a child with ASD.

From these studies, we see evidence that EFT helps couples with children with ASD and other special needs to improve their relational adjustment. Gordon-Walker et al. (1996), Cloutier et al. (2002), and Lee et al. (2017) discussed improvements in marital adjustment in their participants, while couples studied by Ramisch et al. (2013) discussed improvements in areas surrounding conflict patterns, communication, trust, and emotions. Below we will discuss specifically how this was done and how therapists can use EFT to help couples with children with ASD improve their relational adjustment.

Treatment Logistics and Modifications to Treatment

Gordon-Walker et al. (1996) highlighted the accommodations they made to their study to better serve couples with children with chronically ill children. They reported they educated their therapists about the different disabilities represented in the study, and they provided information about the stressors and needs of the families raising children with chronically ill children. During therapy, they highlighted the impact of the child's illness on the individuals and on the relationship. Specifically, they addressed different styles of coping and moving through grief associated with their child's illness.

Another reflection from Gordon-Walker et al. (1996) included that couples in their study were about five years past the initial diagnosis stage and that benefits from early intervention were unknown. Couples reported they would have liked the EFT intervention to have been offered during the initial stages when the child was in the process of being diagnosed.

At the end of their article, the researchers involved with Ramisch et al.'s (2013) in-home study reflected on how working with couples with children with

ASD might affect the EFT process. First, they noticed that going through de-escalation was a difficult process for the couples. Couples varied in their communication patterns and interactional cycles and did not all fit the pursuer-withdrawer model. They recommended therapists take extra time to work with the couples to explore their interactional patterns, learn about their history, identify problematic patterns, and have a thorough idea of areas the couple wished to improve. Another recommendation was to explore all of the reasons for couple distress rather than assuming that the child with ASD is the primary reason for stress and conflict. It is also important to make sure that EFT is a good fit and the most appropriate model for couples depending on their needs. Finally, the authors recommended that therapists consider in-home therapy to help address some of the barriers of clinic-based or office-based treatment.

Practice Recommendations

When offering treatment to couples with children with ASD, it is important to assess the appropriateness of EFT. Hock et al. (2012) reported that parents in the ASD crucible phase might need assistance with contextual demands (such as gaining access to resources). Ramisch et al. (2013) noted that some couples may need other types of help (such as behavioral management strategies) in addition to EFT. It may be helpful to supplement EFT with other models, or with attention to pragmatic concerns.

When applying EFT, one of the first steps is to figure out the negative interaction cycle and to reframe the negative interactions in terms of the cycle, the underlying feelings, and attachment needs (Johnson, 2004; Greenberg & Johnson, 1988). As Ramisch et al. (2013) highlighted, not all interactional patterns will have to do with parenting a child with ASD. Additionally, depending on where the family is at on their journey through diagnosis and intervention, concerns and problems might be different.

The second key to successful therapy using EFT is restructuring the couple's interaction cycle so partners clearly understand one another's attachment longings and emotional cues and could respond accordingly. With couples raising a child with ASD, the therapist may need to go extra slow with evoking and expressing emotions. If communication or identifying feelings is difficult, they may need additional assistance in identifying what they're feeling or understanding the emotional cues of their partner. For example, when the therapist sets up an enactment to help partners reach for or respond to each other in a new way, the therapist may have to "slice it thinner" than usual, meaning making a risky enactment smaller, breaking it into parts, and focusing on longings and fears (Johnson, 2013). For example, with Sasha and Marc, the therapist first asks, "Sasha, can you turn to Marc and tell him about how sad you feel when he does not acknowledge your feelings?" But Sasha says no, since she has not been accustomed to being so vulnerable with Marc, so the therapist "slices it thinner," and takes a less risky route a second time around. The therapist says, "That's okay, Sasha, it feels like too much to tell him all that. Can you tell me instead, what comes up for you when you *think* about telling Marc how sad his lack of acknowledgment makes you feel?" Sasha responds with, "It's too risky. He will just dismiss me again." The therapist takes the new information from Sasha and sets up another, thinner enactment now: "Ahh, it feels risky, like 'maybe he will only dismiss me again, and I couldn't bear that,' is that right? Can you tell him that it feels too risky, that you're concerned he will just dismiss you again?" This time, Sasha is able to tell Marc her "thinner" experience, and as a result, is able to take a successful step in opening up a bit more with her husband instead of retreating into silence.

Conclusion

Emotionally Focused Therapy, with techniques such as evocative reflections, heightening, and enactments, can help partners share vulnerable, primary emotions with each other. Couples who would initially express criticism and blame can learn to clearly express how they feel lonely and distant. Therapists help to restructure interactions so partners can be empathetic, comforting, and patient with each other during these vulnerable expressions. In this way, couples are able to achieve closeness and intimacy. Practicing EFT with couples raising a child with ASD can look very similar to EFT with couples in any other context. However, it would also include an emphasis on paying attention to how couples interpret the impact of ASD on their relationship. As always, good couples therapy is tailored to each client, and as therapists go from this chapter and back into their work, we encourage therapists to "have relentless empathy," and watch the magic of EFT unfold.

If therapists are interested in more focused, advanced training in EFT, visit www.iceeft.com to find a listing of all the Externship trainings offered for the coming year.

References

Bowlby, J. (1956). Mother-child separation. *Mental Health and Infant Development, 1*, 117–122.

Bowlby, J., Ainsworth, M., Boston, M., & Rosenbluth, D. (1956). The effects of mother-child separation: A follow-up study. *Psychology and Psychotherapy: Theory, Research and Practice, 29*(3–4), 211–247.

Cloutier, P. F., Manion, I. G., Gordon-Walker, J., & Johnson, S. M. (2002). Emotionally focused interventions for couples with chronically ill children: A 2-year follow-up. *Journal of Marital and Family Therapy, 28*(4), 391–398.

Gordon-Walker, J., Johnson, S., Manion, I., & Cloutier, P. (1996). Emotionally focused marital intervention for couples with chronically ill children. *Journal of Consulting and Clinical Psychology, 64*(5), 1029–1036.

Greenberg, L. S., & Johnson, S. M. (1988). *Emotionally focused therapy for couples*. New York, NY: Guilford Press.

Hock, R. M., Timm, T. M., & Ramisch, J. L. (2012). Parenting children with autism spectrum disorders: A crucible for couple relationships. *Child & Family Social Work, 17*(4), 406–415.

Johnson, J., & Piercy, F. P. (2017). Exploring partner intimacy among couples raising children on the autism spectrum: A grounded theory investigation. *Journal of Marital and Family Therapy, 43*(4), 644–661. doi:10.1111/jmft.12247.

Johnson, S. M. (2003). Attachment theory: A guide for couple therapy. In S. M. Johnson, V. E. Whiffen (Eds.) *Attachment processes in couple and family therapy* (pp. 103–123). New York, NY: The Guilford Press.

Johnson, S. M. (2004). *The practice of emotionally focused couple therapy* (2nd ed.). New York, NY: Taylor & Francis Group, LLC.

Johnson, S. M. (2013). *Externships in Emotionally Focused Couple Therapy: Creating connection seminars for couples.* Training Manual for Externship Training in Emotionally Focused Therapy. Ottawa, Canada: International Centre for Excellence in Emotionally Focused Therapy.

Johnson, S. M., Hunsley, J., Greenberg, L., & Schindler, D. (1999). Emotionally focused couples therapy: Status and challenges. *Clinical Psychology: Science and Practice, 6*(1), 67–79.

Lee, N. A., Furrow, J. L., & Bradley, B. A. (2017). Emotionally focused couple therapy for parents raising a child with an autism spectrum disorder: A pilot study. *Journal of Marital and Family Therapy, 43*(4), 662–673. doi:10.1111/jmft.12225.

Makinen, J. A., & Johnson, S. M. (2006). Resolving attachment injuries in couples using emotionally focused therapy: Steps toward forgiveness and reconciliation. *Journal of Consulting and Clinical Psychology, 74*, 1055–1064.

Millikin, J. W. (2000). *Resolving attachment injuries in couples using emotionally focused therapy: A process study.* Unpublished doctoral dissertation, Virginia Polytechnic Institute and State University.

Ramisch, J. L., Timm, T. M., Hock, R. M., & Topor, J. A. (2013). Experiences delivering a marital intervention for couples with children with autism spectrum disorder. *The American Journal of Family Therapy, 41*(5), 376–388.

Ramisch, J. L., Onaga, E., & Oh, S. M. (2014). Keeping a sound marriage: How couples with children with autism spectrum disorders maintain their marriages. *Journal of Child and Family Studies, 23*(6), 975–988.

11 Using Bowen Family Systems Theory with Families

Carlos Perez

Introduction

Murray Bowen developed a theory known today as "Bowen family systems theory." Bowen was part of a paradigm shift in the 1950s that moved the clinical focus from the individual to the entire family unit. Bowen's theory is heavily based on the idea of family as a multigenerational emotional system (Bowen, 1978; Titelman, 2015), meaning that each generation has significant influence on those that follow. Rather than only focusing on individual pathology, Bowen therapists are concerned with how families, across generations, create patterns of behaving and responding to stress (Ramisch & Nelson, 2014). Although Bowen had a family-oriented framework, he often worked with couples, and sought to help children by strengthing their parents. He believed children's difficulties were due to parents innapropriately involving them in their marriage (Ramisch & Nelson, 2014). This chapter will focus on using Bowen family therapy with couples raising a child with ASD.

Key Concepts of Bowen

Differentiation of self. A key concept of Bowen's theory is differentiation of self, which is defined in two parts: (1) one's ability to separate emotional reactivity from logical thought, and (2) the ability to balance a healthy sense of autonomy in relationships (Kerr & Bowen, 1988). A well differentiated person will have a strong sense of autonomy and is good at managing anxiety (Ramisch & Nelson, 2014). Additionally, this person is able to consider the opinions and advice of others, but ultimately make decisions independently (Ramisch & Nelson, 2014). Differentiation should not be viewed as a personality characteristic, but rather, a process and an important part of family dynamics. For example, a differentiated parent raising a child with ASD is able to consider advice from family members or friends regarding their child's challenges with eating and is able to make an independent, non-reactive decision about how to handle the situation.

Fusion. An individual who is not differentiated is likely to be fused with others. Individuals who lack autonomy are likely to not be able to think for themselves and are swayed by other people's opinions and wishes (Ramisch & Nelson, 2014). For example, after trying to spend the day at a family reunion, a father of a child with ASD may become very anxious and upset after other family members provide parenting advice. While seeing this father struggle with fusion, a Bowen therapist would encourage him to be responsive rather than reactive in order to make more thoughtful decisions.

Nuclear family emotional process. The "nuclear family emotional process" describes typical patterns in a family unit that deal with stress in order to reduce anxiety. The four main patterns of dealing with stress are: conflict, development of symptoms, distancing, or triangling, which includes involving a third party in a dyadic conflict (Ramisch & Nelson, 2014). When used in moderation and in a flexible way, these patterns can be helpful and can be used to de-stress a situation. However, when individuals are more reactive and use patterns rigidly or exclusively, they become problematic.

Family projection process. The concept of family projection is that parents can project their unresolved differentiation issues onto one or more of their children (Ramisch & Nelson, 2014). Family projection occurs in the form of a triangle, but tends to occur more naturally than a conflictual triangle (Baker, 2015). Children who are given this "honor" are usually special to one or both parents. Like any child, a child with ASD may be a recipient of this projection for several reasons. For example, the child may have been born after a period of infertility or have a physical vulnerability. Children with ASD may receive a lot of positive or negative attention because of their diagnosis. Family projections may look like a parent who is overly anxious about their child's future or peer relationships, or overly relies on their child for emotional validation.

Rational for Using Bowen Family Systems

Considering all of the challenges and struggles experienced by families which are reported in other chapters, we can begin to conceptualize why a therapist would use Bowen family systems theory when working with couples raising a child with ASD. First, treatment is provided from a family framework rather than an individual lens. This notion is very different from other forms of treatment that primarily specialize in working with only the child with ASD. Using a Bowen prespective, parents will be able to see their own patterns of behavior and learn to identify how their patterns affect the emotional stability of their family.

Next, although Bowen experimented with different formats of family treatment, he found it most effective to begin treatment with the parental unit since parents establish the emotional functioning for their family system (Baker, 2015). Past studies found that parents' mental health (i.e., increased anxiety and stress) impacts their child's symptomatic behaviors (Brobst, Clopton, & Hendrick, 2009; Hastings & Johnson, 2001). For example, parental stress and marital dissatisfaction are associated with deficits in social skills and increased self-injurious behaviors (Hastings & Johnson). Working with the parental unit would allow them to increase their differentiation and work on emotional functioning, skills that could potentially help them better manage their child's challenging behaviors.

Treatment Using Bowen Family Systems

The primary goal in Bowen family systems therapy is differentiation of self. This goal helps people increase their ability to think and choose responses rather than reacting and using automatic behaviors. As couples discuss the emotional functioning between them and their families-of-origin, it is the role of the therapist to monitor reactivity and help them maintain a manageable level of emotional engagement while processing this information. Specifically, with issues around diagnosis, stress, symptoms, or adjusting to a change in lifestyle because of the diagnosis, the goal is for the couples to remain calm without becoming emotionally reactive. Parents raising a child with ASD may experience a great deal of stress and anxiety (see Chapter 4). Using Bowen family therapy can help parents learn how to manage their anxiety, regardless of the situation, and learn to proactively respond to situations rather than impulsively reacting.

The couple's ability to make long-term relationship changes depends on their openness to work on their own levels of differentiation of self (Baker, 2015; Titelman, 2015). Making changes to differentiation of self comes from two processes: understanding the emotional process from previous generations, and wanting to rationally change the emotional trend into the next generation. Couples must be willing to see the parts they play in their immediate and extended family's dysfunction. Couples must also have the capacity to change their behaviors to provide a different emotional atmosphere for the following generation. For example, instead of engaging in conflict with each other when their child with ASD begins to have a meltdown, parents are encouraged to alter the atmosphere by remaining calm and helping the child do the same.

The most helpful way for couples to be able to see themselves within their own family systems is to "think systems" (Baker, 2015). A helpful strategy to "thinking systems" is to remain emotionally neutral. According to Kerr and Bowen (1988), becoming emotionally neutral means having the ability to see both sides of a relationship process and looking past the back and forth exchange of emotions. As one becomes emotionally neutral they will be able to recognize their own emotional reactivity and how they have contributed to their family's emotional state.

Becoming emotionally neutral also involves awareness of other's emotional exchanges, including their children, typically developing or not. When parents begin to recognize their own contribution to the family's emotional functioning, they can then recognize how each child's emotional exchange also contributes to the overall functioning of the unit. After parents learn to become emotionally neutral, they can help neurotypical siblings and the diagnosed child practice the same functioning.

Therapist's Use of Self

One of the primary techniques is the therapist's use of him- or herself. Bowen therapists believe that families seek therapy because their typical way of handling stress and anxiety are not working (Kerr & Bowen, 1988). A Bowen therapist working with a family raising a child with autism is advised to not get "pulled into" the anxiety of the family system. For example, when a parent becomes visually upset when discussing their child's meltdowns, a therapist should remain calm and not mirror the client's stress levels. A differentiated therapist helps a family remain calm and does not become triggered by the client's anxiety. For example, when a child with ASD begins to engage in self-harming behaviors, such as head-banging, a therapist should advise the parent to intervene in the behavior in a calm manner rather than becoming visually anxious or fearful.

Genograms

Genograms are a hallmark intervention to Bowen family systems theory (Bowen, 1978; Kerr & Bowen, 1988). A genogram can provide both the therapist and each individual with a better understanding of family patterns – it is the role of the Bowen therapist to help their clients see their family dynamics within their own families-of-origin. By completing a genogram, couples are able to identify triangles, patterns of reacting to stress, and types of relationships (i.e., cut-offs, overinvolved relationships, conflict, and distance). If needed, a Bowen therapist can split up the couple to work on family-of-origin issues individually, eliminating any potential reactivity from discussing the partner's families-of-origin (Baker, 2015).

When helping the couple to analyze their genograms, it is important to ask process questions regarding adapting to the diagnosis and emotional functioning of the family using prompts that include "what," "where," "when," and "how." For example: "What happened in the generation before yours that your family has adapted to certain stress this way?" "How would the generation before you have adapted to Sammie's meltdowns?" "Where was your family living when you received the diagnosis?" "How is/was that important to your family's support system?" "How can you adjust differently or better than the generation before you would have to raising a child with ASD?" "What was going on in your lives when this happened?" "Why" is not considered a process question in the Bowen approach as it tends to place blame instead of helping members emotionally process and become differentiated.

Asking these questions will allow the couple to explore the multigenerational process of their own emotional functioning. After observing their family processes, the couple can begin exploring strategies of changing emotional functioning. The changes can include reducing the couple's anxiety and increasing differentiation of self. Reducing a couple's anxiety can allow them to approach their family system, their child, and the diagnosis itself in a calm, non-reactive way, and respond to symptoms with more emotional composure.

Detriangling

While analyzing each partner's genograms, certain triangles will become apparent. Triangles form when two individuals are engaged in a stressful or anxiety-provoking situation, and one or both people draw in a third entity in order to alleviate their anxiety. Undoing these trianges, or "detriangling," is another key intervention used by a Bowen therapist. Like all parents, those raising a child with ASD may unintentionally triangulate their neurotypical child or their child with ASD in order to reduce the anxiety or stress. For example, parents may argue about finances. When this conflict comes up, they may refocus their attention to the behavior of one or both of their children, therefore triangling them into their conflict. Depending on the child, the child may absorb the anxiety and stress or may develop behavioral problems as discussed above. The therapist can help the couple to realize this pattern of behavior and stay focused in order to eventually resolve their conflict. A Bowen therapist should continuously assess for such triangles and attempt to detriangulate the pattern.

Bowen and Play Therapy

A Bowen family therapist may find it helpful to include children in family therapy sessions. Although play therapy is not purely Bowen, these interventions allow a Bowen therapist to observe and assess the level of functioning within a family. For example, as therapists instruct families to engage in play, they can monitor levels of differentiation of self as they observe children's initiation in play, parents over functioning or lack of engagement in play, or the family's ability to work together in play. It is important for the therapist to take opportunities to correct and guide interactions that reflect an unhealthy level of differentiation of self for children and parents. Around a child's diagnosis, it is important for parents to take the initiative where they see opportunities for engagement, emotional cues, or relationship structures. With siblings, it is also important for parents to guide them through play that is directed toward their sibling with ASD, targeting emotions, social cues, and general engagement.

A play therapy technique that reflects the family's emotional process is the sandtray. In this exercise, the family is encouraged to create their family structure within the sandtray. The therapist then observes the structure, interactions, and how each family member works with each other. This process provides insight to the family's emotional engagement and the emotional patterns of both the parents and children (Nims & Duba, 2011). The sandtray exercise can also help externally display their new desired way of interacting with their family system. The sandtray can provide a place for the family to live out their desired way of emotionally interacting with each other, providing the emotional atmosphere they want to live in. All family members are encouraged to take part in this exercise, especially the diagnosed child, allowing them to participate in the family's construction of their desired functioning.

Puppets are another excellent tool for identifying and working with multigenerational processes (Nims & Duba, 2011). It is useful for the therapist to videotape families conducting their own spontaneous puppet show. The therapist gives the family little direction so the parents can organically show their emotional processes with their children through puppets. The therapist then shows the parents the videotape of the family puppet show, and points out certain interactions that are seen in the multigenerational process. Having parents view themselves projecting behaviors that they inherited from their parents is a very useful tool. The video of puppet work can also show parents the different functioning and thought processes of the diagnosed child. Since children with ASD tend to think in more literal terms, it would be useful for the therapist to help parents read their child's interactions with the use of puppet work.

Conclusion

Bowen family systems theory helps couples identify their own patterns of behavior and learn how family patterns affect their family. Through this process couples hopefully learn about concepts such as differentiation and triangling and how to better handle and resolve conflict calmly and directly. Using different techniques such as a genogram or puppet show, a therapist can help couples see family patterns and trends that are either helpful or harmful to family functioning. Through better managing their own anxiety and conflict, couples will hopefully be able to better manage the stresses and strains that come when raising a child with ASD.

References

Baker, K. G. (2015). Bowen family systems couple coaching. In A. S. Gurman, J. L. Lebow, & D. K. Snyder (Eds.) *Clinical handbook of couple therapy* (246–267). New York: Guilford.

Bowen, M. (1978). *Family therapy in clinical practice.* New York: Jason Anderson.

Brobst, J. B., Clopton, J. R., & Hendrick, S. S. (2009). Parenting children with autism spectrum disorders: The couple's relationship. *Focus on Autism and Other Developmental Disabilities, 24*(1), 38–49.

Hastings, R., & Johnson, E. (2001). Stress in UK families conducting intensive home-based behavioral intervention for their young child with autism. *Journal of Autism and Developmental Disorders, 31,* 327–336.

Kerr, M. E., & Bowen, M. (1988). *Family evaluation: An approach based on Bowen Theory.* New York: W. W. Norton.

Nims, D. R., & Duba, J. D. (2011). Using play therapy techniques in a Bowenian theoretical context. *The Family Journal, 19,* 83–89.

Ramisch, J. L., & Nelson, T. S. (2014). Transgenerational family therapies. In J. Wetchler & L. Hecker (Eds.) *An introduction to marriage and family therapy* (319–356). New York: The Haworth Press.

Titelman, P. (Ed.) (2015). *Differentiation of self: Bowen family systems theory perspectives.* New York: Routledge.

12 Decoding the Puzzle of Fairness

Using Contextual Family Therapy with Families

Kathleen Nash

"It's not fair!" This statement is proclaimed by thousands of parents and siblings related to a child diagnosed with ASD. As these families enter therapy seeking help, strategies, and guidance, systemic therapists offer a unique perspective of their situation. Contextual family therapy is a systemic model that offers an effective approach to empower families and help them cope with feelings of confusion, unfairness, and frustration. Ivan Böszörményi-Nagy, a Hungarian American psychiatrist, created contextual family therapy and is recognized as one of the innovators in systemic therapies. He founded his contextual approach on the principles of systems theories, psychiatry, philosophy, and psychoanalysis (Gangamma, Bartle-Haring, & Glebova, 2012). "Relational ethics" make this approach unique and focuses on each family member's perspectives of fairness, loyalty, trust, and giving.

Contextual therapy offers these families something that behavioral interventions, schedules, and medications cannot: the opportunity for healing through fair relating and giving (Ducommun-Nagy, 2003). Similar to other systemic therapies, contextual therapy values understanding generational patterns of interaction, rules, communication styles, beliefs, and assumptions. In this sense, each child is born into a different family created by these changing generational boundaries and narratives. However, contextual therapy is unique in its belief that family relationships are built upon a legacy of trustworthiness across generations, known as relational ethics (Böszörményi-Nagy & Krasner, 1986). In order to increase trustworthiness, therapy focuses on how relational values and ethics are transmitted across generational boundaries and acquired by members today and in future generations. Contextual therapy interventions derive from principles of ethical relationships, fairness, accountability, family legacies, loyalties, or entitlement earned from trustworthiness (Böszörményi-Nagy & Krasner, 1986; Glebova & Gangamma, 2017). Furthermore, the desire to give to and show concern for future generations makes contextual family therapy distinctively systemic.

Contextual family therapy's emphasis on relational ethics remains a unique contribution to family therapy. As Glebova and Gangamma (2017) explained, therapists consider each member's past experiences, especially those that involve unfair relational injury, along with their present needs, and strive to

understand each family's balance or imbalance of fairness within these relationships. Children acquire their legacy by taking on the roles relative to their
experience in the family, in an attempt to earn credit (Becvar & Becvar, 2013).
A son may be entitled to approval, but his family may only give him blame
because he is diagnosed with ASD. A child diagnosed with ASD may experience the injustice of becoming the family scapegoat, labeled as the family
outcast and reason family members are unhappy. The family legacy becomes one
of unfairness for the child with ASD (Böszörményi-Nagy & Ulrich, 1981). Contextual therapists facilitate change in families by instilling a sense of balance
between relational give-and-take.

Rationale for Using Contextual Family Therapy

Contextual family therapy incorporates individual and systemic approaches with
a fundamental goal of healing clients' pain while also promoting change within
the family system (Goldenthal, 1996). A four-dimensional framework is used to
assess, organize, and provide care to families. As described by Böszörményi-Nagy
and Krasner (1986), the interrelated and essential dimensions are: (1) facts
about the family, (2) individual psychology, (3) systemic transactions, and
(4) the history of the relational patterns and the distinctive dimension of
relational ethics. Parents raising a child with ASD enter therapy seeking
helpful interventions and strategies to address behavioral, sensory, and relational issues. Research reports there are distinct features of ASD (i.e., social deficits, communication delays, stereotypic behaviors and restricted interests), each
with their own unique deficits and genetic characteristics (Neely, Amatea,
Echevarria-Doan, & Tannen, 2012). These parents need help understanding
their child's unique behaviors from a clinician with existing knowledge about
the complexities of ASD and the ability to encourage healing within the family
system.

Parents Feel Empowered

Sensory processing issues, for example, are highly misunderstood. Children are
often punished instead of being understood when they experience sensory overload. A child who screams and runs away when they hear loud sounds, refuses to
eat certain food textures, or has meltdowns when they have to wait to leave the
house is often viewed as having behavior problems rather than sensory problems. Contextual therapists help facilitate mutual understanding between
parents and children, so that parents feel empowered to offer the trust and
comfort their child with ASD is entitled to.

Children Feel Empowered

Additionally, the fundamental convictions of contextual therapy contend that
even the most incapacitated clients have a capacity to care about others and try

to help, even if only in a limited fashion (Ducommun-Nagy, 2003). Thus, contextual therapy takes into consideration the strengths and positive contributions children with ASD can make to their families.

Other Accommodations

Home, school, and community activities are often taken for granted by parents of neurotypical children. However, adaptations in the family of a child with ASD are necessary at multiple levels. The child with ASD interacts not only with family and neighbors, who make up the microsystem, but also with the exosystem of teachers, doctors, and specialists, and the macrosystem of culture, healthcare, and beliefs (Ravindran & Myers, 2012). Each level interacts and influences the other. For instance, family members might learn to accommodate for sensory triggers that could arise at places such as the grocery store or learn to adapt to having various therapists, specialists, and other resources in and out of their home and schedule. Ravindran and Myers (2011) explain that this interconnected relationship between children and their ecosystems, as described by Bronfenbrenner (1994), influences families' narratives, apprehensions, and behaviors as they navigate through unpredictable communities.

Facts About the Family

The first dimension of interaction involves the family. The therapist engages the family in conversations about each member's age, health, employment, religion, education, major illnesses, gender, ability, adoption, and cultural and racial factors (Böszörményi-Nagy & Krasner, 1986). During the exploration of facts, the therapist may unearth crucial details that contribute to family discord. For example, a parent may have an illness that causes stress, or a family culture that views a disability as shameful. Additionally, there could be a history of infertility or other health issues related to the context of having a child with an ASD diagnosis.

Individual Psychology

Dimension two focuses on individual psychology, which includes family members' personalities, as well as their mental health diagnoses and related emotional health. Contextual therapy acknowledges individuals' gifts, needs, talents, personalities, feelings, hopes, and cognitions (Goldenthal, 1996). In this dimension, clinicians discuss the individual diagnoses of each member of the family and provide information and clarification of the ASD diagnosis. Dimension two goes beyond a basic DSM 5 or ICD 10 diagnosis. Contextual therapists explore and give credit for each family member's contributions and psychology, in a fair process known as multidirected partiality, which helps provide a balance of strengths and challenges for each individual family member (Shaham, 2005).

Systemic Transactions

Parents raising a child with ASD experience an array of prolonged and severe stressors that can slowly change patterns of marital and family functioning (Solomon & Chung, 2012). The third dimension of contextual therapy, the exploration of family transactions, provides important guidance on addressing these patterns of functioning and interactions. Therapists will need to understand a family's generational patterns and fairness transactions in the context of the ASD diagnosis. For example, a family may have a history of bias or prejudice toward individuals with a disability, or have values of perfection and family obedience that may have been passed down through multiple generations, but need to be modified in the unique circumstances related to ASD.

Parents and extended family may have feelings of anger or sadness related to the ASD diagnosis, or may show various types of favoritism, which can leave children feeling conflicted, angry, or guilty (Magistro, 2014). This can result in new transgenerational patterns of unfairness, mistrust, and destructive entitlement, which is a contextual term explaining that people who are mistreated tend to pass down mistreatment toward others.

Transactions among and between family members and generations can be viewed and understood using a comprehensive genogram. As a multigenerational model, contextual therapy asserts that interactions between family members are often the consequences of events, beliefs, and ledgers of past generations (Macleod et al., 2014). Information in a contextual genogram includes, but is not limited to, who is loyal to who, who makes final decisions for the family, and who gives more than others (Goldenthal, 1996). Genograms help the therapist and the family members recognize the needs and motivations of others and learn to accept each other as they are (Macleod et al., 2014). The information obtained in the framework of dimensions one through three leads the clinician to the pinnacle of the model – relational ethics.

Relational Ethics

Contextual therapy is the only systemic approach to focus on the construct of relational ethics. Dimension four brings together the concepts of trust, loyalty, and entitlement, which inspire justice and fairness in relationships, and are passed through each generation (Glebova & Gangamma, 2017). In dimension four, the therapist conveys the idea that all members of the family have the right to expect that their well-being will be appreciated and respected in a context of fairness (Adams & Maynard, 2004). The central therapeutic strategy in this dimension is multidirected partiality. This stance provides therapists with the ability to consider every family members' perspective and decide who needs their learning at that moment. Multidirected partiality aids families in seeing the benefits of giving and increases their willingness to give more than they take (Neely et al., 2012). When family members refuse to give, or take too much from others, patterns of destructive or constructive entitlement are unearthed.

To function effectively, family members need to be held ethically account-able for their interactions as they learn to equalize a ledger of what family members are due or have earned (Adams & Maynard, 2004). Balancing a fami-ly's ledger of entitlements and indebtedness creates a foundation to raise a child with ASD upon.

Use with Parents Raising a Child with an ASD

The application of contextual family therapy is illustrated in the following case conceptualization. The fictional Trust family presents in family therapy with a 7-year-old son, Theo, diagnosed with ASD. Theo's mother, Maggie, and father, Jake, are both 43 years old. Theo also has a ten-year-old sister, Abby. Their therapist employs contextual family therapy to address their presenting issues.

The First Dimension – Facts about the Family

Maggie and Jake Trust are a Caucasian, middle-income couple living in subur-ban Philadelphia. Both parents are 43-years-old. Maggie has a bachelor's degree in special education, but has not worked outside the home since Theo was diag-nosed with ASD at age five. Jake is a mechanical engineer in the medical device industry. He holds a bachelor's degree in engineering. The couple grew up and started dating in a small socioeconomically depressed town in Ohio, where their families still live. They attended the same university and after graduation, Jake accepted a job near Philadelphia and they quickly moved. The couple shared additional facts about their family and friends in Ohio. They were described as undereducated, living in poverty, and abusers of alcohol. The couple's family and friends want them to move back to their hometown, despite the lack of employment and educational opportunities.

Their daughter, Abby, is in fourth grade in their local public school. She has been tested and received a gifted Individualized Education Program (IEP). Abby enjoys drawing and spending time with her friends. Theo is seven years old and was presented as the identified patient.

Maggie and Jake describe their relationship as conflictual, often arguing about who does the most around the house. They also disagree about the best ways to help Theo. They were told Theo is high functioning and has tactile and auditory sensory issues that result in behavioral issues. He also lacks safety awareness, and sometimes runs away in public and flees from school. The parents state they are entering therapy because, "we want to all get along better and stop arguing about Theo."

Second Dimension – Individual Psychology

Theo is presented as the main concern because of issues related to his ASD dia-gnosis. Abby said her parents changed after he was diagnosed, and the therapist picked up on a sense of loss from Abby for her parents and the life before the diagnosis (Sousa, 2011). The family was able to describe a loss of the dreams they had for their diagnosed child and the life they should have had.

The psychology of the family includes Maggie's diagnosis of generalized anxiety, which has included anxiety and panic attacks since her freshman year of college. Maggie described her father as a physically abusive alcoholic, and her mother as passive and an enabler. Individual psychology in this dimension is subjective and embraced concepts such as motives, ambitions, and defense mechanisms (Macleod et al., 2014). Maggie shared that she wanted to move to another state to get away from her father and forget all about him.

Third Dimension – Transaction and Generational Patterns

The therapist completed a genogram to gather initial information about Maggie and Jake's families-of-origin and past generations. The therapist discovered how each member within the system related to one another, in subsystem alliances, cut-offs, or competitions for power (Macleod et al., 2014). The therapist also explored Maggie's conflictual relationship with her father and mother, and the alliance Maggie and her mother formed against her father. This relational triangle relieved some stress, but did not address the real problem of her father's unemployment, drinking, and violence. Maggie also did not trust her mother because she could not keep her safe.

In her current relationship with Jake, Maggie seeks to fix problems that arise because she could not fix her nuclear family. Until Theo was diagnosed, Maggie believed she was successful in her role as family fixer and hero. However, her impractical attempts to "fix" Theo have increased her anxiety and panic attacks. Jake does not feel entitled to share his thoughts and concerns with his wife because when he does Maggie obsesses about her perceived failures. This relational pattern has threatened the balance of the family system (Macleod et al., 2014).

Abby has repeated her mother's pattern of trying to be perfect and fix problems. This has resulted in frustration and anger when she does not get all As or when she cannot stop Theo's meltdowns. The pattern is that Jake tries to calm her, but Abby retreats, goes to her room and draws. Abby says she loves Theo and has tried to spend time playing with him and his trains. She has learned that she cannot raise her voice during play, or break any of Theo's "rules," including the position of his trains and wearing his favorite blue shirt.

Fourth Dimension – Relational Ethics

The focus of the therapeutic process for the Trust family was their history of giving and receiving, fairness, entitlements, credits, and loyalty. Contextual therapy emphasizes the need to create interpersonal trust, achieved by means of caring acts (Horowitz, 2009). Abby attempts to be loyal to her parents by earning good grades, so they don't have to worry about her. This is a trustworthy act, but can also be overcompensating to try and make up for the family stress of

Theo's diagnosis. Abby's efforts to spend time with Theo, learn his rules, and follow his lead in play is another act to gain her parents' credit. In order to understand the history and impact of these acts, the therapist asked questions to understand the motivations of each family member. Is the family able to perceive each other's hurts and needs? Abby states she knows why her parents spend most of their time with Theo and she wants to help. In general, she is acting out of loyalty, which is a form of constructive entitlement.

However, Abby has not received credit for what she gives, causing a relational imbalance. Parentification is the contextual term that describes Abby's attempts to heal her mother's unmet needs (Böszörményi-Nagy & Krasner, 1986). Abby feels compelled to ease Maggie's distress by becoming a model child, attempting to balance the family ledger by compensating for Maggie's relationship with her mother (Shaham, 2005). Maggie relies on Abby to tell her she is a good mom and check in on her emotional state. Mom does not give Abby credit for making sure that she is okay and not feeling overwhelmed by Theo. The therapist addresses Maggie's destructive entitlement resulting from the lack of safety and credit she received from her mother.

The focal point of Maggie and Jake's feelings of unfairness is Theo's diagnosis of ASD. Their sense of injustice is viewed in their attempts to try to treat Theo like a "normal" kid. They have not told their extended family about his diagnosis and make excuses to neighbors about his loud meltdowns, telling them, "He just gets overly excited sometimes. He just needs a nap." Maggie feels it is unfair that she has a son with a disability because she worked so hard as a special education employee working with adults with intellectual disabilities. "I don't know if I have anything left," she said, "to admit that Theo has autism."

The therapist employed multidirected partiality to offer Maggie credit for all she had done, saying,

> I know it will not mean as much coming from me, but I think you deserve a lot of credit for the care and patience you gave the individuals you worked with. I wonder if you were so good at your job because of your legacy of giving to your childhood family?

This was helpful for Maggie to consider. She said, "I didn't think of it that way. I don't know if I could have been as patient with the individuals at the workshop and with Theo if I didn't have my childhood experiences."

Multidirected partiality decreases family members' reliance on blame and helps them increase understanding of each other, which benefits everyone (Ducommun-Nagy, 2003). Jake also gave his wife credit for the time and care she gives to their family. He said, "I know you get frustrated and do more than your share of work for Theo, but I really appreciate you."

The therapist also explored the ways in which Jake gave to the family. She discovered that Jake taught Theo a gesture of emotional connection. Since Theo does not like to be hugged, he taught Theo to touch his forehead to Jake's as a way to say, "I love you and it's going to be okay." He taught Theo to do the same with Maggie and Abby. The therapist gave Jake credit for this transaction of expressing love, care, and affection within the Trust family. Theo also was given credit for his giving to the family through love, small jobs, and even by having "rules" that decrease his sensory distress and keep him calm.

The therapist also explored Jake's invisible loyalty to his father. When Jake's mother was upset or in a bad mood, his father would spend more time at work and make excuses to be out of the house, and Jake does the same out of a sense of being loyal to his father. He had a close relationship with his father, but now feels guilty because he moved to another state. The therapist explored alternative ways for Jake to make his loyalty to his father visible. They agreed that Jake's childhood memory of going on walks with his father to talk would be a good alternative and a way to spend quality time with Abby or Theo. Exonerations is a contextual process of understanding and finding compassion for a parent who was not able to give in the past (Frank, 1984). This was a step toward Jake exonerating his father for abandoning him as a way to deal with his mother's anger.

Conclusion

Maggie and Jake were encouraged to earn credit by creating a narrative about Theo to explain his diagnosis to their family and neighbors. As explained by Adams and Maynard (2004), the family can only function effectively when they are held ethically accountable for their actions to balance a ledger of entitlements. Inviting family and friends to support them in raising Theo is a wonderful way to balance their ledger. Theo is entitled to have truthful information shared about his needs and strengths. The consideration of dimension four cleared the way for Theo's parents and sister to give him credit for what he gives to the family. Theo provided a consistent schedule and routine to an otherwise chaotic home. He also provided information about what makes him feel safe and calm. Theo also deserves credit for having the family seek help from the contextual family therapist. Even if Theo was not diagnosed with ASD, based on the information obtained in the first three dimensions, his family needed motivation to heal transgenerational wounds, embrace the significance of relational justice, and experience empathic consideration to create a legacy of trust, today and for future generations.

References

Adams, J., & Maynard, P. (2004). Contextual therapy: Applying the family ledger to couple therapy. *Journal of Couple & Relationship Therapy*, 3(1), 1–11.

Becvar, D., & Becvar, R. (2013). *Family therapy: A systemic integration*. 8th ed. Boston: Pearson Education.

Böszörményi-Nagy, I, & Krasner B. (1986). *Between give and take: Clinical guide to contextual therapy*. New York: Brunner/Mazel.

Böszörményi-Nagy, I., & Ulrich, D. (1981). Contextual family therapy. In A. S. Gurman, & P. Kniskern (Eds.), *Handbook of family therapy*. (pp. 159–186). New York: Brunner/Mazel.

Bronfenbrenner, U. (1994). Ecological models of human development. In T. Husen & T. N. Postlethwaite (Eds.), *The International encyclopedia of education*. Oxford, UK: Pergamon.

Ducommun-Nagy, C. (2003). *Can giving heal? Contextual therapy and biological psychiatry. In family therapy as an alternative to medication: An appraisal of pharmland*. New York: Brunner-Routledge.

Frank, C. (1984). Major constructs of contextual therapy: An interview with Dr. Ivan Böszörményi-Nagy. *The American Journal of Family Therapy, 12*(1), 7–14.

Gangamma, R., Bartle-Haring, S., & Glebova, T. (2012). A Study of Contextual Therapy Theory's Relational Ethics in Couples in Therapy. *Family Relations, 61*(5), 825–835.

Glebova, T., & Gangamma, R. (2017). Contextual family therapy. In J. Carlson & S. Dermer (Eds.), *The sage encyclopedia of marriage, family, and couples counseling* (Vol. 1, pp. 352–356). Thousand Oaks, CA: SAGE Publications, Inc.

Goldenthal, P. (1996). *Doing contextual therapy*. New York: W. W. Norton.

Horowitz, H. (2009). The Healing Power of Giving: A Contextual Therapy Case Study. *Journal of Spirituality in Mental Health, 11*(3), 213–217.

Macleod, D. J., Sadewa, A. B., Authur, R., Collins, K. L., Hand-Breckenridge, T. L., Runstedler, Y., & Van Hooren, K. A. (2014). The balance of fairness in family relations: A contextual family therapy case study. *Consensus, 35*(2), 1–12.

Magistro, C. A. (2014). Relational Dimensions of Environmental Crisis: Insights from Böszörményi-Nagy's contextual therapy. *Journal of Systemic Therapies, 33*(3), 17–28.

Neely, J., Amatea, E. S., Echevarria-Doan, S., & Tannen, T. (2012). Working with families living with autism: Potential contributions of marriage and family therapists. *Journal of Marital and Family Therapy, 38*, 211–226.

Ravindran, N., & Myers, B. (2012). Cultural influences on perceptions of health, illness, and disability: A review and focus on autism. *Journal of Child & Family Studies, 21*(2), 311–319.

Shaham, O. (2005). An illustration of contextual family therapy. *Family Therapy Magazine, 4*(5), 34–37.

Solomon, A. H., & Chung, B. (2012). Understanding autism: How family therapists can support parents of children with autism spectrum disorders. *Family Process, 51*(2), 250.

Sousa, A. C. (2011). From refrigerator mothers to warrior heroes: The cultural identity transformation of mothers raising children with intellectual disabilities. *Symbolic Interaction, 34*(2), 220–243.

13 Parent-Child Interaction Therapy with Families

Joshua Masse

Parent-Child Interaction Therapy (PCIT) is an evidence-based behavioral parent training (BPT) intervention for children aged two to seven years designed to decrease challenging behaviors (e.g., noncompliance, aggression, emotion dysregulation) while also enhancing caregiver-child relationships. Up until about 2007, cases of children with ASD were not commonly treated with PCIT as it was assumed that the intervention would not be effective with this population because of the reliance on social contingencies. However, accumulating clinical and research outcomes examining PCIT with the ASD population, coupled with the increased prevalence rate of ASD and a more thorough understanding of the secondary behavioral issues associated with ASD, has resulted in a proliferation of referrals to PCIT therapists. Given PCIT's behavioral underpinnings and a strong family-centered approach, the intervention is aligned with the evidence-base on how best to treat young children with ASD with co-occurring behavioral problems. This chapter provides a clinical and research overview of PCIT, a theoretical rationale outlining the utility of the treatment with the ASD population, and examples of clinical modifications of the model tailored for the ASD population and their families.

Overview of PCIT

PCIT was developed over 40 years ago by Dr. Sheila Eyberg at the Oregon Health and Science University and has since been widely researched and disseminated. The therapy is based on Hanf's (1969) two-stage treatment model and combines social learning theory, play therapy, and attachment theory (Eyberg & Funderburk, 2011; McNeil & Hembree-Kigin, 2010).

Similar to other behavior parenting training programs predicated on Hanf's model, PCIT includes two phases: a caregiver-child relationship enhancement phase (Child Directed Interaction [CDI]) and a structured discipline phase (Parent Directed Interaction [PDI]). Each phase of treatment begins with a didactic session, at which a therapist teaches, models, and role plays the PCIT skills with caregivers. Subsequent sessions begin with a brief check-in and a discussion of home practice. Next, behind a one-way mirror, a therapist uses the Dyadic Parent-Child Interaction Coding System (DPICS) to code parents for five minutes in the use of the PCIT skills. Based on the coding data, therapists establish goals for the sessions and live coach caregivers using a bug-in-the-ear microphone device while the parent and child play together. By way of active coaching, the therapist helps the parents master the skills by providing support, reinforcement, and corrective feedback. Caregivers are then assigned to practice the skills at home for five minutes daily.

The first phase of PCIT, CDI, is a form of therapeutic play in which the child leads the activity (if engaged in appropriate play) as parents are taught to provide support in an effort to enhance the parent-child relationship. Specifically, care-givers learn to follow the child's lead in play by using positive parenting skills, referred to as the PRIDE skills: **P**raising the child for a specific behavior (labeled praise), **R**eflecting the child's statements, **I**mitating the child's play, **D**escribing their child's behavior, and using **E**njoyment throughout the play. Parents also learn to avoid asking questions, criticizing, and giving commands as these behaviors prevent the child from leading the play and may create conflict.

With regard to behavior management in CDI, parents learn to use selective attention by responding to appropriate behaviors with the PRIDE skills while ignoring negative behaviors. In order to move onto the next phase of treatment (i.e., PDI), caregivers must demonstrate mastery of the skills. Mastery is defined as ten descriptions of child behavior, ten labeled praises, and ten reflections, while providing three or less commands, questions, and criticisms in a five-minute play situation without assistance from the therapist.

After the parents have mastered the CDI skills, they progress to PDI, the second phase of PCIT. In this phase, parents continue to use the skills taught in CDI while also learning skills to increase child compliance and pro-social behaviors and decrease inappropriate behaviors. In this phase, caregivers learn ways to give effective instructions and to consistently provide consequences for child compliance (i.e., contingent labeled praise) and noncompliance (i.e., standardized timeout procedure). PDI progresses in a gradual fashion as children learn to comply with increasingly more challenging requests. Additionally, parents learn strategies for enforcing house rules and controlling their child's behavior in public settings. PDI mastery is met when a caregiver administers effective (i.e., direct, clear) commands for 75 percent of the total commands given during a five-minute observation and 75 percent appropriate follow through (i.e., labeled praise for compliance, warning then timeout for noncompliance) to those commands. Graduation occurs when caregivers demonstrate mastery of CDI and PDI skills, Eyberg Child Behavior Inventory (ECBI; Eyberg & Ross, 1978) scores are below clinical cutoff, and caregivers feel confident to manage challenging behaviors across situations (for more information on PCIT, including training guidelines, visit www.pcit.org).

Treatment Outcomes of PCIT

PCIT research trials have been conducted since the 1990s and have shown the treatment to be effective in ameliorating a wide range of behavioral and emotional challenges. Although PCIT was originally devised for families of children with externalizing behaviors, several investigations have examined its usefulness with diverse populations, across settings, and with various clinical disorders. PCIT has been disseminated to children with developmental disorders and intellectual disability (Bagner & Eyberg, 2007), chronic illness (Bagner, Fernandez, & Eyberg, 2004), internalizing disorders (Pincus, Choate, Eyberg, & Barlow, 2005), and child maltreatment populations (Urquiza & McNeil, 1996). PCIT has been researched with a variety of cultural groups including Puerto Rican families (Matos, Torres, Santiago, Jurado, & Rodriguez, 2006), Mexican-American families (McCabe, Yeh, Garland, Lau, Chavez, 2005), Spanish speaking families (Borrego, Anhalt, Terao, Vargas, & Urquiza, 2006), and African American families (Capage, Bennett, & McNeil, 2001; Fernandez, Butler, & Eyberg, 2011). Also, PCIT has been shown to be effective in home-based settings and community outpatient centers (Fowles et al., 2017; Ware, McNeil, Masse, & Stevens, 2008) Finally, research has shown that treatment gains are maintained up to three to six years post-treatment (Hood & Eyberg, 2003).

With respect to PCIT with the ASD population, cases of ASD had historically been excluded from research trials as it was assumed that the treatment would not be effective due to PCIT's reliance on social contingencies. As such, although PCIT has been researched for decades, empirical investigations determining the effectiveness of PCIT with the ASD population are a fairly recent undertaking which started approximately ten years ago with a theoretical article (Masse, McNeil, Wagner, & Chorney, 2007) and has gained empirical momentum since. Presently, less than 15 articles have been published with the large majority of research constituting of case studies or small *n* designs. Although still accumulating, outcomes are strongly encouraging, demonstrating reductions in disruptive behavior and increases in positive parenting skills and expressive language (Hansen & Shillingsburg, 2016). Also, outcomes have demonstrated a positive impact on core ASD symptoms such as social awareness (Ginn, Clionsky, Eyberg, Warner-Metzger, & Abner, 2015), social relatedness and imitative skills (Masse & Warner-Metzger, in press; Masse, McNeil, Wagner, & Quetsch, 2016), and shared positive affect (Solomon, Ono, Timmer, & Goodlin-Jones, 2008; for a complete overview of PCIT and ASD research, see Lieneman, Brabson, Highlander, Wallace, & McNeil, 2017).

Rationale for Conducting PCIT with Families Raising a Child with ASD

As widely noted, there has been an increase in the prevalence rate of ASD in the past decade with current estimates suggesting one in 68 children are now identified with the disorder (Centers for Disease Control and Prevention [CDC], 2014). In addition, secondary conditions commonly co-occur and younger children are more likely to present for treatment due to concerns related to oppositional behaviors, aggression, self-injury, hyperactivity, or inattentive symptoms. Indeed, research has shown that up to 80 percent of children with ASD often present with at least one comorbid diagnosis and up to 37 percent meet diagnostic criteria for a disruptive behavior disorder (Kaat & Lecavalier, 2013; Simonoff et al., 2008). Left untreated, behavioral problems within the ASD population can lead to a wide-range impairment across domains including learning issues, social deficits, increased psychotropic medication use, and less success with ASD-related services such as speech therapy or occupational therapy (Butter, Wynn, & Mulick, 2003). As such, parents often place more emphasis on initially treating challenging behaviors rather than targeting the core symptoms of ASD (Shawler & Sullivan, 2015).

With respect to the family, behavioral challenges have been associated with difficulties with sibling relationships and poorer overall family functioning (Rao & Beidel, 2009). Given the chronicity of the disorder and prevalence of secondary conditions, raising a child with ASD can be burdensome on the family unit. Research shows that parents with children with ASD experience a significantly greater amount of stress in comparison to non-ASD children or even other children with other chronic disabilities (Hayes & Watson, 2013). Also, parents with children with ASD experience increased marital strain, and an increased risk for depression (Burrell & Borrego, 2011). Moreover, some parents may perceive challenging behaviors as chronic and less amendable to change, which may contribute to a more permissive or conflict-avoidant parenting style. For example, a caregiver ensures adherence to a strict schedule in an effort to prevent temper tantrums (e.g., "walking on eggshells"). As a result, the opportunities for social and behavioral development are disallowed and behavioral issues may go unmanaged or may intensify, thus increasing the likelihood of the number of deleterious consequences associated with negative behaviors, and increasing subsequent parent-child related stress.

PCIT is beneficial to families in that the treatment targets childhood disruptive behaviors and has been shown to reduce parenting stress for caregivers of children with ASD. Specifically, Ginn et al. (2017) found a positive trend on the difficult child subscale of the Parenting Stress Index (PSI) following the CDI portion of PCIT. Likewise, Agazzi and colleagues (2017) showed reductions in total stress on the PSI at post-treatment across three caregivers, and Masse (2010) demonstrated the parent-child dysfunctional interaction scale of the PSI dropped to below significant levels for two of three dyads at post-treatment, while the other dyad reported a low level at pre-treatment.

From a therapeutic background perspective, BPT models such as PCIT compare favorably to ASD-focused interventions as taking an integrative approach by involving family members in therapy (Strauss et al., 2012). As noted, PCIT empowers caregivers to be the primary agent of change in shaping their child's behavior and being able to provide ongoing treatment across settings. Research has demonstrated that outcomes for children with ASD are more positive and generalizable with family involvement in treatment compared to sole interventionists (Burrell & Borrego, 2011). Furthermore, research has revealed that shared core components of both PCIT and ASD-focused approaches result in the largest effects on outcomes with children with ASD.

These include parental involvement, behavioral-based techniques grounded in learning principles, a focus on improving communication, teaching appropriate play and social skills (e,g. imitation, turn taking), and skill building in a natural setting (Masse, McNeil, Wagner, & Chorney, 2007; Rogers & Vismara, 2008). In sum, as evidenced by a recent meta-analysis demonstrating the effectiveness of BPTs (Postorino et al., 2017), parent training models serve a critical function in the treatment of young children with autism.

From a treatment standpoint, given the diagnostic increase of ASD and the common co-occurring behavioral issues, there has been an increase in the number of children with ASD referred to outpatient clinics for behavioral treatment. Although long-proven treatments for ASD (e.g., Lovaas' ABA approach; Rogers & Vismara, 2008) exist, they are oftentimes unavailable in particular areas of the country, are too intensive (e.g., 40 hours/week) or too expensive for families, namely those who are low-resourced (Ginn et al., 2017). Therefore, in the past several years, PCIT has presented as an affordable, short-term intervention to treat children with ASD in community settings.

Theoretical Considerations for Conducting PCIT with ASD

A crucial consideration when conducting PCIT with the ASD population is determining whether social attention is reinforcing to a child given that PCIT is predicated upon the supposition that a child's behavior is responsive to caregiver attention. To assess the impact of social reinforcement, PCIT allows for continuous functional analysis of behavior. For example, when a caregiver is told to remove attention for child disruptive behaviors, a therapist is able to observe – in real time – the consequence of that behavior and make a determination of its reinforcing value. These types of contingencies occur numerous times throughout a coaching session. At present, there are a lack of research findings or definitions of a particular subset of children with ASD who respond more favorably to PCIT skills than others. However, the general recommendation is to make a determination after caregivers have consistently used the breadth of CDI skills at a high rate. This way a child is experiencing an obvious contrast of caregiver attention in response to positive or neutral behavior versus disruptive behavior and a stronger conclusion of whether treatment is effective can be drawn.

Clinical Modifications to PCIT for the ASD Population

Research has demonstrated that PCIT is a robust and versatile treatment requiring minimal change to realize optimal outcomes across settings and diagnoses. However, ASD is unique given the wide range of clinical impairment. Although formal clinical parameters for PCIT with ASD have not yet been developed, some tailoring may be necessary, as determined by functional level. For example, a child with ASD and Level 1 functioning likely would require fewer modifications to the protocol as compared to a child with a more pervasive and severe behavioral presentation. As such, it's important to focus on symptom severity in determining whether modifications to the protocol are needed. It's imperative to note that changes to the core components (e.g., coaching, coding, relying on behavioral principles) of the treatment are never warranted and adaptations should not be applied in a generic manner, but rather after careful assessment and consideration (Masse & Warner-Metzger, in press).

One illustration of clinical tailoring is exemplified by way of stereotyped or repetitive verbal behaviors (e.g., echolalia). For children who demonstrate lower instances of echolalia, average to above average language capabilities, and are noticeably motivated by social reinforcement, differential attention (e.g., ignoring the echolalia and attending to other vocalizations) may be an appropriate technique to coach caregivers to reduce this verbal behavior. However, for some children with more severe symptoms and less developed verbal skills, this form of language may serve as a functional bridge as they develop their communicative repertoire. Therefore, PCIT coaches should not ignore this behavior but use the occurrence as an opportunity to *meet* their child at their functional level and *expand* the child's language capabilities (e.g., vocabulary, concepts) through scaffolding (Masse & Warner-Metzger, in press). The following exchange demonstrates the meet and expand approach:

CHILD: This train moves fast! *(delayed echolalia)*
CAREGIVER: The train does move fast! *(Reflection and meeting child at level of functional language)*
CHILD: This train moves fast!
CAREGIVER: I like how you're being gentle with the train. *(Label Praising and expanding appropriate play behaviors)*
CHILD: This train moves fast!
CAREGIVER: You're putting a lion on the train car. *(Behavior Description and expanding vocabulary)*
CHILD: This train moves fast!
CAREGIVER: I'll put an animal on the train car, too. *(modeling extension of play behaviors and scaffolding perspective of others)*
PARENT: I like playing with you. *(Label Praise and encouraging pro-social skills in context of stereotyped speech)*

In addition to stereotyped verbal behaviors, the meet and expand approach can also be applied to repetitive play. For example, many children with ASD prefer to continually line up specific toys or are overly focused on parts of objects thereby diminishing functional play opportunities. While PCIT therapists are encouraged to retain preferred toys in the therapy session, introducing novel play activities is warranted in an effort to expand a child's play repertoire. The following is another example of the meet and expand and approach applied to repetitive behavior interests: *You're lining up the dinosaurs* (Behavior Description). [Parent picks up Legos] *I'm going to make a tree the dinosaur can eat from* [places the tree right next to dinosaur's mouth]. *Oh, you're helping the dinosaur eat* (Behavior Description)!

Although CDI – with slight variations contingent upon functioning level – is appropriate and beneficial for the great majority of children with ASD, more consideration is needed about the appropriateness of the PDI phase. For example, PCIT may not be warranted for all children with poor receptive language (< 24 months) who do not understand simple instructions. As a general rule, if a child is unable to identify ten common objects or follow single-step instructions, it is not appropriate to administer the PDI sequence (Masse & Warner-Metzger, in press). In addition, some children may benefit from an additional teaching phase before introducing the timeout. As outlined in Lesack, Bearss, Celano, and Sharpe (2014), one method is a three-step "errorless learning" prompting sequence that begins with a caregiver combining a command with a gesture, followed by modeling compliance while repeating the command, and then physically guiding the child to comply. Once mastery is attained, defined as compliance with three consecutive commands needing only a verbal or model prompt, the timeout sequence is taught to the child. Other PDI modifications may include truncated commands to as few words as possible (e.g., "put block here"), and shaping the timeout to shorter time increments. Again, these adaptations should be considered in the context of functional ability and should not be applied universally with all ASD cases.

As noted, given the chronicity and range of behavioral difficulties connected to ASD, family factors such as caregiver stress and sibling conflict is an important variable to continually monitor and address throughout PCIT. In terms of caregiver stress, a PCIT clinician may consider dedicating several more minutes at the outset or at the end of the session (to protect coaching time) to allow parents the opportunity to discuss stressors (both related and unrelated to the child's behavior). Likewise, caregivers could be instructed to delineate additional concerns or stressors regarding their home practice for their therapist to review at the upcoming session. Alternatively, a phone or email check-in during the week may be appropriate. As stress can impact psychological functioning, a mental health referral for a caregiver may be appropriate. Also, perhaps due to the intense nature of the behavioral challenges and chronicity of ASD, research has shown that some families may need more sessions, particularly during PDI (Masse et al., 2016).

With regard to siblings, the PCIT protocol (Eyberg & Funderburk, 2011) includes sessions dedicated to implementing the skills with the identified client and his/her siblings (if applicable). These sessions range in objectives, but the overall focus is typically increasing pro-social and reciprocal relationship skills. For a child with ASD, specific skills could include sharing, eye contact, showing an interest in a sibling's play, expanding play themes and types of toys with a sibling, and basic conversational skills. During sibling sessions, PCIT therapists coach parents to remain vigilant of social behaviors that are typically difficult for children on the spectrum. These behaviors may include engaging in less preferred (e.g., the sibling's preferred) activities, utilizing toys with the sibling that do not inherently complement one another (such as trucks and dolls), allowing for inclusion in the play (e.g., the sibling puts a Lego on the same wall the target child is building), or making polite requests of the siblings (asking sibling for a piece of paper to draw on). In summary, ongoing assessment and monitoring of family stressors should be of primary importance when conducting PCIT with the ASD population (Masse & Warner-Metzger, in press).

Conclusion and Future Directions

The proliferation of ASD has led to the greater need of evidence-based, readily available, and affordable interventions for young children with ASD and their families. It is critical that community providers are informed about and trained in proven, research-driven, family-based treatments to ensure children and their families are receiving optimal care. As ASD impacts both the child and his/her family, providing parents with specific techniques to manage behavior across settings is critical in the treatment approach. PCIT is a family-based model originally developed to reduce challenging behaviors while improving caregiver-child relationships for children without ASD. However, accumulating research has shown PCIT, without major adaptation and while maintaining its core components, produces comparable outcomes with children on the autism spectrum by ameliorating behavioral challenges and reducing caregiver stress. Going forward, PCIT practice guidelines will continue to evolve as informed by the bi-directional relationship of clinical experience and empirical findings.

References

Agazzi, H., Yin Tan, R., Ogg, J., Armstrong, K., & Kirby, S. (2017). Does Parent–Child Interaction Therapy (PCIT) reduce maternal stress, anxiety, and depression among mothers of children with autism spectrum disorder? *Child and Family Behavior Therapy, 39*(4), 283–303.

Bagner, D. M., Fernandez, M. A., & Eyberg, S. M. (2004). Parent–child interaction therapy and chronic illness: A case study. *Journal of Clinical Psychology in Medical Settings, 11*, 1–6.

Bagner, D. M., & Eyberg, S. M. (2007). Parent–child interaction therapy for disruptive behavior in children with mental retardation: A randomized controlled trial. *Journal of Clinical Child and Adolescent Psychology, 36*, 418–429.

Borrego, J., Anhalt, K., Terao, S. Y., Vargas, E. C., & Urquiza, A. J. (2006). Parent–Child Interaction Therapy with a Spanish speaking family. *Cognitive and Behavioral Practice, 13*, 121–133.

Burrell, T. L., & Borrego, J. (2011). Parent's involvement in ASD treatment: What is their role? *Cognitive and Behavioral Practice, 19*, 423–432.

Butter, E. M., Wynn, J., & Mulick, J. A. (2003). Early intervention critical to autism treatment. *Pediatric Annals, 32*, 677–684.

Capage, L. C., Bennett, G. M., & McNeil, C. B. (2001). A comparison between African American and Caucasian children referred for treatment of disruptive behavior disorders. *Child & Family Behavior Therapy, 23*, 1–14.

Centers for Disease Control and Prevention (2014). Prevalence of autism spectrum disorders among children aged 8 years: Autism and developmental disabilities monitoring network, 11 sites, United States, 2010, *MMWR Surveillance Summaries, 63*(2), 1–22.

Eyberg, S. M., & Funderburk, B. (2011). *Parent–Child Interaction Therapy Protocol.* Gainesville, FL: PCIT International.

Eyberg, S. M., & Ross, A. W. (1978). Assessment of child behavior problems: The validation of a new inventory. *Journal of Clinical Child Psychology, 7,* 113–116.

Fernandez, M. A., Butler, A., & Eyberg, S. M. (2011). Treatment outcome for low socioeconomic status African American families in Parent–Child Interaction Therapy: a pilot study. *Child and Family Behavior Therapy, 33,* 1, 32–48.

Fowles, T., Masse, J., McGoron, K., Beveridge, R., Williamson, A., Smith, M., & Parrish, B. (2017). Home-based vs. clinic-based Parent–Child Interaction Therapy: comparative effectiveness in the context of dissemination and implementation. *Journal of Child and Family Studies,* Advance online publication. https://doi.org/10.1007/s10826-017-0958-3.

Ginn, N. C., Clionsky, L. N., Eyberg, S. M., Warner-Metzger, C., & Abner, J. P. (2017). Child-directed interaction training for young children with autism spectrum disorders: Parent and child outcomes. *Journal of Clinical Child & Adolescent Psychology, 46*(1), 101–109.

Hanf, C. (1969). *A two-stage program for modifying maternal controlling during mother–child (M–C) interaction.* Paper presented at the meeting of the Western Psychological Association, Vancouver, British Columbia, Canada.

Hansen, B., & Shillingsburg, A. (2016). Using a modified Parent–Child Interaction Therapy to increase vocalizations in children with autism. *Child and Family Behavior Therapy, 38,* 4, 318–330.

Hayes S. A., & Watson S. L. (2013). The impact of parenting stress: a meta-analysis of studies comparing the experience of parenting stress in parents of children with and without autism spectrum disorder. *Journal of Autism and Developmental Disorders, 43*(3), 629–642. doi:10.1007/s10803-012-1604-y.

Hood, K. K., & Eyberg, S. M. (2003). Outcomes of parent–child interaction therapy: Mothers' reports of maintenance three to six years after treatment. *Journal of Clinical Child and Adolescent Psychology, 32,* 419–429.

Kaat, A. J., & Lecavalier, L. (2013). Disruptive behavior disorders in children and adolescents with autism spectrum disorders: A review of the prevalence, presentation, and treatment. *Research in Autism Spectrum Disorders, 7,* 1579–1594.

Lesack, R., Bearss, K., Celano, M., & Sharp, W. G. (2014). Parent–child interaction therapy and autism spectrum disorder: Adaptations with a child with severe developmental delays. *Clinical Practice in Pediatric Psychology, 2*(1), 68–82.

Lieneman, C. C., Brabson, L. A., Highlander, A., Wallace, N. M., & McNeil, C. B. (2017). Parent–child interaction therapy: Current perspectives. *Psychology Research and Behavior Management, 10,* 239–256.

Masse, J. J. (2010). Examining the efficacy of parent–child interaction therapy with high-functioning autism. Dissertation Abstracts International: Section B: The Sciences and Engineering, Vol 70(10-B) p. 6558; ProQuest Information & Learning.

Masse, J. J., McNeil, C. B., Wagner, S. M., & Chorney, D. B. (2007). Parent–child interaction therapy and high-functioning autism: A conceptual overview. *Journal of Early and Intensive Behavior Intervention, 4*(4), 714–735.

Masse, J. J., McNeil, C. B., Wagner, S., & Quetsch, L. B. (2016). Examining the efficacy of parent-child interaction therapy with children on the autism spectrum. *Journal of Child and Family Studies, 25*(8), 2508–2525.

Masse, J., & Warner-Metzger, C. (in press). Melding of two worlds: Lessons learned about PCIT and autism spectrum disorders. In C. McNeil, Quetsch, L., & Anderson, C. (Eds.),

Handbook of parent-child interaction therapy for children on the autism spectrum. New York, NY: Springer.

Matos, M., Torres, R., Santiago, R., Jurado, M., & Rodriguez, I. (2006). Adaptation of parent-child interaction therapy for Puerto Rican families: A preliminary study. *Family Process, 45,* 205–222.

McCabe, K. M., Yeh, M., Garland, A. F., Lau, A. S., & Chavez, G. (2005). The GANA program: A tailoring approach to adapting parent–child interaction therapy for Mexican Americans. *Education and Treatment of Children, 28,* 111–129.

McNeil C. B., & Hembree-Kigin, T. L. (2010). *Parent–child interaction therapy.* New York, NY: Springer.

Pincus, D. B., Choate, M. L., Eyberg, S. M., & Barlow, D. H. (2005). Treatment of young children with separation anxiety disorder using parent–child interaction therapy. *Cognitive and Behavioral Practice, 12,* 126–135.

Postorino, V., Sharp, W., McCracken, C., Bearss, K., Burrell, T. L, Evans, A. N., & Scahill, L. (2017). A systematic review and meta-analysis of parent training for disruptive behavior in children with autism spectrum disorder. *Clinical Child and Family Psychology Review, 20,* 391–402.

Rao, P., & Beidel, D. (2009). The impact of children with high-functioning autism on parental stress, sibling adjustment, and family functioning. *Behavior Modification, 33*(4), 437–451.

Rogers, S. J., & Vismara, L. A. (2008). Evidence-based comprehensive treatments for early autism. *Journal of Clinical Child & Adolescent Psychology, 37*(1), 8–38.

Shawler, P., & Sullivan, M. (2015). Parental stress, discipline strategies, and child behavior problems in families with young children with autism spectrum disorders. *Focus on Autism and Other Developmental Disabilities, 32*(2), 142–151.

Simonoff, E., Pickles, A., Charman, T., Chandler, S., Loucas, T., & Baird, G. (2008). Psychiatric disorders in children with autism spectrum disorders: prevalence, comorbidity, and associated factors in a population-derived sample. *J Am Acad Child Adolesc Psychiatry, 47*(8), 921–929.

Solomon, M., Ono, M., Timmer, S., & Goodlin-Jones. (2008). The effectiveness of parent-chile interaction therapy for families of children on the autism spectrum. *Journal of Autism and Developmental Disorders, 38,* 1767–1776.

Strauss, K., Vicari, S., Valeri, G., D'Elia, L., Arima, S., & Fava, L. (2012). Parent inclusion in early intensive behavioral intervention: the influence of parental stress, parent treatment fidelity and parent-mediated generalization of behavior targets on child outcomes. *Research in Developmental Disabilities, 33*(2), 688–703.

Urquiza, A. J., & McNeil, C. B. (1996). Parent–child interaction therapy: Potential applications for physically abusive families. *Child Maltreatment, 1,* 134–144.

Ware, L. M., McNeil, C. B., Masse, J. J., & Stevens, S. B. (2008). Efficacy of in-home parent–child interaction therapy. *Child and Family Behavior Therapy, 30*(2), 127–135.

Part IV
ASD through the Lifespan

14 Empowering Parents After a Recent Diagnosis

Jennifer Jones and Kami Gallus

It is often said that no two people with autism are alike. The same is true of families. If you have met one parent of a child with ASD, you have met one parent of a child with ASD. Even parents of the same child are likely to have distinct, individual processes. The goal of this chapter is to sensitize clinicians to parents' experiences of obtaining and receiving a diagnosis and the fear, worry, and stress that often accompanies their child's new diagnostic label. The chapter will also discuss meaning making as an important and effective coping strategy. Finally, this chapter will provide clinicians with principles for practice when supporting parents coping with loss and beginning the process of meaning making. Clinicians' work with families indicates the meaning making journey does not have clear starting or ending points, rather the threads of meaning are woven into the fabric of parents' unique narratives that often includes more questions than answers.

The Missing Piece: The Quest for a Diagnosis

While every parent's experience is unique, the quest for a diagnosis is often accompanied by common questions, concerns, and emotions that something "just isn't right." For Kelli, that realization came before her son Logan's first birthday,

> ... all seemed to be going well and on track for Logan throughout the first months of his sweet life. One day, when he was about 10½–11 months of age, he just stopped saying words. We began noticing how he engaged and played with toys – he would watch the wheels spin on cars, he loved (and still loves) fans. With other toys, he would hold them in his lap and slap or hit at them. We realized something wasn't right. And so the journey began with a lot, I mean a lot of doctor visits, assessments and tests.

Research suggests parents of children with ASD often experience many obstacles on their quest for a diagnosis (Howlin & Moore, 1997). Even though parents frequently begin reporting concerns around the age of two years or earlier, children with ASD are oftentimes not diagnosed until around the age of four years (Center for Disease Control and Prevention, 2012). Depending on the complexity of ASD, parents may be told by professionals to "wait and see" or that their child is "likely to outgrow it" despite expressing their concerns for months or even years (Perry, Koudys, Dunlap, & Black, 2017). During this frustrating period of doubt and anxiety, parents experience higher levels of distress as they attempt to convince professionals that their concerns lie well beyond one phase of development (Goin-Kochel, Mackintosh, & Myers, 2006).

Rearranging the Pieces: The New Puzzle

After months or years of seeking answers to explain their child's behavior and development, the receipt of a formal diagnosis of ASD is always a unique and deeply personal experience for parents. Reflecting on the day she received Logan's diagnosis more than 20 years earlier, Kelli said:

> I remember the visit like it was yesterday. The doctor said, "Logan will probably never talk or be able to attend a public school." What were we supposed to do with this information? We were first-time parents – scared, worried, confused, angry at what we just heard, and very overwhelmed.

Logan's father, Pat, shared his thoughts about the day they received Logan's diagnosis:

> Although not much was known about autism at that time, I had a strong feeling that would be the diagnosis. I never really became depressed or anxious about his diagnosis; I just wanted to make sure we did everything we could for him. I remember a small amount of shock to actually hear the doctor give us the diagnosis, but I really knew what the outcome was going to be for several months.

Similar to Pat and Kelli, research indicates parents experience a variety of emotions in response to receiving a formal diagnosis, including worry, fear, sadness, anger, and guilt (Myers, Mackintosh, & Goin-Kochel, 2009). Parents also face their own unique set of stressors based on a child's distinct challenges, required accommodations, and co-occurring diagnoses (Herring et al., 2006). The stress parents of children with ASD experience comes from a variety of factors, with parents of children with more severe impairment reporting higher stress (Hastings & Johnson, 2001). Research has repeatedly found that parents of children with ASD report significantly higher levels of stress and aggravation than parents of typically developing children or children with other developmental disabilities (Dabrowska, 2010; Estes et al., 2009; Schieve, Blumberg, Rice, Visser, & Boyle, 2007). Sharpley, Bitsika, and Efremidis (1997) found that more than 80 percent of parents of a child with ASD reported feeling stretched beyond their limits. The three most stressful factors reported by parents involve concern over the permanency of the condition, poor acceptance of behaviors by society and family members, and low levels of social support (Sharpley et al., 1997).

The unknown regarding their child's future may also weigh heavily on parents. With early diagnosis and intervention some individuals with ASD are able to meet typical adult milestones (e.g., financial independence); however, many also have intellectual disability and/or mental health and behavioral disorders that require long-term services and supports (Perry et al., 2017). Furthermore, financial hardships, child behaviors that are disruptive or hard to manage, strained extended family relationships, inadequate supports and services, and social stigma and discrimination may lead to parents who are socially isolated and struggling to make meaning particularly in the months and years immediately following their child's diagnosis.

Making Meaning of the Puzzle

While it is common to wrestle with a sense of loss surrounding their child's diagnosis, how parents cope with this unique loss varies widely. Research suggests that parents' use of coping strategies that rely on cognitive problem-solving and social support networks yields more positive adjustment outcomes (Glidden, 2012). Likewise, positive reappraisal and reframing results in greater well-being and positive perceptions among parents of children with disabilities (Glidden, Billings, & Jobe, 2006; Hastings, Allen, McDermott, & Still, 2002). Meaning making is an important and constructive process of coping for parents rearing a child with ASD (Pakenham, Sofronoff, & Samios, 2004). Theoretical models of meaning making emphasize two fundamental tasks of recovery and resolution: sense making and benefit-finding (Davis, Nolen-Hoeksema, & Larson, 1998).

The sense making construal of meaning making involves developing explanations for the loss or stressful life event within one's existing schemas or worldviews. Qualitative studies of parents of children with an ASD diagnosis report prominent and consistent themes of searching for meaning (Bayat, 2007; King et al., 2006). Parents' discourse regarding sense making encompasses a broad range of ongoing attempts to understand autism, including possible causes, anticipated cures, and religious explanations as well as themes of accepting the diagnosis or reframing ASD in terms of differentness and strengths (Huws, Jones, & Ingledew, 2001; Pakenham et al., 2004). Pat shared the role of his faith in making sense of Logan's diagnosis, "I fully believe God doesn't make mistakes and every situation happens for a reason. Logan brings joy and happiness to everyone he encounters, which is his gift."

Deriving benefit from loss or stressful life events involves the process of assigning positive value or significance to the event for one's own life. Benefit-finding does not negate the challenges associated with parenting a child with ASD; rather it is a coping mechanism that parents may employ on their journey to meaning making. Researchers have found that parents of children with ASD report benefits such as positive changes in personality and/or life priorities, greater understanding of children with disabilities, increased knowledge, new opportunities, strengthened relationships and growth in faith/spirituality (Pakenham et al., 2004). Both Pat and Kelli articulate specific benefits to being

Logan's parents. Kelli shared, "Parenting a child with ASD has taught me how to celebrate and appreciate the small victories. It has changed the way I teach, how I see others and their challenges." Similarly, Pat shared:

> Logan had a huge influence in the person I have become. I am a much more patient and giving person because of him. For our family, Logan has brought us closer together as we all try to come up with ways to improve his life.

The quality of parents' relationships with family members, mentors, doctors, therapists, teachers, and other professionals within their social networks also stands out as key to the process of making meaning after adversity and loss. Parents with strong social support through good relationships with professionals report more positive experiences of diagnosis (O'Brien & Daggett, 2006). Further, researchers found that parents who reported greater connection and satisfaction with a social support network derived more benefits from and engaged in more sense making discourse regarding their child's ASD diagnosis (Pakenham et al., 2004). For Kelli, relationships with other parents served a crucial role in her meaning making process:

> It has been so comforting to share these years with other parents of children with disabilities and know we speak the same language! It's a blessing knowing Logan has a buddy to spend the night with – a place to go and hang out where he is understood and loved for all of his quirks and endless conversations about monster trucks, the fair, and every holiday.

Principles of Practice for Supporting Families

The following principles reflect the values we believe professionals must subscribe to when working alongside parents of children with ASD as they navigate meaning making across the lifespan. We are keenly aware there is not a one-size-fits all approach that will guarantee success. It is our hope that these four broad principles will empower helping professionals to engage parents who are navigating their own journeys following their child's diagnosis.

Understand your values. Recognizing that the mental model of helping professionals carry into their work with individuals and families greatly impacts the helping process, it is important for professionals to identify and acknowledge their personal values and beliefs regarding ASD. As professionals, we hold working mental models of ASD that serve to define our understanding of the diagnosis, determine the terminology we use, and ultimately provide the basis upon which we devise strategies for providing supports and services. All professionals must be aware of the mental model they bring to the helping relationship and how their own working model impacts meaning making processes. Professionals must check their biases, including believing the common myths that having a family member with ASD is solely a liability or blessing to marriage and family relationships. Strategies applied when working with families of individuals with challenges, and resources of each family member, including the individual with ASD.

Recognize resilience. While the ASD diagnosis is bestowed upon an individual, all members and the family system as a whole are impacted. Professionals working alongside individuals with ASD and their families would benefit from an understanding of general system theory (Satir, 1967; von Bertalanffy, 1968) and family quality of life (Zuna, Summers, Turnbull, Hu, & Xu, 2010). Professionals who adhere to these systemic approaches exhibit a richer understanding of families as systems whose parts are interdependent and open to change.

Helping professionals need to be empathetic listeners and creative problem solvers when addressing the unique needs of parents. Utilizing a strengths-based approach that promotes individual and family resilience is essential. Engaging in the meaning making process empowers families to acknowledge their strengths, utilize their resources, and recognize their own capacity for resilience. Bayat (2007) uncovered four resilience enhancing processes among parents of children with ASD: making positive meaning of disability, mobilizing resources, finding greater appreciation of life in general, and gaining spiritual strength. Informed helping professionals must recognize when to intervene on natural resilience processes. For example, if parents do not seem to be engaging in meaning making process but neither are they experiencing distress, there may be no clinical utility in engaging in meaning making work. However, for parents reporting or experiencing distress following a child's ASD diagnosis, helping professionals can partner with families by exploring and enhancing these known resilience processes as parents engage with their unique ASD narratives.

Help families engage with their unique narratives of ASD. Narratives are the life stories we tell ourselves about ourselves. Parents' meaning of their children's ASD diagnosis is embedded in these narratives and can be evoked by assisting parents to share their life stories in their own words. As parents engage with their unique narratives (Michie & Skinner, 2010) they begin to reframe their understanding of the diagnosis in a manner that enhances meaning making, well-being, and acceptance of ASD as a part of life. Helping professionals working with parents of children recently diagnosed with ASD can borrow from meaning making interventions like those originally developed to assist trauma survivors (Grossman & Lee, 1998) and later adapted to work with patients following a cancer diagnosis (Lee, Cohen, Edgar, Laizner, & Gagnon, 2006). Key strategies of meaning interventions consist of utilizing Socratic questioning (Carey & Mullan, 2004) and "lifeline" interventions (Tracz & Gehart-Brooks, 1999) to initiate story-telling and assist with breaking the story into manageable facts. Once the story of diagnosis and unfolding life with ASD has been told, helping professionals can then help parents identify underlying assumptions and beliefs that have emerged while reviewing the stressors from different perspectives. Meaning making interventions are directed primarily at parents' inner worlds, assisting parents in reflecting on their thoughts, feelings, and behaviors experienced as a result of the diagnosis and ultimately exploring alternative explanations and storylines.

Parents also need time and support to reimagine a future that includes ASD for themselves and their child. Particularly in the early years after diagnosis, parents may wrestle with finding hope and seeing possibilities. Reflecting on what she needed most in the days, months, and years following Logan's diagnosis, Kelli explained, "I desperately needed to find someone who had 'been there, done that.' I needed someone to tell me Logan would be OK and where to go from here, but first, someone who would let me cry." Helping professionals must provide a safe haven for parents to honestly and accurately describe the joys, losses, celebrations, and setbacks that occur along their meaning making journey by validating the rewards and challenges associated with parenting a child with ASD. Once parents begin to understand and validate the assumptions and beliefs that developed as a result of their children's diagnosis, helping professionals can assist parents with rearranging life priorities and making personal decisions necessary to live a meaningful life in the present that provides hope for the future.

Help parents reimagine a future. Parents of individuals with ASD seemingly face one marathon after another beginning with their quest for a diagnosis and then seeking treatment, supports, and services for their child – all while simultaneously assimilating the meaning and experience of ASD into their own personal and social identity. Following their child's diagnosis, parents may feel a sense of urgency to find answers for the never-ending questions each day brings. Clinicians can play a valuable role in setting the pace for the marathons parents are just beginning. Each family's journeys to meaning making will be unique, but all families will benefit from helping professionals who acknowledge and validate the impact and permanency of ASD while also giving parents permission to maintain their individual identity as they assimilate their new role as a parent of a child with ASD. Parents may also need time and support to cope with the loss of one future and reimagine a new future for themselves and for their child.

For Pat and Kelli, the meaning making journey continues even 20 plus years after Logan was diagnosed with ASD. The challenges continue and are often heightened around times of transition. Yet, they both recount numerous benefits. Pat and Kelli's narratives reflect how they have coped with the losses associated with ASD and the support systems that helped them capitalize on Logan's unique abilities. Logan has far exceeded the doctor's original prognosis. Logan works three days a week at the zoo doing what he loves most – greeting people and making them smile. He also volunteers at the Children's Hospital each week. Pat and Kelli are so proud of his independence:

Logan makes his own breakfast; packs his lunch and medicine; picks out what to wear; and communicates with family and friends on his cell phone through calls, texting and social media! Logan loves life and never ceases to amaze us as he continues to work hard and accomplish some pretty awesome stuff!

Conclusion

If you've met one family of a child with ASD, you've met one family of a child with ASD. Understanding and appreciating the unique characteristics and experiences of each family is foundational for clinicians as they assist families with coping strategies following their child's diagnosis. There is not a singular therapeutic method approach guaranteed to ensure success. However, four broad principles – understand your values, recognize resilience, help families engage with their unique narratives of ASD, and help families reimagine a future – can empower helping professionals to engage parents as they navigate their meaning making journeys.

Acknowledgment

The authors would like to express their sincere appreciation to Pat and Kelli for sharing their meaning making journey as Logan's parents.

References

Bayat, M. (2007). Evidence of resilience in families of children with autism. *Journal of Intellectual Disability, 51*, 702–714.

Carey, T. A., & Mullan, R. J. (2004). What is Socratic questioning? *Psychotherapy: Theory, Research, Practice, Training, 41*(3), 217–226. doi:10.1037/0033-3204.41.3.217.

Center for Disease Control and Prevention. (2012). Prevalence of autism spectrum disorders – Autism and Developmental Disabilities Monitoring Network, 14 sites, United States, 2008. *MMWR Surveillance Summaries, 61*, 1–19.

Dabrowska, A. (2010). Parenting stress and coping styles in mothers and fathers of preschool children with autism and Down syndrome. *Journal of Intellectual Disability Research, 54*(3), 266–280.

Davis, C. G., Nolen-Hoeksema, S., & Larson, J. (1998). Making sense of loss and benefiting from the experience: Two construals of meaning. *Journal of Personality and Social Psychology, 75*, 561–574.

Estes, A., Munson, J., Dawson, G., Koehler, E., Zhou, X., & Abbott, R. (2009). Parenting stress and psychological functioning among mothers of preschool children with autism and developmental delay. *Autism, 13*(4), 375–387.

Glidden, L. M. (2012). Family well-being and children with intellectual disability. In J. A. Burack, R. M. Hodapp, & G. Iarocci, & E. Zigler (Eds.). *The Oxford Handbook of Intellectual Disability and Development.* (pp. 303–317). Oxford University Press: New York.

Glidden, L. M., Billings, F. J., & Jobe, B. M. (2006). Personality, coping style, and well-being of parents rearing children with developmental disabilities. *Journal of Intellectual Disability Research, 50*, 949–962.

Goin-Kochel, R. P., Mackintosh, V. H., & Myers, B. J. (2006). How many doctors does it take to make an autism spectrum diagnosis? *Autism, 10*(5), 439–451.

Grossman, M., & Lee, V. (1998). Meaning intervention manual. Unpublished manuscript. McGill University, Montreal, Quebec, Canada.

Hastings, R. P., Allen, R., McDermott, K., & Still, D. (2002). Factors related to positive perceptions of mothers with children with intellectual disabilities. *Journal of Applied Research in Intellectual Disabilities, 15*, 269–275.

Hastings, R. P., & Johnson, E. (2001). Stress in UK families conducting intensive home-based behavioural intervention for their young child with autism. *Journal of Autism and Developmental Disorders, 31*, 327–336.

Herring, S., Gray, K., Faffe, J., Tonge, B., Sweeney, D., & Einfeld, S. (2006). Behaviour and emotional problems in toddlers with pervasive developmental disorders and developmental delay: Associations in parental mental health and family functioning. *Journal of Intellectual Disability Research, 50*, 874–882.

Howlin, P., & Moore, A. (1997). Diagnosis in Autism: A survey of over 1200 patients in the UK. *Autism, 1*(2), 135–162.

Huws, J. C., Jones, R. S. P., & Ingledew, D. K. (2001). Parents of children with autism using an email group: A grounded theory study. *Journal of Health Psychology, 6*(5), 569–584.

King, G. A., Zwaigenbaum, L., King, S., Baxter, D., Rosenbaum, P., & Bates, A. (2006). A qualitative investigation of changes in the belief systems of families of children with autism or Down syndrome. *Child: Care, Health, and Development, 32*, 353–369.

Lee, V., Cohen, S. R., Edgar, L., Laizner, A. M., & Gagnon, A. J. (2006). Meaning-making intervention during breast or colorectal cancer treatment improves self-esteem, optimism, and self-efficacy. *Social Science & Medicine, 62*(12), 3133–3145. doi:org/10.1016/j.socscimed.2005.11.041.

Michie, M., & Skinner, D. (2010). Narrating disability, narrating religious practice: Reconciliation and Fragile X syndrome. *Intellectual and Developmental Disabilities, 48*, 99–111.

Myers, B. J., Mackintosh, V. H., & Goin-Kochel, R. P. (2009). "My greatest joy and my greatest heart ache:" Parents' own words on how having a child in the autism spectrum has affected their lives and their families' lives. *Research in Autism Spectrum Disorders, 3*, 670–684.

O'Brien, M., & Daggett, J. A. (2006). *Beyond the autism diagnosis – a professional's guide to helping families.* Baltimore, MD, USA: Paul H Brookes Pub Co.

Pakenham, K. I., Sofronoff, K., Samios, C. (2004). Finding meaning in parenting a child with Asperger syndrome: correlates of sense making and benefit finding. *Research in Developmental Disabilities, 25*, 245–264.

Perry, A., Koudys, J., Dunlap, G., & Black, A. (2017). Autism spectrum disorders. In M. L. Wehmeyer, I. Brown, M. Percy, K. A. Shogren, & W. L. A. Fung (Eds.), *A Comprehensive Guide to Intellectual and Developmental Disabilities* (2nd ed., pp. 219–230). Baltimore, MD: Paul H. Brooks Publishing Co.

Satir, V. (1967). *Conjoint family therapy* (2nd ed.). Palo Alto, CA: Science and Behavior Books.

Schieve, L. A., Blumberg, S. J., Rice, C., Visser, S. N., & Boyle, C. (2007). The relationship between autism and parenting stress. *Pediatrics, 119*, S114-S121.

Sharpley, C. F., Bitsika, V., & Efremidis, B. (1997). Influence of gender, parental health, and perceived expertise of assistance upon stress, anxiety, and depression among parents of children with autism. *Journal of Intellectual and Developmental Disability, 22*, 19–28.

Tracz, S. M., & Gehart-Brooks, D. R. (1999). The lifeline: Using art to illustrate history. *Journal of Family Psychotherapy, 10*, 61–63.

von Bertalanffy, L. (1968). *General system theory: Foundations, developments, applications.* New York, NY: George Braziller.

Zuna, N., Summers, J. A., Turnbull, A. P., Hu, X., & Xu, S. (2010). Theorizing about family quality of life. In R. Kober (Ed.), *Enhancing the quality of life of people with intellectual disabilities: From theory to practice* (pp. 241–278). Amsterdam, The Netherlands: Springer Netherlands.

15 Empowering Families During Early and Middle Childhood

Von Poll and Christa Clayton

Early Intervention

The earlier a child with ASD receives early-intervention services, the better the outcomes are for that child (Jagan & Sathiyaseelan, 2016; Roberts, Williams, Smith, & Campbell, 2016; Warren et al., 2011). For example, pervious research has found a positive relationship between early interventions and improvements in communication abilities, fewer meltdowns, and more proactive parental involvement (Jagan & Sathiyaseelan, 2016). Early intervention should be family-centered and strengths-based. Families prefer to work with providers who are collaborative, non-judgmental, and supportive (Coogle & Hanline, 2014; Roberts et al., 2016).

Clinicians may begin treatment by helping the family increase their understanding of the diagnosis and typical characteristics and behaviors of children with ASD. Although there may be some similarities between children with this diagnosis, symptom presentation and temperaments are unique to each child. It is vital for clinicians to be open to parents' interpretations of behavior, as they are the experts of their children's lives. Although psychoeducation may be warranted, it is important to meet the parents where they are in their understanding of ASD and their child's behaviors. As discussed in Chapters 4 and 14, it is important to assist the parents in making meaning of the child's diagnosis, providing a safe environment to cope with the loss of raising a typically developing child and processing the stressors associated with raising a child with ASD. Research suggests families raising a child with ASD exhibit resilience processes, including mobilizing resources, increasing family cohesion, and employing spirituality as a source of strength (Bayat & Schuntermann, 2012). Clinicians should be cognizant of a family's strengths and resources as they conduct treatment.

There are other professionals who will be involved in the treatment process, including applied behavior analysis (ABA) therapists, occupational therapists (OT), physical therapists (PT), and speech and language pathologists (SLP). It is important to have a basic understanding of the skills and services other professionals provide for a child with ASD so that clinicians can work as a team to provide the best care (please see Chapter 24 for more information about collaborating with other professionals). It is advantageous to network and to have a reference list of professionals in the area for various therapies or services. It is also beneficial to obtain releases of information from the child's parents to help when speaking to other providers and coordinating care. This coordination of care allows parents and staff members to effectively navigate challenges the child faces.

School Readiness and Individualized Education Programs (IEPs)

Parents of children with disabilities report higher levels of anxiety regarding their child's transition to attending school (McIntyre, Eckert, Fiese, DiGennaro, & Wildenger, 2010). Mental health clinicians can assist parents in initiating school visits and planning meetings with faculty and school staff as ways to ameliorate anxiety and foster a sense of collaboration with the child's school. It is invaluable for clinicians to understand and know what services are available to families, as many parents do not have the opportunity to work in a system or extensively research what opportunities are available. Although it may take a great deal of additional research and time on the clinician's part, learning about general services that children with ASD and their parents can request can drastically determine the outcome of what services are provided to a child within the school. It is best practice for clinicians to use continuing education opportunities to educate themselves about relevant laws and evidence-based services and interventions for individuals with ASD.

Individualized education programs (IEPs) are a vital service for children with developmental disabilities. Knowing and understanding the function of an IEP is important when working with families with a child with ASD, as they detail the services and accommodations a child will receive in school. Parents are stakeholders in the IEP process; they have the right to actively advocate for the services their children will receive. Clinicians can aid parents in exercising their autonomy and asserting their needs during IEP meetings, which are often stressful and anxiety provoking. As parents gain more experience advocating for the child to various assistance programs, social service agencies, and school boards, their self-perception shifts from that of a parent of a child with autism to an expert about their child's diagnosis and individualized needs (Edwards, Brebner, McCormack, & MacDougall, 2018). Clinicians can help parents navigate the process of identity evolvement and challenges that occur as they interact with outside systems. In addition to advocating for children's educational needs, parents need to be aware of the social challenges that emerge during early childhood.

Navigating and Encouraging Peer Relationships

During early childhood, peer relationships may not seem important to a child with ASD. Children may have difficulty developing socioemotional skills due to less time spent interacting with peers, repetitive stereotyped "stimming" behaviors, and a lack of appropriate social and behavioral responses when peer interaction occurs (Hampshire & Hourcade, 2014). As children grow older, more emphasis is placed on peer relationships; therefore, it is critical that young children begin learning social skills. Peer-mediated interventions are the most effective method of increasing social skills for children with ASD (McConnell, 2002). Peer-mediated interventions use social situations found within the child's immediate, natural context to teach social competence and expand the child's social networks (Shivers & Plavnick, 2015).

Regardless of the setting and the context that mental health professionals work in, clinicians can incorporate social skills within their curriculum and treatment plan. For example, clinicians can create social skills games or develop group therapy classes within their professional setting. Clinicians can foster interactions between children by encouraging play initiation and requests as well as playing beside children to help them interact with others. Professionals can also hold integrated classes or groups that include neurotypical children to help children with ASD work on social skills. Neurotypical children may be reluctant to engage with children with ASD, leading to peer neglect and bullying.

Preventing and Handling Bullying

Parents may undermine the seriousness of bullying during early childhood, but early bullying prevention is necessary. Approximately one in ten students are victims of bullying on a daily basis during school (Chamberlain, George, Golden, Walker, & Benton, 2010). Students with ASD were found to be four times more likely to report being bullied versus their typically developing peers (Wainscot, Naylor, Sutcliffe, Tantam, & Williams, 2008). Various research samples found that between 57 percent and 75 percent of students with ASD self-reported being bullied at school (Kowalski & Fedina, 2011; Little, 2002).

In order to begin decreasing the chance of being bullied, clinicians can help parents educate children about recognizing and responding to various forms of bullying behaviors, including physical and verbal bullying and social exclusion (Hwang, Kim, Koh, & Leventhal, 2018). Friendship bonds have been found to be a protective factor against peer victimization, but forming and maintaining connections may be difficult for children with ASD. Parents are advised to help create peer relationships with positive and influential friends. Parents can also connect with other parents and teachers in their child's life to identify the compassionate and caring children that can be a positive friend in the child's life. Clinicians should also assess bullying experienced by individuals with ASD by asking about the child's friendships and interactions with peers. Finally, social skills training can help buffer some of the negative consequences associated with peer victimization. The transitions associated with school and peer interactions in early childhood can create stress with any family system; for individuals with ASD, transitions can create extreme discomfort and increase tension within the family.

Managing Day-to-Day Routines and Schedule Changes

Day-to-day routines and schedule changes can create stress and anxiety for individuals with ASD (American Psychiatric Association, 2013). Clinicians can help parents identify ways to help children develop a fairly consistent routine. Storyboards, which are pictures of the child's schedule, can help children understand the day's event sequence and prepare for transitions.

When life becomes unpredictable, clinicians can help families process their child's behaviors and employ behavioral interventions to help the child learn self-regulation skills. Parents can reduce their stress by planning out the day and activities that encourage their child with ASD to participate with the larger family. Researchers suggest creating a picture exchange communication system (PECS) with pictorial symbols representing the child's wants and needs as well as a feelings chart to teach children about emotional expression (Dogoe, Banda, & Lock, 2010). Even in the face of expected schedule changes, there is always a possibility for a meltdown. It is important for clinicians to help parents prepare for that possibility and establish sensory supports. Understanding the child's triggers (i.e., certain smells and lighting) can help parents reduce the potential for meltdowns due to schedule changes. Research suggests handling stressful sensory experiences by minimizing exposure to light, strong scents, loud sounds, and providing fidget materials to distract children in the midst of a meltdown (Grandin, 2015).

Middle Childhood

The social aspect of the lives of children is not as prevalent in early childhood as it becomes during middle childhood. Children begin to become more aware of other people and begin to learn how to interact socially with peers, a learning process that can be challenging for children. It is an increasingly difficult time for children with ASD as they try to navigate friendships without the mastery of some of the social development tasks that other children seem to have mastered in early childhood.

Navigating and Encouraging Peer Relationships

One way to help encourage peer relationships in children with ASD is by setting up playdates with other children. When children with ASD are in a school setting, they may become very overwhelmed due to the amount of peers and additional stimuli. Playdates allow children the opportunity to learn social skills in a smaller environment. Playdates have the potential to create stress due to parents' concerns about their child's unpredictable behavior. One way to help parents alleviate some of their concerns is by scheduling a short, structured playdate including a task or game their child enjoys. For example, Hu, Zheng, and Lee (2018) analyzed a peer-mediated Lego activity wherein three children successfully interacted through the pre-structured roles of engineer (child who gives building directions), supplier (child who finds the correct pieces), and builder. This intervention demonstrates the need for many children with ASD to engage in highly structured play activities to achieve social engagement. One challenge of structured play is that it may be developmentally below the child's peer group. Research suggests increasing symbolic play over functional play for children with minimal verbal ability by identifying toys children enjoy, providing visual aids and cues about how to use the toy, and generalizing play by adding additional toy materials, modeling new ways of interacting with the toys, reducing visual aids, and involving peers in the play process (Chang, Shih, Landa, Kaiser, & Kasari, 2017; Hampshire & Hourcade, 2014).

Additionally, enrolling children into groups where they can learn and practice social skills in a safe and supportive setting has been proven to increase communication in children with ASD (Brock, Dueker, & Barczak, 2017; Platos & Wojaczek, 2017). Although children are able to learn listening and communication skills, the main objective of many social interventions is to decrease isolation and peer exclusion. Platos and Wojaczek (2017) suggest implementing a buddy program that partners children with ASD with a highly motivated, emotionally mature peer who is trained to deliver social interventions and engage in structured play activities. In their review of a peer-mediated recess intervention, Brock and colleagues (2017) trained buddies to help children with ASD meet small goals, including eye contact or sustained attention toward another person and listening to and following directions. Through modeling and compliments, this intervention increased peer interaction and appropriate engagement with other students. Socialization skill development may be a key process in reducing externalizing behaviors in children with ASD, thereby resulting in improved peer relationships and decreased peer victimization (Shea, Payne, & Russo, 2018).

Preventing and Handling Bullying

Bullying and victimization usually peaks between the ages of nine and 15, where children are targeted based on being younger, weaker, or exhibiting slower development than their peers (Carney & Merrell, 2001). Children with ASD often respond to victimization with aggression and behavioral outbursts, which may perpetuate further victimization (Schroeder, Cappadocia, Bebko, Pepler, & Weiss, 2014). Many children with ASD are mistakenly labeled by teachers as perpetrators of bullying in the absence of peer interaction due to their aggression (Hwang et al., 2018). Comorbid difficulties such as hyperactivity and conduct problems are associated with bullying behavior, which may become a treatment focus for clinicians (Hwang et al., 2018). Rex, Charlop, and Spector (2018) created the Skills Acquisition Assessment Session (SAAS) video intervention to teach children with ASD how to respond to bullying appropriately. Their intervention group generalized and demonstrated competence regarding the skills depicted in the videos, including assertive responses and telling a trusted adult.

Due to the high rates of bullying for children with ASD, it is necessary to talk to parents about prevention and what steps they can take if their child is being bullied. Educating typically developing children about ASD did not result in more positive attitudes toward children with ASD (Swaim & Morgan, 2001; Morton & Campbell, 2007). However, when typically developing children had direct personal contact with a child with ASD their attitudes improved (Mavropoulou & Sideridis, 2014). Parents can also help teachers understand ASD and have the teacher present some educational materials to their child's class. Students listen and engage at higher levels when teachers speak to the class about ASD instead of a parent guest speaker (Mavropoulou & Sideridis, 2014). They also recommend introducing some of the behaviors that the class may see from the child in order to normalize ASD.

Managing Day-to-Day Routines and Schedule Changes

Many older children with ASD desire increased autonomy and control in their lives. It is important for parents to establish rules, routines, and plans to manage challenging behaviors including irritability and noncompliance. Problems often occur for children in the absence of desired parental attention or activities (Hodgetts, Nicholas, & Zwaigenbaum, 2013). Clinicians can help parents discover reinforcing factors that maintain problematic behavior sequences. For example, a child's meltdown may be reinforced by receiving a parent's attention for exhibiting the behavior. In a meta-synthesis of how parents of children with ASD manage challenging behaviors several themes were discovered, including: accommodating the child or modifying their environment, creating and maintaining structure and routines, responding to behavior with prompting and monitoring, and managing distress via safety planning (O'Nions, Happé, Evers, Boonen, & Noens, 2017).

Depending upon the developmental and chronological age of the child and their level of severity, accommodations and preventative factors will greatly vary. For example, some children with ASD who enter junior high or high school may struggle with the transitions into different classrooms and possibly new schedule changes every day. Clinicians should be cognizant of each individual they are working with and ask various questions about the individual's routine and how the individual's routine impacts their mood and abilities.

Conclusion

Early and middle childhood are significant transition periods for families, especially those with children diagnosed with ASD. An ASD diagnosis impacts school-aged children's academic transitions and performance, peer relationships, and daily routines. Clinicians must be aware of larger systemic barriers to accessing services and school support for children with ASD, as well as family dynamics and life cycle transitions associated with increased stress levels.

References

American Psychiatric Association. (2013). Neurodevelopmental disorders. In *Diagnostic and statistical manual of mental disorders* (5th ed.). Arlington, VA: American Psychiatric Publishing.

Bayat, M., & Schuntermann, P. (2012). Enhancing resilience in families of children with autism spectrum disorder. *Handbook of Family Resilience*, 409–424.

Brock, M. E., Dueker, S. A., & Barczak, M. A. (2017). Brief report: Improving social outcomes for students with autism at recess through peer-mediated pivotal response training. *Journal of Autism and Developmental Disorders*, 48(6), 2224–2230.

Carney, A. G., & Merrell, K. W. (2001). Bullying in schools: Perspectives on understanding and preventing an international problem. *School Psychology International*, 22(3), 364–382.

Chamberlain, T., George, N., Golden, A., Walker, F., & Benton, T. (2010). *Tellus4 National Report (DCSF-RR218)*. London: National Foundation for Educational Research.

Chang, Y., Shih, W., Landa, R., Kaiser, A., & Kasari, C. (2017). Symbolic play in school-aged minimally verbal children with autism spectrum disorder. *Journal of Autism and Developmental Disorders*, 48(5), 1436–1445. doi:10.1007/s10803-017-3388-6.

Coogle, C. G., & Hanline, M. F. (2014). An exploratory study of family-centered helpgiving practices in early intervention: Families of young children with autism spectrum disorder. *Child & Family Social Work*, 21(2), 249–260. doi:10.1111/cfs.12148.

Dogoe, M. S., Banda, D. R., & Lock, R. H. (2010). Acquisition and generalization of the picture exchange communication system behaviors across settings, persons, and stimulus classes with three students with autism. *Education and Training in Autism and Development Disabilities*, 45, 216–229.

Edwards, A. G., Brebner, C. M., McCormack, P. F., & MacDougall, C. J. (2018). From "parent" to "expert": How parents of children with autism spectrum disorder make decisions about which intervention approaches to access. *Journal of Autism and Developmental Disorders*, 48(6), 2122–2138. doi:10.1007/s10803-018-3473-5.

Grandin, T. (2015). Understanding sensory behavior. In S. Blyth (Ed.). *Boosting learning in the primary classroom: Occupational therapy strategies that really work with pupils* (pp. 88–100). London: Routledge.

Hampshire, P. K., & Hourcade, J. J. (2014). Teaching play skills to children with autism using visually structured tasks. *TEACHING Exceptional Children*, 46(3), 26–31.

Hodgetts, S., Nicholas, D., & Zwaigenbaum, L. (2013). Home sweet home? Families' experiences with aggression in children with autism spectrum disorders. *Focus on Autism and Other Developmental Disabilities*, 28(3), 166–174.

Hu, X., Zheng, Q., & Lee, G. T. (2018). Using peer-mediated LEGO® play intervention to improve social interactions for Chinese children with autism in an inclusive setting. *Journal of Autism and Developmental Disorders*, 48(7), 2444–2457.

Hwang, S., Kim, Y. S., Koh, Y., & Leventhal, B. L. (2018). Autism spectrum disorder and school bullying: Who is the victim? Who is the perpetrator? *Journal of Autism and Developmental Disorders*, 48(1), 225–238. doi:10.1007/s10803-017-3285-z.

Jagan, V., & Sathiyaseelan, A. (2016). Early intervention and diagnosis of autism. *Indian Journal of Health & Wellbeing*, 7(12), 1144–1148.

Kowalski, R. M., & Fedina, C. (2011). Cyber bullying in ADHD and Asperger syndrome populations. *Research in Autism Spectrum Disorders*, 5, 1201–1208.

Little, L. (2002). Middle-class mothers' perceptions of peer and sibling victimization among children with Asperger's syndrome and nonverbal learning disorders. *Issues in Comprehensive Pediatric Nursing, 25*, 43–57.

Mavropoulou, S., & Sideridis, G. D. (2014). Knowledge of autism and attitudes of children towards their partially integrated peers with autism spectrum disorders. *Journal of Autism and Developmental Disorders, 44*(8), 1867–1885.

McConnell, S. (2002). Interventions to facilitate social interaction for young children with autism: Review of available research and recommendations for educational interventions and future research. *Journal of Autism and Developmental Disorders, 12*, 351–372.

McIntyre, L. L., Eckert, T. L., Fiese, B. H., DiGennaro, F. D., & Wildenger, L. K. (2010). Family concerns surrounding kindergarten transition: A comparison of students in special and general education. *Early Childhood Education Journal, 38*(4), 259–263.

Morton, J. F., & Campbell, J. M. (2007). Information source affects peers' attitudes toward autism. *Research in Developmental Disabilities, 29*(3), 189–201.

O'Nions, E., Happé, F., Evers, K., Boonen, H., & Noens, I. (2017). How do parents manage irritability, challenging behaviour, non-compliance and anxiety in children with autism spectrum disorders? A meta-synthesis. *Journal of Autism and Developmental Disorders, 48*(4), 1272–1286. doi:10.1007/s10803-017-3361-4.

Płatos, M., & Wojaczek, K. (2017). Broadening the scope of peer-mediated intervention for individuals with autism spectrum disorders. *Journal of Autism and Developmental Disorders, 48*(3), 747–750. doi:10.1007/s10803-017-3429-1.

Rex, C., Charlop, M. H., & Spector, V. (2018). Using video modeling as an anti-bullying intervention for children with autism spectrum disorder. *Journal of Autism and Developmental Disorders, 48*(3), 1–13. doi:10.1007/s10803-018-3527-8.

Roberts, J. M. A., Williams, K., Smith, K., & Campbell, L. (2016). *Autism spectrum disorder: Evidence-based/evidence-informed good practice for supports provided to preschool children, their families and carers.* National Disability Insurance Agency: Australia.

Schroeder, J. H., Cappadocia, M. C., Bebko, J. M., Pepler, D. J., & Weiss, J. A. (2014). Shedding light on a pervasive problem: A review of research on bullying experiences among children with autism spectrum disorders. *Journal of Autism and Developmental Disorders, 44*(7), 1520–1534. doi:10.1007/s10803-013-2011-8.

Shea, N., Payne, E., & Russo, N. (2018). Brief report: Social functioning predicts externalizing problem behaviors in autism spectrum disorder. *Journal of Autism and Developmental Disorders, 48*(6), 2237–2242. doi:10.1007/s10803-017-3459-8.

Shivers, C. M., & Plavnick, J. B. (2015). Sibling involvement in interventions for individuals with autism spectrum disorders: A systematic review. *Journal of Autism and Developmental Disorders, 45*(3), 685–696. doi:10.1007/s10803-014-2222-7.

Swaim, K. F., & Morgan, S. B. (2001). Children's attitudes and behavioral intentions toward a peer with autistic behaviors: Does a brief educational intervention have an effect? *Journal of Autism and Developmental Disorders, 31*, 195–205.

Wainscot, J. J., Naylor, P., Sutcliffe, P., Tantam, D., & Williams, J. V. (2008). Relationships with peers and use of the school environment of mainstream secondary school pupils with asperger syndrome (high-functioning autism): A case-control study. *International Journal of Psychology and Psychological Therapy, 8*(1), 25–38.

Warren, Z., McPheeters, M. L., Sathe, N., Foss-Feig, J. F., Glasser, A., & Veenstra-VanderWeele, J. (2011). A systematic review of early intensive intervention for autism spectrum disorders. *Pediatrics, 127*, e1303–e1311.

16 Empowering Families Transitioning into High School

Hsu-Min Chiang and Lauren Andersen

In a review of the studies focusing on the transition to high school for individuals without disabilities, Benner (2011) reported that students may experience academic, social, and emotional challenges during this transition process. Ninth graders, for example, used to be the most senior students in middle school, but they become the most junior population as they enter high school. Also, compared to middle schools, high schools may have a greater number of students and a larger campus to navigate. Finally, students often feel the level of support that they receive from their high school teachers and principals is less than that from their middle school personnel (Barber & Olsen, 2004).

When transitioning from middle school to high school, the new school environment, school personnel, and peers may bring substantially more stress to individuals with ASD than typically developing children (Strnadová & Cumming, 2016). The transition process from middle school to high school will vary depending on the individual's level of functioning as well as educational needs and supports. Individuals with ASD have been reported to show high levels of emotional and behavioral difficulties during the transition to high school (Mandy et al., 2016). Effective transition supports can result in reducing emotional issues and behavioral challenges for these individuals (Mandy et al., 2016). This chapter will review frequent challenges that children with ASD and their families face while transitioning from middle to high school. The chapter will also provide recommendations for how families can support their child during this time.

The Differences between Middle Schools and High Schools

There are various classroom setting options (e.g., general education classrooms, inclusion classrooms, resource rooms, self-contained classrooms) and school options (e.g., public schools, private schools) for individuals with ASD. Typically, children with ASD will have the same classroom setting from middle school to high school. However, some teens may be placed in a different setting in high school. Some parents may prefer a private school for their children. Because of the same school environment, these individuals may experience less difficulties during transition. However, given that the majority of the individuals with ASD in the United States attend public schools, the information provided in this section is mainly for this population.

When transitioning to high school, individuals with ASD may have the most difficulty adjusting to: school structure, teachers' expectations, grading policies and behavior management systems, scheduling, and class transitions.

School Structures

High school campuses are typically bigger than middle school campuses. The size of the buildings and classrooms in high schools are also typically bigger than those in middle schools. It may take some time for individuals with ASD to become comfortable walking around a new high school campus and participating in a new environment.

Teachers' Expectations

High school students are older and (usually) more mature than middle school students. They are expected to participate in post-secondary education and/or employment after graduating from high school. Thus, high school teachers expect their students to be more independent, take more responsibility in managing homework and school projects, act maturely, and receive lower levels of support than middle school students. The different expectations from high school teachers and middle school teachers may make individuals with ASD feel high school teachers are not as supportive as their middle school teachers.

Grading Policies and Behavior Management Systems

Many middle schools have "teams" of teachers, where multiple teachers work together to plan and organize curricula and implement teaching around the same time. These teachers may offer one concise grading policy and adopt one specific behavior management system so it is easy for students to understand what is expected across various classes. However, in high schools, each teacher typically comes up with his/her own grading policy and may have his/her own behavioral expectations for his/her class. Individuals with ASD may find it difficult to acclimate to multiple grading policies and behavior management systems across classes in high schools.

Scheduling

The duration of a class may be different between middle school and high school. A middle school model is usually student-centered and may have more flexible scheduling, whereas a high school model is typically subject-centered and adopts a fixed period schedule. In middle schools, a school may offer a block schedule, which provides a longer duration of instructional time without interruption. In high schools, a school may utilize a period schedule in which every class meets for the same amount of time. It may take time for individuals with ASD to acclimate to their new high school schedules.

Class Transitions

In middle school, students transition to different classrooms with the same group of students. If a student gets confused with class schedules and locations, his/her peers can help in getting to the right classroom on time. Whereas in high school, students typically move from one class to another independently. If an individual with ASD does not have the right information about the class meeting time and the location of the classroom, it is likely that he/she may not arrive in the right classroom on time or miss the class.

It is important to educate individuals with ASD to understand the differences between middle schools and high schools. If teens with ASD are not well prepared for these differences, it may result in anxiety regarding the transition.

How Can Families Prepare Their Child with ASD for Transitioning into High School?

With supports from families, the transition process for individuals with ASD can be easier. Several strategies may be used for parents to prepare their child with ASD for transitioning into high school. Clinicians can help families with children with ASD by walking through these strategies with them.

Encourage a Child with ASD to Express His/Her Preferences

Children with ASD should be given the opportunities to express their school preference and the supports they need for a successful transition. Additionally, parents should understand their child's strengths and weaknesses and help guide the child toward a decision that focuses on his/her strengths. If the child with ASD shows more interest in learning vocational skills, parents should seek vocational training for their child. Many public schools today offer individuals with ASD the opportunity to develop career-related skills. If the child with ASD aims to go to college after high school, a traditional high school focusing on academics would be ideal.

Parents should allow their child to express their high school preference and post-high school goals openly and discuss the pros and cons for their preference and goals. If there are differences between parents' and child's preferences and goals, parents should allow time to have discussions with their child. If parents think their child may have unrealistic goals, they should provide detailed explanations and redirect their child to set up appropriate goals. It is important to let the child with ASD understand why parents do not support his/her goals.

Once the ideal high school has been determined, the child with ASD should then be encouraged to express what supports and services he/she may need during the transition process. Parents can provide a list of possible transition support ideas to their child and have their child select the one(s) that he/she thinks can benefit him/her in the transition process.

Visit the High School while Class is in Session

Families can work with their child's middle school special education teachers or support team to plan a visit to the high school for their child with ASD. Middle school personnel can collaborate with high school personnel to schedule times for the graduating middle school students to attend classes in high schools. The high school visits can begin in the spring semester before the students enter high school. Each student visits the high school that he/she will be attending individually, with or without the support of a teacher assistant. When a new student visits, the high school special education teacher for the class can have current students introduce themselves, participate in activities that students typically do, and go on a tour to see all of the classrooms. The high school special education teacher can design activities for incoming and ongoing students to work together. For example, they can do academic work together and share information about each other's interests and dislikes. Typically, high school special education teachers will try to make their classrooms warm and inviting so the incoming students will like the new environment. Given that having a successful transition is important, families can work with high school personnel to discuss ways to have their child be familiar with their new school before a new semester starts.

Have a Good Transition Plan

Transition plans are essential to seamless transitions. Parents should attend their child's transition meetings and collaborate with their child's current and future special education teachers as well as school administrators to create a plan that specifies when the transition will begin and how the student will integrate into his/her new school. Having a solid plan at least six months before the transition ensures that the transition to high school is a successful one for both the student and his/her family. The student's needs at the high school and how the new school will support the student should be clearly stated in the transition plan. If parents and teachers have different views in terms of academic plans (e.g., what courses to take, what activities to participate in), parents should advocate for their child (Connell, Hutnick, Glover, & Glover, 2012).

It may take some time for a child with ASD to learn the fact that they may not see their beloved middle school teachers at school anymore. It also may take some time for a child with ASD to feel comfortable with their new high school teachers. The changes in teachers during the transition process may influence the behaviors and mood of individuals with ASD. Thus, how to prepare a child for new teachers should also be discussed during transition planning.

Have a Good Communication System with Teachers

Teachers are good resources for obtaining needed support and information. Collaborating with middle school and high school teachers is key for a successful transition. Parents should have a good communication system with their child's teachers. Parents should allow time to communicate with each of the school personnel who will be involved in their child's transition to let each of the transition team members understand their child's needs and how they want the middle school and high school to help their child.

Conduct a Transition Intervention

Preparing a child with ASD for high school should begin as early as possible, especially for the child who has a strong tendency to attach to routines and be resistant to change. Parents can conduct a transition intervention to help their child with ASD to smoothly transition to high school. The transition intervention can include activities such as understanding the differences between middle schools and high schools, gradually familiarizing the child with the new school environment, scheduling, transportation, and school personnel, setting appropriate high school goals, learning how to make new friends, and determining plans to maintain the friendship with the friends from middle school.

Practice Being a High School Student

Parents can get a school calendar from the high school that their child with ASD will attend as well as a weekly class schedule and homework assignments from a freshman from the high school so their child can have a clear idea how his/her new high school life and daily schedule will look. Parents can arrange some high school days at home for their child with ASD. During those days, they can have their child practice waking up at the time he/she will need to for arriving at school on time. They can also practice going to and from the high school. Additionally, the family can pretend as if different rooms at home are different classrooms in the new high school and practice following a typical high school freshman's daily schedule transitioning from one class to another one. Parents can also assist their child to work on a high school freshman's homework assignment so their child can know what their high school homework may look like.

Find a Peer Partner for a Child with ASD

Individuals with ASD can benefit from their peers' support. Parents can find a child who lives in the same neighborhood and will go to the same high school with their child to be a peer partner for transitioning to the new school. They can share the same transportation to school and come home together. They can be each other's support in the new school environment. Parents can also find a neighborhood child who is a current student at the new school to guide their child and his/her peer partner to be familiar with the new high school life and provide support when needed.

Help a Child with ASD Develop Coping Skills

Transitioning from middle school to high school requires a student to utilize coping skills and implement strategies to calm himself/herself when experiencing negative emotions, such as fear and anxiety. Children with ASD may be anxious about transitioning to high school because they have negative impressions about high school. If this is the case, parents can emphasize on the positive aspects of attending a high school (e.g., making new friends, learning new skills and knowledge, getting a high school degree).

Have Family Meetings

Both parents should discuss each other's expectation for their child going to a high school and whether they perceive their child going to a new school will have any negative impacts on his/her jobs and family responsibilities. They can brainstorm strategies for foreseen issues and seek outside supports if necessary. Both parents should be on the same page for the transition plan for their child with ASD.

If there are other siblings in the family, parents can have family meetings to discuss everyone's concerns about their sibling with ASD going to a new school and how everyone can be supportive in the transition process.

Find Outside Support

It might be helpful to ask other families about their experiences with their child's transition to high school. Learning from the experiences shared by other parents who have children with ASD can greatly help parents understand what difficulties their child may experience. They can learn how other parents had prepared their child for transitioning to a high school and receive useful advice.

Conclusion

Transitioning from middle school to high school is not easy for individuals with or without disabilities. Transition brings uncertainty; however, it also brings new hopes and connections to new dreams. Going to high school allows individuals with ASD to develop new friendships, learn new skills, and participate in extra-curricular clubs and/or sports teams. High school offers transition programs to help teens with ASD transition to their post-secondary education programs and/or jobs. To have a successful transition requires parents to collaborate with middle school and high school teachers to design an effective transition plan. To make the transition seamless, individuals with ASD should be encouraged to actively participate in their transition planning. Their strengths and needs should be carefully addressed. Parents are the key for their child's successful transition.

References

Barber, B. K., & Olsen, J. A. (2004). Assessing the transitions to middle and high school. *Journal of Adolescent Research, 19*(1), 3–30. doi:10.1177/0743558403258113.

Benner, A. D. (2011). The transition to high school: Current knowledge, future directions. *Educational Psychology Review, 23*(3), 299–328. doi:10.1007/s10648-011-9152-0.

Connell, D., Hutnick, M., Glover, S., & Glover, C. (2012). Helping Children on the Autism Spectrum Make a Successful Transition from Middle School to High School and Beyond. *Exceptional Parent, 42*(2), 21–23.

Mandy, W., Murin, M., Baykaner, O., Staunton, S., Hellriegel, J., Anderson, S., & Skuse, D. (2016). The transition from primary to secondary school in mainstream education for children with autism spectrum disorder. *Autism, 20*(1), 5–13. doi:10.1177/1362361314562616.

Strnadová, I., & Cumming, T. (2016). *Lifespan transitions for individuals with disabilities: A holistic perspective*. London: Routledge.

17 Empowering Families Transitioning into Early Adulthood

Rachita Sharma and Kimberlee Flatt

The process of planning for adult life for an individual with ASD involves providing attention to numerous areas, including ones that are educational, vocational, independent living, and social in nature. Consequently, transitioning to adulthood can be a challenging phase of life for most individuals. This is especially true for youth with ASD, a group that often encounters unequal opportunities in areas of educational and vocational transition in comparison to neurotypical adolescents. When compared to their peers with other disabilities, individuals with ASD lag behind their peers in achieving employment, independent living, and community participation (Billstedt, Gillberg, & Gillberg, 2005; Luftig & Muthert, 2005; National Organization on Disability, 2004). For example, only 55.1 percent of young adults with ASD held competitive employment (paying jobs) during their first six years out of high school (Shattuck et al., 2012). This was the lowest percentage among all of the disability categories examined in the study. Not surprisingly, several researchers have provided evidence of the struggle encountered by adolescents with ASD and their families during the transition to adulthood (Blacher, Kraemer, & Howell, 2010; Neece, Kraemer, & Blacher, 2009). This chapter examines the different areas related to transition that require special consideration when working with individuals transitioning into early adulthood.

The Process of Transition Planning to Adulthood

Transition planning is an immensely beneficial process for individuals with ASD. Researchers have suggested that parents who are actively involved in transition planning report greater satisfaction with transition outcomes for their children (Cooney, 2002; Neece et al., 2009; Test et al., 2009). Therefore, including the family in transition planning enhances the process. A transition plan is formulated with input from both the individual with ASD and his or her family. The plan will focus on the individual developing skills linked with desired life outcomes and will connect the individual to adult service agencies in the community (Alwell & Cobb, 2006; Test, Aspel, & Everson, 2006). In other words, facilitating engagement of persons with ASD into their own transition planning can increase their success beyond the education setting.

Typically, transition planning begins around the age of 14.4 years, an age when students are significantly less likely to have goals related to post-secondary education or employment (e.g., college, vocational training, and competitive employment) and more likely to have goals related to maximizing functional independence and social relationships. This means that transition plans for students with ASD typically do not include plans for college or employment, two important areas of a person's life that contribute to his or her overall self-efficacy and independence.

Among the most critical factors that are predictive of post-secondary success is a student's functional independence (Wei, Wagner, Hudson, Yu, & Javitz, 2016). To more accurately assess a student's functional independence, we must have an awareness of the current supports that are in place. Many of these supports are unknown or unintentional (e.g., a predictable school day with a bell schedule and access to familiar classmates). Then, we thoughtfully anticipate the demands of the new environment and begin to plan for supports, accommodations, or the teaching of new skills that may be needed to promote success as they take the next step.

While formal transition planning from a public school setting requires key members (i.e., parents, student, general and special education teachers, administrator, and a member with specialized training in career and technology education), each student's transition should be individualized and should incorporate expertise from a variety of professionals. Studies show that coordinating services with representatives from vocational rehabilitation and/or post-secondary educational institutions often improves outcomes of independent living (Fabian, Dong, Simonsen, Luecking, & Deschamps, 2016). The saying "it takes a village to raise a child" is never more fitting than during these unique years of transition.

Stakeholders in the Process

Parents. Whether the child's future goals are academic or vocational in nature, having the support of parents can make a world of a difference. Williams (2017) found that parents' expectations for their child on the spectrum had a positive correlation with successful employment. Considering the length and breadth of transition planning, it is no surprise that many parents and children find themselves overwhelmed by the information. However, at its core, the transition planning process is a blueprint for the path the child will embark on after graduating from high school. Although overwhelming in nature, it is important for all stakeholders involved in the process (including the teachers, parents, and the children) to focus on the needs of the child thereby leading to a transition plan that is individualized for that child, in that time, based on his/her aspirations, goals, and needed supports for the future.

While transition planning requires the parents to wear the hat of an advocate for their child, post-transition goals typically require that the parents wear the hat of an advisor. This role conversion is essential so that when younger, children have the backing of parents who advocate on their behalf. When they are adults, they have the backing of parents who are still invested in their success by being advisors who offer direct support only when required, thereby respecting the autonomy of their adult child with ASD.

Teachers. When reflecting on the typical process of transition planning, teachers reported that individuals with ASD were more likely to be identified as needing specialized training in the areas of speech communication, mental health, behavioral intervention, occupational therapy, and mobility. Collaborations and connections provided to the community for individuals with ASD included agencies that provide vocational rehabilitation, supported employment programs, vocational training programs, social service agencies, job placement programs, supervised residential support facilities, mental health agencies, sheltered workshops, colleges, potential employers, and adult day care programs (Fabian, et al., 2016; Heller, Gibbons, & Fisher, 2015).

Vocational vs. Post-secondary Settings

Section 504 of the Rehabilitation Act of 1973 works together with the Americans with Disability Act (ADA) of 1990 and IDEA to protect children and adults with disabilities from exclusion and unequal treatment in schools, jobs, and the community. These protective legislations have resulted in greater opportunities than previously available for individuals with all disabilities, including ASD, in various areas of life such as employment, post-secondary education, and independent living. Overall, when comparing the differences between educational and vocational planning, it is important to recognize that while educational planning draws on entitlement, vocational planning is based on eligibility.

Vocational Settings. Competitive work requires certain socially appropriate behaviors and abilities of any adult, including adults on the spectrum. The list includes (1) the ability to perform the essential functions of a job, (2) the ability to operate independently (with minimal to no prompts), (3) the ability to manage one's own time (including arrivals, breaks, and departures) and, (4) the ability to perform activities of daily living (such as grooming, transportation, and meal preparation). Individuals with ASD who are interested in pursuing competitive employment need to be actively involved in the process.

In vocational settings, ADA prevents employers from asking about an individual's disability and related impairments. However, if work-related accommodations (such as frequent breaks and reminders) are required on-site then the individual will need to disclose the nature of the disability in order to obtain approved accommodations. Oftentimes individuals with ASD will begin working with a Vocational Rehabilitation Counselor (VRC) provided by the State's Department of Assistive and Rehabilitation Services prior to completion of primary education. Once approved for services, individuals with ASD collaborate with their assigned VRC to explore vocational options. Once an area of vocational interest has been determined, VRCs can help with the job search, application and interview process, and also provide on-the-job training if required. Rehabilitation counselors can also serve as a liaison between the employer and the employee with ASD to suggest possible accommodations based on the individualized need of the employee.

Educational Settings. In post-secondary educational settings, the numbers of individuals with ASD have increased tremendously in the past decade. Current estimates suggest that students with ASD comprise between 0.7 percent to 1.9 percent of the college population. The number of college students with ASD is growing at a rate faster than nearly any other demographic including individuals with other disabilities. By the year 2020, nearly 433,000 individuals with ASD will be enrolled in post-secondary educational settings (Cox, 2017). Nonetheless, while individuals with ASD often have the cognitive and intellectual capacity required to perform well in post-secondary academic settings, they often experience challenging barriers that hinder their academic success.

While the numbers of individuals on the spectrum have risen in colleges and universities, current estimates suggest that they have a high incompletion rate that stands at approximately 80 percent. However, recent studies evaluating the success of college students on the spectrum describe that individuals with ASD achieve academically at the same or higher levels than their typical peers, and are more likely to succeed at the college level with appropriate supports. In particular, those with ASD may be particularly well-suited for success in STEM fields due to their ability to observe, identify, construct, and apply logical systems of reasoning (Cox, 2017).

The need for providing adequate support services to individuals with ASD on college campuses has become imperative. Due to the disability disclosure protection provided by the ADA, people with ASD all too often gain admission without ever identifying their diagnosis. Consequently, the struggles of these students are frequently not noticed by their professors until their sensory, social, learning, and organizational challenges contribute to their academic failure (Gobbo & Shmulsky, 2014). Thus, it becomes important that college students with ASD who need academic accommodations (such as testing in a distraction-free room) actively engage in the process of obtaining accommodations by registering with the office for disability accommodations on campus. Such offices are available in the majority of two and four-year colleges and universities within the United States.

Special Areas of Consideration when Planning for Transition of Students with ASD

The collaboration of primary stakeholders plays a crucial role in planning the transition of individuals with ASD. Careful, collaborative, comprehensive, and intentional planning allows for the development of a successful plan for transition. Additionally, the best-laid plans include mindful consideration of special areas that may impact the self-efficacy of individuals with ASD. These areas include foci on mental health symptoms, executive functioning deficits, social skills development, exploration of romantic relationships, and transportation needs. Each of these areas is briefly explored in the ensuing section.

Mental Health

Anxiety and depression can be challenges faced by individuals with ASD whether in post-secondary or vocational settings (Gelbar, Smith, & Reichow, 2014). Symptoms of depression and anxiety require special attention because even symptoms that do not meet clinical levels of impairment still cause impairment in daily life activities of individuals, thus posing a threat to their accomplishment of transition goals (Gotham, Brunwasser, & Lord, 2015). Researchers have found that symptom levels in females with ASD increase at a faster rate throughout adolescence, while males with ASD appear to have elevated levels of depressive symptoms in school ages that persist well into young adulthood. Thus, parents and other stakeholders of individuals with ASD are encouraged to identify and address these symptoms while planning for transition.

Executive Functioning

Executive functions are a set of cognitive skills that allow individuals to engage in goal-focused tasks and everyday decision-making skills. Typically, these tasks require inhibition, reduced distractions, planning, and working memory. Individuals with ASD who demonstrate difficulties in executive functioning may struggle with engaging in the goal-related objectives of their individual transition plan (Hill, 2004). Thus, if required, executive functioning deficits may require special attention from the stakeholders involved in the transition planning process.

Social Skills

Adults with ASD report having friends, but being less close to their friends when compared to adults who are not on the spectrum (Baron-Cohen & Wheelwright, 2003). Additionally, adults with ASD are less likely to enjoy interactions with friends for the sake of social interaction (Tobin, Drager, & Richardson, 2014). Participation in social skills or social support groups will increase skills and provide social opportunities. Participants in social support groups describe the feeling of a welcoming community that permits them to be themselves as they share strategies for coping with stress or anxiety, an activity that gives them something to do and provides access to potential interaction partners (Jantz, 2011). In addition to social skill support as a formal intervention option, some studies suggest the use of family members, neighbors, community members, or work colleagues to improve social interactions (Hughes et al., 2013).

Romantic Relationships

Navigating the social world for friendship can be challenging for individuals with ASD, and electing to partake in romantic relationships can prove to be even more challenging. A study by Strunz and colleagues (2017) found that the vast majority of persons with ASD were interested in having a romantic relationship: It was most often not a lack of interest, rather individual social difficulties that created hardships in their ability to obtain and maintain these relationships. Character traits common with persons with ASD such as reliability, stability, and loyalty are found to promote successful partnerships (Myhill & Jekel, 2008). Some individuals with ASD choose relationships with partners that do not have autism while others elect partnerships with someone who is also on the spectrum. The findings of this study suggested increased satisfaction in relationships where both partners had ASD, citing fewer issues as both parties were likely to understand the challenges they face in everyday social interactions.

Transportation

Some researchers have reported that transportation is the most prominent barrier for individuals with disabilities in terms of independence (Friedman & Rizzolo, 2016). Through transportation, individuals can access medical care, necessities related to daily living, employment, and leisure opportunity. Young people with autism often depend on others for their transportation needs (Cox, 2017). The toll of the financial and emotional commitment to being the primary means of transportation for adult children with ASD was discussed in a study done by Lubin and Feeley (2016). Adults with ASD who participated in the focus groups organized by Lubin and Feeley (2016) reported that knowledge and understanding of transit services were the most valuable areas of improvement required in transition planning. Additionally, adults with ASD and their parents expressed a consistent theme of a desire for increased independence with transportation (Lubin & Feeley, 2016).

One alternative parents may have in providing transportation for their adult children with ASD is the use of public transportation. Access to public transportation varies significantly based on the local community and the options that are made available. Some communities have adopted specialized transportation for persons with disabilities, and at times Medicaid waiver programs can offset some of the financial burdens of the families (Friedman & Rizzolo, 2016). When using public transportation, families must consider, plan, and teach for the complexity of their local public transportation system including time management, transfer requirements, unfamiliar destinations, and more (Lubin & Feeley, 2016).

Driving comprises a complex set of skills far more involved than merely complying with a static set of rules; drivers are required to plan and execute actions quickly based on their moment-to-moment environments. Additionally, drivers share the road with others creating social situations in which understanding point of view is beneficial. Currently, there are no specific educational materials or programming specific to teaching driving or driver's safety to individuals with ASD (Daly, Nicholls, Patrick, Brinckman, & Schultheis, 2014).

Conclusion

Transitioning to post-secondary life is challenging and these challenges are often magnified for persons with ASD. Supporting the process of transition to post-secondary life requires collaboration and involvement from a wide range of stakeholders including parents and teachers. Successful transition outcomes for individuals with ASD typically include focus on vocational as well as post-secondary transition. Regardless of the type of transition intended, the areas of executive functioning, social skills, romantic relationships, and transportation must be considered in the planning process. Although planning the transition of youth with ASD has become more systematic in recent years, current areas of deficit indicate we have a long way to go before transition planning for individuals with ASD becomes seamless. It is through active collaboration, elevated standards, and intentional planning that we can continue to help those impacted by autism find their best personal outcomes in this journey.

References

Alwell, M., & Cobb, B. (2006). A map of the intervention literature in secondary special education transition. *Career Development for Exceptional Individuals*, 29(1), 3–27.

Americans with Disabilities Act of 1990, Pub. L. No. 101–336, §2, 104 Stat. 328 (1991).

Baron-Cohen, S., & Wheelwright, S. (2003). The friendship questionnaire: An investigation of adults with Asperger syndrome or high-functioning autism, and normal sex differences. *Journal of Autism and Developmental Disorders*, 33, 509–517.

Billstedt, E., Gillberg, C., & Gillberg, C. (2005). Autism after adolescence: population-based 13- to 22-year follow-up study of 120 individuals with autism diagnosed in childhood. *Journal of Autism and Developmental Disorders*, 35(3), 351–360.

Blacher, J., Kraemer, B., & Howell, E. (2010). Family expectations and transition experiences for young adults with severe disabilities: does syndrome matter? *Advances in Mental Health and Learning Disabilities*, 4(1), 3–16.

Cooney, B. F. (2002). Exploring perspectives on transition of youth with disabilities: Voices of young adults, parents, and professionals. *Mental Retardation*, 40(6), 425–435.

Cox, B. E. (2017). Autism Coming to College (Issue Brief). Tallahassee, FL: Center for Postsecondary Success.

Daly, B. P., Nicholls, E. G., Patrick, K. E., Brinckman, D. D., & Schultheis, M. T. (2014). Driving behaviors in adults with autism spectrum disorders. *Journal of Autism and Developmental Disorders*, 44, 3119–3128.

Fabian, E., Dong, S., Simonsen, M., Luecking, D. M., & Deschamps, A. (2016). Service system collaboration in transition: An empirical exploration of its effects on rehabilitation outcomes for students with disabilities. *Journal of Rehabilitation*, 82, (3).

Friedman, C., & Rizzolo, M. C. (2016). The state of transportation for people with intellectual and developmental disabilities in medicaid home and community-based services 1915 (c) waivers. *Journal of Disability Policy Studies*, 27, 168–177.

Gelbar, N. W., Smith, I., & Reichow, B. (2014). Systematic review of articles describing experience and supports of individuals with autism enrolled in college and university programs. *Journal of Autism and Developmental Disorders*, 44(10), 2593–2601.

Gobbo, K., & Shmulsky, S. (2014). Faculty experience with college students with autism spectrum disorders: A qualitative study of challenges and solutions. *Focus on Autism and Other Developmental Disabilities, 29*(1), 13–22.

Gotham, K., Brunwasser, S. M., & Lord, C. (2015). Depressive and anxiety symptom trajectories from school age through young adulthood in samples with autism spectrum disorder and developmental delay. *Journal of the American Academy of Child & Adolescent Psychiatry, 54*(5), 369–376.

Heller, T., Gibbons, H. M., & Fisher, D. (2015). Caregiving and family support interventions: crossing networks of aging and developmental disabilities. *Intellectual and Developmental Disabilities, 53*(5), 329–345.

Hill, E. L. (2004). Executive dysfunction in autism. *Trends in Cognitive Sciences, 8*(1), 26–32.

Hughes, C., Harvey, M., Cosgriff, J., Reilly, C., Heilingoetter, J., Brigham, N., ... Bernstein, R. (2013). A peer-delivered social interaction intervention for high school students with autism. *Research and Practice for Persons with Severe Disabilities, 38*, 1–16.

Jantz, K. M. (2011). Support groups for adults with Asperger syndrome. *Focus on Autism and Other Developmental Disabilities, 26*, 119–128.

Lubin, A., & Feeley, C. (2016). Transportation issues of adults on the autism spectrum: Findings from focus group discussions. *Transportation Research Record: Journal of the Transportation Research Board, 4*, 1–8.

Luftig, R. L., & Muthert, D. (2005). Patterns of employment and independent living of adult graduates with learning disabilities and mental retardation of an inclusionary high school vocational program. *Research in Developmental Disabilities, 26*(4), 317–325.

Mayhill, G., & Jekel, D. (2008). Asperger marriage: Viewing partnerships thru a different lens. The National Association of Social Workers Massachusetts (NASWM). Focus CE Course, 1–11.

National Organization on Disability. (2004). *NOD/Harris Survey of Americans with Disabilities: Landmark survey finds pervasive disadvantages.* Washington, DC: Author.

Neece, C. L., Kraemer, B. R., & Blacher, J. (2009). Transition satisfaction and family well being among parents of young adults with severe intellectual disability. *Intellectual and Developmental Disabilities, 47*(1), 31–43.

Shattuck, P. T., Narendorf, S. C., Cooper, B., Sterzing, P. R., Wagner, M., & Taylor, J. L. (2012). Postsecondary education and employment among youth with an autism spectrum disorder. *Pediatrics*, peds-2011.

Strunz, S., Schermuck, C., Ballerstein, S., Ahlers, C. J., Dziobek, I., & Roepke, S. (2017). Romantic relationships and relationship satisfaction among adults with Asperger syndrome and high-functioning autism. *Journal of Clinical Psychology, 73*, 113–125.

Test, D. W., Mazzotti, V. L., Mustian, A. L., Fowler, C. H., Kortering, L., & Kohler, P. (2009). Evidence-based secondary transition predictors for improving postschool outcomes for students with disabilities. *Career Development for Exceptional Individuals, 32*(3), 160–181.

Test, D. W., Aspel, N. P., & Everson, J. M. (2006). Best practices and future issues in transition. *Transition Methods for Youth with Disabilities*, 32–59.

Tobin, M., Drager, K. D., & Richardson, L. F. (2014). A systematic review of social participation for adults with autism spectrum disorders: support, social functioning, and quality of life. *Research in Autism Spectrum Disorders, 8*, 214–229.

Wei, X., Wagner, M., Hudson, L., Yu, J. W., & Javitz, H. (2016). The effect of transition planning participation and goal-setting on college enrollment among youth with autism spectrum disorders. *Remedial and Special Education, 37*, 3–14.

Williams, J. E. (2017). Parental factors related to the successful employment of adults with autism spectrum disorder (Doctoral dissertation). Retrieved from ProQuest Dissertations Publishing.

18 Empowering Families Deciding Between Home or Placement and Coping with Placement Decisions

Jeffry B. Jackson

One of the most difficult decisions families affected by autism may face is whether or not to place their family member with autism in some form of out-of-home care (e.g., group homes, residential treatment center). These families often face multiple stressors that tend to be exacerbated when autism symptoms are more severe and when barriers prevent access to support and resources (Blacher, 1994); these stressors typically have negative impacts on family relationships and family member well-being (Mirfin-Veitch, Bray, & Ross, 2003). Disruptions in family and individual functioning may lead families to consider placing the member with autism in out-of-home care for the perceived benefit of the *entire* family including the child with autism, siblings, and parents (Martin & Colbert, 1997).

Most parents who have placed their child in out-of-home care, also known as "placed," recommend psychotherapy to others who are considering placement or who have placed. For instance, a father of a son with autism who was placed at 16 years of age said the following about psychotherapy:

> The most traumatic part for any family is giving up the child and putting him in the system and placing him. If you can do something to ease that transition for the parents by informing them more, helping them go through that transition, offering parents counseling to help them through that transition so you don't go through the guilt and all the other things you do when you give up a child basically to put them into that system.
>
> (Jackson, 2004, p. 171)

However, families often report that clinicians lack the expertise to help them navigate decisions regarding placement, manage associated stressors, and process their experience if they decide to place (Jackson & Roper, 2014). Specifically, parents indicate that therapists frequently (a) minimize family members' stresses and concerns surrounding their loved one with autism, and (b) are not sufficiently knowledgeable about the issues and circumstances that they encounter around placement decisions and adapting to post-placement life. The purpose of this chapter is to assist clinicians in working with families who are considering placement as well as families who have placed.

Unless otherwise indicated, the recommendations in the chapter are based on research I conducted with Dr. Susanne Olsen Roper on parents who had placed their child with severe or profound developmental disabilities – more than half of whom had autism – in some form of out-of-home care (Jackson, 2004; Jackson & Roper, 2014; Roper & Jackson, 2007). Given parents typically remain in a more parental role when a child with autism is an adult (particularly in cases of severe autism), I use the term *child with autism* in this chapter to describe a person's position in the family (e.g., parents, children), not to describe the person's age.

Families Considering Placement

When families who are considering placement request psychotherapy, it may be helpful to have the first session with the parents and without the child with autism or any siblings present. This provides an opportunity to assess for their potential involvement in subsequent sessions. Given that people with more severe autism are more likely to both be placed and have communication abilities that might limit their ability to participate in discussions about placement, it often makes sense to help parents first work through the placement decision, and then, if parents lean toward placement or decide to place, discuss the potential involvement of the child with autism and how to address placement with their child.

One of the primary reasons parents opt for placement is that the level of care necessary to help their child with autism makes it difficult to provide the quality of care they want for their other children. A recent meta-analysis on functioning among siblings of people with autism found that siblings of those diagnosed were up to twice as likely to have more negative outcomes than comparison groups. These siblings were more likely to have lower psychological functioning, social functioning, and sibling relationship quality, and were twice as likely to have symptoms of anxiety and depression (Shivers, Jackson, & Mcgregor, under review). Siblings often have additional responsibilities directly related (e.g., helping the sibling with autism) and indirectly related (e.g., taking over parental responsibilities at home such as making dinner and helping other siblings with homework so that parents can provide care to the child with autism) to the diagnosed child.

The older the siblings are, the more their involvement is typically merited in making the placement decision; in fact, it is important to note that adult siblings may also be faced with placement decisions if parents are incapacitated or deceased.

Siblings may have inaccurate thoughts on placement or have adverse reactions to placement (e.g., anger at their parents, sadness, fear they could also be placed, belief that placement is in some way their fault). If parents decide to place, clinicians should be sure to work with parents on how to talk to their children about placement. For example, clinicians can ask questions like the following: *What things would be important to consider when planning how to talk to your children about placement? How could you go about addressing placement with your children in a sensitive and thoughtful way? How would you like to go about asking your children what they think about placement?*

Therapy for families evaluating whether or not to place should focus on (a) validating and normalizing the stressors that lead them to consider placement, and (b) exploring the pros and cons of placement to help them make a well-informed decision. Parents who are considering placement are often in crisis and feel stressed, exhausted, worried that they are failing their children, and ashamed that they are considering placement. It is important to elicit and then validate how they are feeling, the types of challenges they have been dealing with, and the efforts they have made to manage their challenges.

Family member well-being – of the child with autism and the other family members – is at the center of making a decision about placement. Helping family members identify likely pros and cons for placement can help them figure out how to best support everyone in the family. Open-ended questions about how placement might positively affect (pros) and negatively affect (cons) the child with autism, the other children, and the parents can start the process of exploration. Finding out how parents think their child would like placement and manage placement is an important factor for parents to consider. The following recommended prompts are for clinicians to use with parents; however, they can be easily adjusted for situations in which the child with autism is able to participate in the discussion, as well as situations in which siblings are older or have a more active role in the decision-making process.

Placement Pros

- Child with autism
  - "Would placement ...
    - potentially provide your child with quality or better quality care?"
    - provide services that your child does not have now that might increase growth, development, and potential?"
    - help your child become more independent?"
    - make it so your child will be well-taken care of in the event that something should happen to you (e.g., unexpected death, severe cognitive impairment)?"
    - help your child feel like he/she is developmentally on-track (e.g., going to college or moving in with roommates if the child is an adult)?"
    - provide your child with a meaningful social network of other residents with autism?"
    - increase your child's safety?"
      - "Are there challenging or violent behaviors (e.g., biting, hitting, getting into cupboards and refrigerators, running away, harmful self-stimulation) that might be better managed by staff supervision?"

- "How might age, physical strength, and physical size be factors? (e.g., would family-provided caregiving become more difficult and more physically demanding as the child ages?)"
    - be something your child could understand?"
- Siblings of child with autism
    - "Would placement ...
        - help you provide more time, attention, and care for your other children?"
        - reduce significant extra responsibilities related to your child with autism?"
        - increase the safety of your other children?"
        - improve relationships between siblings?"
- Parents
    - "In what ways would placement improve family life?"
    - "Would placement ...
        - reduce caregiving stress and concerns related to child with autism?"
        - improve your relationship with your child's other parent and, in situations like divorce and remarriage, your relationship with your current spouse/partner?"
        - minimize or prevent resentment due to caregiving responsibilities?"
        - decrease any feelings of isolation?"
        - make it easier to be the type of parent you want to be in your interactions with your child with autism and other children?"
        - allow you more personal time to focus on individual pursuits and growth?"
        - increase your safety?"
    - "Who in your life is supportive of placement?"

Placement Cons

- Child with autism
    - "How could you access additional support services (e.g., respite care, in-home behavior management training) to make it possible to keep your child at home?"
    - "Parents who place often report worrying about the quality of care their child receives at the placement, the values of the staff and other residents, and that their child might be forced to leave placement for behavioral problems. What concerns do you have about placement?"
    - "Parents who have placed often find that there are breakdowns in communication with the administration and staff, unresponsiveness to their requests, unfulfilled promises, red tape to navigate, and that staff are unqualified or shorthanded. How might you preemptively avoid some of these problems? How stressful would these types of bureaucratic

problems be for you? How might you manage these types of problems if they were to occur?"

- "Placements often have turnover in staff and other residents. How well do you think your child would manage caretaker and resident turnover?"

- Siblings of child with autism
  - "Siblings often believe that placement was their fault and that if they had done things differently or behaved better that placement would not have occurred. How likely are your other children to believe placement was their fault? If they believe placement was their fault, what things could you do to support them?"
  - "Siblings who are younger may worry that they might also be placed. How likely are your other children to worry that they might be next and how might you talk to them about this?"
  - "Siblings often experience placement as bittersweet because of the associated benefits and challenges, which can be especially difficult for younger children to make sense of. What things might your other children see as disadvantages associated with placement?"
  - "It is not uncommon for siblings to be upset with their parents and other family members who were in support of placement. How likely are your other children to be upset about placement? If they were to be upset, how might you help them?"
  - "Placement typically results in major adjustments for siblings (e.g., getting used to their sibling being gone, shuffling of roles). How well do you think your other children would adapt to placement? What could you do to help them adapt?"

- Parents
  - "In what ways would placement worsen family life?"
  - "Parents who place often feel guilty that they are not (a) parenting their child in the ways they did when the child was at home, (b) fulfilling their responsibility as parents, and (c) visiting enough, especially if their child is not an adult. Do you think you would feel guilty? If so, how would you manage the guilt?"
  - "Parents who place often experience a sense of emptiness, sadness, and sometimes depression because their child is not a part of the family in the same way as in the past. Do you think you might experience emptiness, sadness, or depression? If so, how would you cope with emptiness/sadness/depression?"
  - "Family members often feel relief as a result of placement and then feel guilty for feeling relieved. How likely do you think you are to feel a sense of relief if your child were placed? Do you think you might feel bad for feeling relieved? If so, how might you cope?"
  - "Family members often disagree about whether to place, placement timing, and placement setting. To what degree are members of your family on the same page about placement?"

- "Placement can create financial stress. How would you finance the placement?"
- "Parents who place often feel stigmatized and judged by others who think that the child should have stayed at home. Are there people you are close to who might disagree with your decision to place? How might you manage feeling stigmatized?"

Placement Research

Clinicians should encourage family members to assess the quality of potential placements. Family members can research potential sites then tour them in person, meet with administrators and staff, and ask if there are family members of residents who they can contact to hear about their experiences. Family members should find out about admission criteria, waitlists, financing, and on-site visit and home visit parameters. Family members might also consider the geographic proximity of placements, as this will likely affect visit frequency.

Families Who Have Placed

Family therapy that includes the entire nuclear family can help parents, the child with autism, and her/his siblings cope with and adapt to post-placement life. Families who have placed tend to experience an ambiguous loss, which is an unclear state of grief and stress because the person is both present and absent (Boss, 2004). The family member with autism is there but not there because he/she is present psychologically in the hearts and minds of family members but absent physically outside of visits. The intensity of the ambiguous loss is likely stronger when placement occurs before the child is an adult. Placing a child in out-of-home care may lead to feelings of ambiguity for family members because the member with autism is alive, but not in their lives the way he/she was before. For example, parents may experience a sense of sadness or emptiness as they go through daily routines like walking by their child's empty bedroom, having family dinner with an empty chair at the table, or Tuesdays eliciting the thought, "I used to take my child to occupational therapy today." These experiences of loss are common after the death of a loved one and are part of the normal grieving process. If these losses occur when the family member is still alive, they can create a sense of ambiguity because the feelings of loss are real but may not seem logical given that the person is still living (Boss, 2002).

The ambiguity of the loss is often further complicated by the fact that family members chose placement (and thus the loss), and visitation results in the family member with autism being physically in and out of their lives. Depending on cognitive ability, the child who is placed may also experience ambiguous loss through placement with family members present psychologically but physically absent. The greater the incongruence between the physical family and the psychological family, the greater the family system boundary ambiguity and risk for compromised stress management and well-being (Boss, 2006; Boss, Caron, Horbal, & Mortimer, 1990).

Because the nature of ambiguous loss makes the loss difficult to resolve, effective treatment for ambiguous loss focuses on increasing resilience and learning to manage the ambiguities (Boss, 1993, 1999). Boss developed six target areas for intervention to assist families in processing the complexities associated with ambiguous loss: finding meaning, normalizing ambivalence, tempering mastery, reconstructing identity, revising attachment, and discovering hope (Boss, 2006). We adapted these recommendations for families who have a family member with profound disabilities who has moved into an out-of-home care situation.

Find Meaning in Family Life after Placement

Thinking about the benefits experienced because of the family member with autism and her/his placement can help bring meaning to the ambiguous loss. Focusing on the ways in which the family member with autism has improved their lives can alleviate some of the emotional stress from placement. Common examples include thinking about how having a family member with autism has helped them (a) learn important lessons about themselves that they might not have learned any other way, (b) learn how to be more caring and empathic, (c) grow as individuals, and (d) feel closer as a family. In trying to reconcile the sometimes conflicting emotions associated with placement, family members can consider the advantages that placement may have for the child, other family members, themselves, and specific aspects of family life. The child may have greater independence, possibly increased potential through placement care services, and the rest of the family knows that the child will be taken care of should something happen to them. Siblings may benefit from increased attention from parents. Parents may find that it is easier to enjoy the time they spend with their child during visits.

Reduce the Need to Feel in Control

Family members will generally cope more easily with ambiguous losses if they realize they cannot be in control of many situations relating to their child with autism. However, this does not mean they should be passive. For example, parents can accept decreased control over the child's well-being at the placement, and they can still find ways to remain involved in the child's life. Continued involvement can occur through visitation, volunteering on placement committees, contributing to decisions about their child's care, and maintaining guardianship. Creating new family routines and rituals around placement is another way to gain a greater sense of control over placement. Family members tend to manage better when they have realistic expectations and recognize what can and cannot be changed. Although there are no perfect solutions to coping with ambiguous loss due to placement, if family members revise their perceptions about placement, reduce self-blame, and continue making decisions that best fit their situation, they will likely manage better.

Redefine the Relationship with the Child

Adapting to life after placement can be furthered by establishing new identities and roles. For instance, parents might consider what they can do to still feel like a parent to their child, even though their child is living outside of their home. Clearly identifying how and when they will have contact with their child and what they will do when they spend time together with their child can help this process. The following questions can be used to help parents (and modified to help siblings) redefine their role with the child. *In what ways can you continue to function as the parent of your child with autism given you are currently not the primary caregiver day in and day out? What parental things are you already doing for your child notwithstanding placement? What additional parental things could you do that might further help you hold on to your role as a parent of your child with autism? Are there ways in which you structure visits that reinforce your parent-child relationship and connection?*

Identify and Accept Conflicting Emotions

Conflicting emotions are common in instances of ambiguous loss due to placement. Helping family members understand that feeling sadness, guilt, and relief as a result of placement can provide validation and normalization of their emotional experience. In addition, family members frequently simultaneously feel love, frustration, joy, and despair with regard to both the child and placement. Helping family members identify their range of emotions and realize that what they are experiencing is not atypical and that it makes sense given their situation can help them manage the complexities of the ambiguous loss created by placement.

Think Dialectically about Placement

Helping clients think dialectically – holding two seemingly contradictory beliefs at the same time (Linehan, 2015) – about placement can help them manage some of the difficulties associated with placement and revise some of the ways they think about their relationship with their child. Examples of placement dialectical thinking derived from our research include the following:

- Because of placement, the child with autism is not in family members' lives in some ways (e.g., physically absent while at placement) AND is in family members' lives in other ways (e.g., psychologically present in their minds and hearts while at placement, physically present during visits).
- Family members may grieve because placement has altered many of the expectations they had about how family life would be AND consider themselves fortunate because the child is still in their life.

- Parents may believe that their child requires and deserves a substantial amount of their time and attention AND they may also believe that it is important to make time to focus on their own needs and the needs of their other children.
- Family members may feel guilty about placing the child AND know that placement is the best thing for the child and the family.
- Family members may simultaneously experience wanting the child to live with them at home AND believing the child is receiving the help that they need from trained professionals at their placement.
- Family members may hope that the child will learn and improve enough from her placement to come home AND also recognize that the child may live the rest of her life in out-of-home care.
- Family members may hope the child's communication skills will improve so that they can feel closer to him and understand how he experiences his placement AND accept that the child's communication may not improve or could even deteriorate and accept the difficult place of not knowing how he experiences his placement.
- Family members can believe that placement is the best current decision AND it may not be the best decision in the future.
- Family members can acknowledge that they did everything they could to keep the child at home AND entertain that things may have worsened without placement.

Hold on to Hope

The process of discovering hope involves figuring out which hopes to cling to and which ones to let go of (Boss, 2006). Hope can be derived from learning how to live with ambiguity and take action toward doing what can be done to increase resiliency (changing what can be changed). It is important for family members to look forward to good things in the immediate and distant future. Knowing that many of the emotional challenges associated with placement decrease over time can provide family members with hope, and this benefits everyone.

Conclusion

One of the most difficult decisions faced by families raising a child with autism is whether or not to place their family member in a type of out-of-home care. Clinicians should be aware of the specific thoughts and concerns reported by parents during transitions. Open-ended questions are a great resource for mental health clinicians to ask each family member involved in potential placement of an individual.

References

Blacher, J. (1994). Placement and its consequences for families with children who have mental retardation. In J. Blacher (Ed.), *When there's no place like home: Options for children living apart from their natural families* (pp. 213–244). Baltimore, MD: Brookes.

Boss, P., Caron, W., Horbal, J., & Mortimer, J. (1990). Predictors of depression in caregivers of dementia patients: Boundary ambiguity and mastery. *Family Process, 29,* 245–254. doi:10.1111/j.1545-5300.1990.00245.x.

Boss, P. (1993). Boundary ambiguity: A block to cognitive coping. In A. P. Turnbull, J. M Patterson, S. K. Behr, D. L. Murphy, J. G. Marquis, & M. J. Blue-Banning (Eds.), *Cognitive coping, families, & disability* (pp. 257–269). Baltimore, MD: Brookes.

Boss, P. (1999). *Ambiguous loss: Learning to live with unresolved grief.* Cambridge, MA: Harvard University Press.

Boss, P. (2002). *Family stress management: A contextual approach* (2nd ed.). Thousand Oaks, CA: Sage.

Boss, P. (2004). Ambiguous loss. In F. Walsh, & M. McGoldrick (Eds.), *Living beyond loss* (2nd ed., pp. 237–246). New York, NY: Norton.

Boss, P. (2006). *Loss, trauma, and resilience.* London, United Kingdom: Norton.

Jackson, J. B. (2004). *Parental coping methods for managing stresses experienced following out-of-home placement of a child with developmental disabilities.* Retrieved from ProQuest Dissertations Publishing. (1419527).

Jackson, J. B., & Roper, S. O. (2014). Parental adaptation to out-of-home placement of children with severe or profound developmental disabilities. *American Journal on Intellectual and Developmental Disabilities, 119,* 203–219. doi:10.1352/1944-7558-119.3.203.

Linehan, M. M. (2015). *DBT skills training manual* (2nd ed.). New York, NY: Guilford.

Martin, C. A., & Colbert, K. K. (1997). Parenting children with special needs. In *Parenting: A life span perspective* (pp. 257–281). New York: McGraw-Hill.

Mirfin-Veitch, B., Bray, A., & Ross, N. (2003). "It was the hardest and most painful decision of my life!": Seeking permanent out-of-home placement for sons and daughters with intellectual disabilities. *Journal of Intellectual & Developmental Disabilities, 28,* 99–111. doi:10.1080/1366825031000147049.

Roper, S. O., & Jackson, J. B. (2007). The ambiguities of out-of-home care: Children with severe or profound disabilities. *Family Relations, 56,* 147–161. doi:10.1111/j.1741-3729.2007.00448.x.

Shivers, C., Jackson, J. B., & Mcgregor, C. (under review). Adjustment among typically developing siblings of individuals with autism spectrum disorder: A meta-analysis.

19 Assisting the Family After Divorce or Separation

Julie Ramisch

When I first started researching couples with children with ASD, it was around the time that the mass media frightened many parents and couples with the 80 percent divorce rate statistic. Researchers were baffled by the statistic and started to investigate. Couples whom I saw in my practice were frightened and scared. It was as if they had been handed divorce paperwork by society. They felt doomed. Additionally, if we look at the research that was published up until that time, we would find a lot of documentation and reports of individual stress and strain from raising a child with ASD (e.g., Benson, 2006; Gray, 2002; Hastings, 2003; Sivberg, 2002).

The truth is that parents with children with ASD do get separated and divorced. It is not 80 percent of couples, though. Researchers have been able to demonstrate that compared to couples with children without disabilities, couples with children with ASD are exposed to a longer risk period for separation and divorce and do get separated and divorced more than couples with children without disabilities. However, when following the same couples with children with ASD over time, most couples stayed together while a smaller percentage become separated or divorced (Baeza-Velasco, Michelon, Rattaz, Pernon, & Baghdadli, 2013; Hartley et al., 2010). Many couples with children with ASD are in long and happy relationships.

Another truth is that couples may get separated or divorced for a variety of reasons. If there is marital distress, it may not have to do with the behaviors or symptoms from the child with ASD. Baeza-Velasco et al. (2013) and Freedman, Kalb, Zablotsky, and Stuart (2011) both reported that symptom severity of the child with ASD did not affect separation or divorce outcomes. Couples with children with ASD may get separated or divorced for the many reasons that couples without children with special needs get separated or divorced (e.g., lack of intimacy, domestic violence, infidelity, unresolvable conflict, financial incompatibility, etc.). It is important to assess all of the possible reasons that a couple may be experiencing stress in their relationship. As clinicians, we must keep in mind that ASD rarely causes separation or divorce, but it does provide a set of special circumstances that clinicians must take into account.

Multiple Pathways to Separation and Divorce

As a clinician, there may be multiple pathways to experiencing a family during or after a separation or divorce. First, an in-tact family (two parents and children) might initiate therapy due to distress and then start the separation or divorce process during treatment. Second, one parent may initiate treatment for him or herself or for the child(ren) during or after the separation or divorce. Finally, there are times when parents are court-ordered to seek co-parenting treatment or family therapy during the divorce process or as part of a divorce settlement. When getting started with any family, beginning questions might include, but are not limited to: *How close is/was the child to each parent? How involved is/was each parent in the child's life? What are the current custody arrangements (if any)? How has the child's behavior altered since the separation or divorce? Have previous problem behaviors altered since the separation or divorce? Has the child regressed in developmental milestones, such as walking, talking, toilet training, etc?* It is also important to get to know what behavioral interventions or systems for the child with ASD the family had in place that were working as it will be important to try to keep things as consistent as possible.

Working with Two Parents

When working with two parents seeking separation or divorce, or parents who have already gone through the process and who are willing to engage in therapy together, hopefully clinicians can help them to maintain or build a co-parenting relationship that will continue past treatment. Children with ASD need the support of both parents through their lifespan as the parenting demands often continue into adolescence and early adulthood (Hartley et al., 2010). As children with ASD become older, parents need to work together to address issues such as school accommodations, post-secondary education or career training, future living accommodations, possible employment or getting involved with community support programs, and so on. I have found that explaining to parents the importance of working together and emphasizing that they are doing it for the child rather than for the other parent will often keep them engaged in the process. Parents who have been court-ordered to co-parenting will often find that this reframe of the purpose of treatment (to help the children and not them/the other person/their relationship) helps them to want to make changes because they are in the best interest of the child.

When a Parent Refuses to Participate in Therapy

I have found that the process of helping families through the stages of separation or divorce is easier when both parents are able and willing to participate in the process. Sometimes, though, one parent may come in alone or bring in the child. I've even had times where a parent has brought in a child for behavioral concerns and we have been able to trace it back to an issue related to the separation or divorce. The situation becomes challenging when one parent refuses to come in (alone or together) or even acknowledge that there might be a problem. I try to remind him or her that we are trying to do what is in the best interest of the child. If they still refuse and I feel it is a big enough concern, I may refer the parent I am seeing to seek help from whatever legal authority may be involved. Of course, I will continue to work with the parent and/or child as best as I can.

Explaining Separation or Divorce to Children with ASD

If given the opportunity, a clinician can be significant when it comes time to explain the separation or divorce to the child or children. There are many resources that are available to help with this experience. Clinicians might want to spend some time on Youtube looking at videos or on Amazon (or the local library) looking for appropriate books. How a clinician might go about this task will highly depend upon the level of functioning of the child with ASD. Specifically, if a child is nonverbal and he or she does not communicate with a device, it will be important to communicate with the parents to find a way to talk about this subject in a way that the child might understand. If the child is able to communicate verbally, I recommend using developmentally-appropriate words and checking for understanding as often as possible. It is important to emphasize that both parents will try to continue to work together to ensure that their routines and activities will continue as normal. Also, I find it valuable to reassure the child that both parents love them and that the divorce is not their fault. Sometimes the child might have questions right away, while other children might take some time to process the information. I always try to have both parents in the room at the same time while having this conversation. If parents are resistant, I remind them that they are doing this because it is what is best for the child.

Parenting Plans

If working with parents in the initial stages of separation or divorce, there may be an opportunity to help parents with children with ASD think of areas that are important to a parenting plan that otherwise might be left out by traditional parenting plans. The following areas are discussed in more detail: residential arrangements and visitation, routines and consistency, and special recreation and hobbies.

Residential Arrangements and Visitation

Children with ASD need structure, routine, and sameness. It can be difficult and stressful to frequently transition from one home to another. Thinking outside of the traditional residential arrangements after a separation or divorce, some parents might plan for the child or children to remain in one home while the parents alternate their own living situations. For example, one week one parent will live in the family home with the children and then on Sunday the other parent will come to live in the family home with the children for a week. The parents switch homes rather than the children. For parents who can and who are willing to coordinate like this, this might also be an economical plan as one parent does not have to immediately purchase furnishings for an entire second home. If this plan is not feasible, it might be better to have the child with ASD have one primary home with visits to the second home. Initially, shorter visits might be recommended, working up to longer visits and eventually overnights. Of course, this all depends on the level of functioning of the child as some children with ASD are able to handle change and transitions better than others.

Not knowing where they are going to stay for the night or who is going to pick them up from school can cause fear and anxiety for a child with ASD. With a schedule that involves transitioning from one home to another, it might be helpful to provide the child with ASD with a schedule or a calendar that they can comprehend. For example, for one child who was often confused and anxious about who was picking him up after school, he found comfort when he had a calendar with pictures of mom's and dad's faces placed on the days that they were coming for him. He knew who to expect and who to look for after school.

Parents who can exhibit flexibility with scheduling will probably have an easier time while everyone is adjusting to new schedules, routines, and accommodations. While many parenting plans will state that the children have to be exchanged at a specific time such as 6 pm on Sunday, it might work better to have a range of time such as 6–7 pm to allow for difficult transitions, trouble with redirection, and possible meltdowns.

Routines and Consistency

For a child with ASD, routines regarding which parent they are spending time with is important, but so are routines when it comes to the day-to-day schedule of their lives. While a child without ASD may easily adapt to doing things one way at mom's house and another way at dad's house, a child with ASD will thrive if both parents can try to keep routines the same at both houses. Morning routines (getting up, getting dressed, eating breakfast, getting items packed for school, etc.), night-time routines (chores, homework, hygiene, bedtime, etc.), and even mealtime routines will go much more smoothly if both parents can coordinate what they are doing. Otherwise, a child with ASD may become confused, irritable, and have additional behavioral problems. For example, a newly divorced parent brought in a nonverbal child with ASD who was refusing to eat dinner at their house, and through asking questions about routines I was able to find out that this parent was having the child eat dinner at the kitchen table (as they always had been doing), while the other parent was having the child eat dinner on the floor in the living room in front of the TV. While a verbal child might have been able to communicate the problem, it can take a bit more questioning to figure out what is going on when a child is nonverbal. If parents are able to maintain consistency and routines, it can eliminate problems from even starting.

Special Recreation and Hobbies

Depending on the community where the family lives, there may or may not be recreational activities for children with special needs. As the child ages and depending on his or her activity level, it might be helpful for clinicians to assist the parents get involved in these activities. If parents agree to sign up a child for an activity, they need to agree to both do what they can to make sure the child attends the activities on a regular basis. If both parents are involved in these activities, they can also have knowledge about how the child is behaving and progressing in the activities. Additionally, many children with ASD have special hobbies or interests. I like to emphasize that, especially in the initial phases of the divorce process, it is helpful for the child to have access to their special interests at both homes.

Conclusion

As discussed in this chapter, when a family is experiencing separation or divorce it is important for the clinician to thoroughly assess all of the possible reasons for such dissolution of the marriage. Investigate all areas of possible stress, from ASD-related stressors to stressors that have nothing to do with ASD. Having a complete view of the situation will help clinicians work with separating families from a broader perspective. Many parents will be willing to attend sessions because they realize it is in the best interests of their children, while some may be a bit resistant. Some may be court-ordered and challenging to work with. Oftentimes a reminder that we are gathering to do what is best for the children will help to bring cooperation. Finally, clinicians knowledgeable in this area can have some influence on the development of parenting plans by making suggestions that may otherwise be left out.

References

Baeza-Velasco, C., Michelon, C., Rattaz, C., Pernon, E., & Baghdadli, A. (2013). Separation of parents raising children with autism spectrum disorders. *Journal of Developmental and Physical Disabilities*, 25, 613–624.

Benson, P. R. (2006). The impact of child symptom severity on depressed mood among parents of children with ASD: The mediating role of stress proliferation. *Journal of Autism and Developmental Disorders*, 36, 685–695.

Freedman, B., Kalb, L., & Zablotsky, B., & Stuart, E. A. (2011). Relationship status among parents of children with autism spectrum disorders: A population-based study. *Journal of Autism and Developmental Disorders*, 42, 539–548.

Gray, D. E. (2002). Ten years on: A longitudinal study of families of children with autism. *Journal of Intellectual & Developmental Disability*, 27, 215–222.

Hartley, S. L., Barker, E. T., Seltzer, M. M., Floyd, F., Greenberg, J., Orsmond, G., & Bolt, D. (2010). The relative risk and timing of divorce in families of children with an autism spectrum disorder. *Journal of Family Psychology, 24*, 449–457.

Hastings, R. P. (2003). Child behavior problems and partner mental health as correlates of stress in mothers and fathers of children with autism. *Journal of Intellectual Disability Research, 47*, 231–237.

Sivberg, B. (2002). Family system and coping behaviors: A comparison between parents of children with autistic spectrum disorders and parents with non-autistic children. *Autism, 6*, 397–409.

Part V
Special Topics

20 Arranging an Appropriate Therapeutic Environment

Lacey Bagley and Brie Turns

The clinical treatment for a family raising a child with an ASD can be greatly influenced by the therapeutic environment. Anything from the location of the building, the smells, lighting, and texture of the environment can influence how a child with ASD behaves in the therapy room. This chapter will discuss various factors that clinicians should be aware of when working with children with ASD and how making slight alterations to the therapeutic setting can help a child feel comfortable during treatment. The authors of this chapter acknowledge that children are raised in a multitude of environments but the language of this chapter will be "parent(s)."

Recommendations for the Intake Session

When a family first starts therapy or counseling, the intake session is often used to gather information about the background and history of the family and the presenting concern(s). When a child has ASD, the intake process helps provide clinicians with vital information about the family and specifically about the child's unique behaviors. As Turns and Springer (2015) have suggested, when a family has children with behavioral challenges, including ASD, the clinician should meet with the parent(s) alone during the intake session. This meeting will allow the clinician and parents to openly discuss the strengths and challenges of the child and family. The clinician can also ask openly about the financial, physical, and psychological strain the family has endured without children listening. Finally, inviting the parents into the therapy room first will allow them to assess the physical environment of the therapy offices to prevent potential challenges when the child enters therapy. For example, during an intake session with a mother, she stated that her son had a negative experience in the same building that my (B.T.) office was located. Knowing that her son would experience a "meltdown," future sessions were held at a different location.

There are vital questions clinicians should ask during the intake session. This is the opportunity for the clinician to learn more about the child and his or her level of functioning. It is important for the clinician to understand the history of the ASD diagnosis. What were the first concerns that the parents had about their child that led them to seek help from a professional? What other therapies or interventions have they tried? What behaviors or symptoms have improved and which ones have become worse? These questions will help clinicians better prepare for how they will involve the child with ASD in sessions.

Similar to treating families raising a typically developing child, a clinician should assess all of the various relationships within the family system. Assessments such as the Double ABCX model (Ramisch, 2012) can be used to determine areas of strengths and resiliency. Clinicians will also need to spend time asking about how the unique behaviors and challenges of the child with ASD impact the family. As clinicians discuss the behavioral challenges parents may be experiencing with their child, scaling questions can be useful to help understand the severity of the challenges (Brockman, Hussain, Sanchez, & Turns, 2016). For example, if a parent states his or her child has meltdowns during their morning routine (getting ready for school, eating breakfast, putting on shoes, and getting into the vehicle), the clinician can then ask: on a scale from 1 to 10 where 1 is the actions are not disruptive to the routine and 10 is the actions are extremely disruptive to the routine, how disruptive would you say the actions of the child have been this week?

It is also important for clinicians to learn about the other services (e.g., speech or occupational therapy) that may be involved with the family. Many families use a variety of care services and clinicians should assess how those relationships and services benefit the family; as clinicians learn about the other care providers, they may want to request a release of information to work more efficiently within their already established care structure (Turns & Springer, 2015). If clinicians are working with families who are unaware of the resources available to them, it would be beneficial to guide them in seeking services available in their community as well as aiding them in assessing the pros and cons of available services (Neely, Amatea, Echevarria-Doan, & Tannen, 2012). Clinicians should also include information about services specifically available to family members of children with ASD – including autism-specific support groups (Ramisch, 2012).

Finally, it is important to identify the parent's therapeutic goals; without assuming his or her goals are focused on their child or the autism diagnosis. As usual, the presenting problem will structure who attends and the duration of therapy (Turns & Springer, 2015). Working with the entire system may prove the most beneficial to the family and their therapy goals. Structuring sessions in a variety of ways can help thoroughly assess how each subsystem functions and how therapy can help each relationship. For example, even when the presenting problem focuses on the child, I (B. T.) will spend sessions with parents to assess their self-care and ensure the parents are spending quality time together.

One of the unique jobs of clinicians is to recognize the uniqueness of each family, being "mindful about the nuances of each family and enter their world with respectful curiosity and sensitivity" (Turns & Springer, 2015, p. 15). This includes having parents assess the facility to see if it meets the needs of their child. The following section provides exercises and suggestions for how to assess the office space.

Assessing the Therapeutic Environment

Many children with ASD have specific sensory sensitivities. For example, I (B.T.) worked with a child who would vomit from the smell of certain foods and aromas. It is important for mental health clinicians to be aware of their therapeutic environments and how a child with ASD could be negatively triggered by certain lights, sounds, smells, and textures. Assessing your office does not require a full remodeling but an attunement to what you currently have and being mindful to small adjustments you can make to your space and facility to fit a client's needs. Individuals with ASD may have their own unique needs, so we strongly recommend having the parents participate in the exercises as well – to ensure all of their child's needs are met.

Throughout this section there are two words that therapists should keep at the forefront of their minds: stimulation and senses. Stimulation meaning the process of taking in information through your senses and senses meaning your five senses: sight, smell, touch, sound, and taste (Leekman, Nieto, Libby, Wing, & Gould, 2007). For many clinicians, using the five senses is a balancing act that comes naturally. For example, people can intake sounds and allow them to pass by without much thought.

> EXERCISE: Close your eyes and listen. What sounds do you hear? If you are in your therapy room, perhaps there is the ticking of the clock or the muffled sounds of other people outside your office. If you have a window, are there sounds from the road or outside environment that you can hear?

When you open your eyes and continue reading, your mind is able to ignore those sounds while you focus on the task at hand. For some of your clients with ASD, this may not be the case as their sensitivity to sound is heightened. You may be able to focus on the therapeutic conversation; however, they are being bombarded with every sound in the environment. If they appear very distracted, consider the extra sounds in the space.

Along with the external sounds, internal acoustics of the therapy space can influence clients with ASD. Larger spaces can quickly become reverberant or resonant, which can overstimulate clients. When doing family therapy, a larger room may be needed to accommodate for more people. When clinicians are in a therapy space and multiple people start talking at once, clinicians can organize and process the noises because of their different voices. However, some clients with ASD may only hear more noise – without the ability to filter, organize, and process different voices (Leekman, Nieto, Libby, Wing, & Gould, 2007). So, increasing the number of people and having the session in a large, potentially reverberant or resonant space may be ineffective and overstimulating.

Another sense to consider is sight. This is essentially what one sees in one's immediate surroundings and space.

> EXERCISE: Stand at the precipice of your doorway, looking into your therapy room. What do you see? Look left, right, up, and down. Is it a nicely organized space with limited clutter? Or, like many busy clinicians, are there loose papers on an already over-cluttered desk and unmanaged shelves?

Sight stimulation is a lot like noise stimulation for clients with ASD. It may be difficult to organize and process thoughts in a space that is as disorganized and cluttered as our minds. Limited sight stimulation provides for an easier canvas to think and process from. As an example, I (B. T.) have an office with three book shelves full of miniatures for use with a sandtray. In order to help clients with ASD and my younger clients from becoming overly stimulated, I hang curtains in front of the shelves in order to cover them when they are not in use.

An important aspect of sight stimulation to consider is the lighting in the waiting room and office. Lighting is significant and may even include the type of light bulbs being used as some clients with ASD are sensitive to fluorescent bulbs (Turns & Springer, 2015). If clinicians only have an overhead light and it is fluorescent, then clinicians are at risk of overstimulating the client. Lamps are an easy solution; multiple lamps are even better.

> EXERCISE: If you turn off the overhead light in your space, what is an adequate amount of lighting (so as to not be too dim)? Start with what you think is best (1–2 lamps) and then practice a session with another clinician as a sit-in client or a parent. You may need to add another lamp or invest in lamps with dimmer switches to provide the best lighting in the space.

The last sense to consider when assessing your office is touch. This sense is less about removing overstimulating items and more about providing interventions that help clients in the de-stimulating process or preventing meltdowns and boredom (Turns & Springer, 2015). When starting off sessions, I (L. B.) like to do a simple check-in with the client. How is today going – has it been an easy day or has it been a hard day? The intention with this exercise is two-fold: first, to acknowledge that the client is the expert of their experience and second, that their answer is a meaningful guide for clinicians to use during the session. If it has been an easy day, clinicians can continue ahead with the session as planned. If it has been a hard day, clinicians may start with a de-stimulating exercise or by using stress-management tools before or during the session. These are items that need to be readily available for the client to use as they need them. Examples include: stress balls, fidget items, Legos, or playdough. Parents will know which activities are best for their children and should be included when considering what items to have available in the clinician's office.

Before concluding this section, it is important to make one quick note about safety. Some clients with ASD may experience outbursts of anger or high energy. It is best to control the space for their safety and that of the clinicians.

EXERCISE: Think about items in your room that may be thrown and may cause harm or damage; this may be the most important exercise to include parents in, as they are the experts of their child's behavior challenges. Ask yourself, do you have a way to easily remove potentially dangerous items (a drawer or place for them on a high shelf)? If you do not have a place of safekeeping then you may need to consider removing them from the space all-together.

In addition to safety, some children with ASD are also "runners," meaning that they may run out of a room when they would like to leave a situation. We advise clinicians to ask parents about their child's potential to run out of the office and create a safety plan to prevent possible injury. Some offices have nearby parking lots or stairs that could be a safety hazard to a child who runs.

Preparing the Child for the First Visit

After clinicians have completed the intake session with the parents, learned about the unique behaviors of the child, and prepared the space to begin therapy, it is time to work in tandem with the parents to prepare their child for his or her first visit to therapy. Some children with ASD may already have multiple weekly appointments with different providers. Parents can help prepare them for this appointment by normalizing the therapy process. One way this can be done is by explaining the similarities and differences between the events. Additionally, this process should also include a description of the facility, the room, and the clinician – highlighting how everything has been prepared to meet their specific needs (when appropriate). Since having the initial intake session with the parents, the therapeutic alliance has been established and an open dialog can be used when they have questions about the process of therapy with their child.

During early sessions, clinicians should spend some time assessing parents' communication skills and then work with them on how to best communicate with their child around the topic of coming to therapy. One common pitfall is when parents use language that is blaming, shaming, or criticizing of the child or the child's ASD diagnosis. It is beneficial to teach parents how to use language that separates the problem from the child's identity. Modern therapy models, such as narrative family therapy, would suggest an approach of externalizing the problem behavior by giving it an entity separate from the child's identity. As ASD is not a temporary "problem" to be overcome but a lifelong diagnosis, families should focus on using the skills provided in narrative therapy by externalizing problem behaviors (i.e., meltdowns, outbursts, and catatonic stupor), which may become potential barriers to attending therapy.

Conclusion

Creating a therapeutic environment is an important but often overlooked aspect of working with individuals with ASD. We first recommend meeting with parents to learn about their families' needs and best hopes for therapy and how clinicians can provide a safe and manageable environment for the individual with ASD. While considering the numerous ways individuals with ASD may experience a sensory overload, clinicians are able to prevent possible outbursts or meltdowns. For clinicians and their clients to have a successful visit, remember these four key things: sound, sight, light, and safety. Lastly, be sure to maintain a relationship with parents so that when their child reacts negatively or positively to an experience, they will communicate how you can adjust your strategies toward success in the therapy room.

Although we recognize that creating a "perfect" environment for every client a clinician will treat is not feasible, making slight adjustments in the setting may help individuals feel more comfortable and thrive in a new environment. As authors, we recognize that as our discipline grows in learning how to work with families raising a child with ASD, we can only meet their unique needs by working and learning best practices from families and from one another. Connect with other clinicians who have worked with individuals with ASD or seek supervision from a trained clinician to provide ethical care to clients.

References

Brockman, M., Hussain, K., Sanchez, B., & Turns, B. (2016). Managing child behavior problems in children with autism spectrum disorders: Utilizing structural and solution focused therapy with primary caregivers. *The American Journal of Family Therapy, 44,* 1–10. Retrieved from http://dx.doi.org/10.1080/01926187/01926187.2015.1099414.

Leekman, S. R., Nieto, C., Libby, S. J., Wing, L., & Gould, J. (2007). Describing the sensory abnormalities of children and adults with autism. *Journal of Autism and Developmental Disorders, 37*(5), 894–910.

Neely, J., Amatea, E. S., Echevarria-Doan, S., & Tannen, T. (2012). Working with families living with autism: Potential contributions of marriage and family therapists. *Journal of Marital and Family Therapy, 38,* 211–226. doi:10.1111/j.1752-0606.20111.00265.x.

Ramisch, J. (2012). Marriage and family therapists working with couples who have children with autism. *Journal of Marital and Family Therapy, 38*(2), 305–316. doi:10.1111/j.1752-0606.2010.00210.x.

Turns, B., & Springer, N. (2015). Families with autism spectrum disorder: Assessment & intervention. *Family Therapy, 14*(2), 12–16.

21 Spirituality and the Family Unit

Erik W. Carter

Equipping families to flourish is at the heart of the work of many clinicians, professionals, and other service providers. The constellation of formal services and informal supports parents receive can play a powerful role in helping them to thrive amidst the ordinary and unexpected challenges of raising their children. Likewise, their absence can be a source of deep frustration and struggle. For many families, their spirituality and congregational involvement represents an important source of strength, support, and social connections as they navigate life together. The same is true for families who have children with ASD. Indeed, faith and flourishing are closely linked in the lives of many families.

The Spiritual Dimensions of Life

Although I use the term spirituality broadly in this chapter to refer to the spiritual beliefs, commitments, connections, and resources individuals possess, distinguishing different aspects of the spiritual dimension of life can be helpful when working with families impacted by ASD. *Religiosity* typically refers to the beliefs and practices associated with organized religion. For example, religiosity can encompass the beliefs and values people hold about God and their religious community, their involvement in congregational activities (e.g., attending worship services, religious education programs, participation in small groups), and a variety of personal practices that take place outside of a faith community (e.g., prayer, devotions). *Spirituality* often refers to those aspects of life that bring meaning, hope, and value – whether they are pursued through or outside of religious contexts. Of course, different expressions of religiosity and spirituality can clearly play different roles at different times in people's lives. Moreover, spirituality is a complex and nuanced aspect of people's lives that is best considered outside of dichotomous terms. In other words, it may be more helpful to know what role spirituality plays in the lives of families than to ask whether or not they are spiritual.

Faith, Families, and Autism Spectrum Disorder

When it comes to the sacred dimensions of life, families who are and are not impacted by autism may be much more alike than different. Indeed, research spanning the last two decades indicates spirituality and congregational involvement is likely to be just as pertinent and prominent in the lives of parents of children with ASD as it is for anyone else (Ault, 2010; Ekas, Whitman, & Shivers, 2009; Salkas, Magaña, Marques, & Mirza, 2016). A substantial proportion of these parents indicate their faith is an important aspect of their lives, say they pray regularly, and report that their faith impacts their daily decisions and provides a sense of purpose. Many report some involvement in the worship, learning, fellowship, and service activities that take place through a local congregation (Luther, Canham, & Cureton, 2005; Twoy, Connolly, & Novak, 2007). Studies also illustrate the varied ways in which involvement in a religious community can provide access to practical supports, foster supportive relationships, shape their understanding of disability, and provide emotional strength for meeting the everyday challenges of raising their children (Carter, Boehm, Annandale, & Taylor, 2016; Speraw, 2006). Moreover, several studies have documented strong associations between the religious faith of parents and higher family quality of life (Boehm, Carter, & Taylor, 2015; Poston & Turnbull, 2004). Such findings align closely with a much larger collection of research documenting the strong association among indicators of religiosity, spirituality, and well-being for the general public (Koenig, King, & Carson, 2012).

Key Challenges for Families

As with any family, spirituality can be an important dimension of the lives of families with members who have ASD. What may be unique for these families are some of the particular challenges they experience and the ways in which their spirituality may be drawn upon or shaped by these life experiences. In the following sections, I highlight several key junctures during which understanding and supporting of the spirituality of families may be especially impactful.

Initial Diagnosis

The window when families first receive an autism diagnosis for their child can be marked by myriad emotions (e.g., confusion, doubt, isolation, blame, guilt, relief). Often described as a defining moment in one's family journey, the responses of individual family members can vary widely. For some parents, their spirituality influences how they interpret and cope with this diagnosis – whether in small or substantial ways. When asked to share their beliefs about their child's disability and its implications, parents have articulated an array of answers. For example, some parents blame God for the diagnosis, perceive they are being punished, assume God has abandoned them, or come to question God's existence or benevolence. Others see their child's disability as a special blessing, a gift from God, a part of God's plan, or an affirmation of God's presence. Indeed, some parents express a combination of both harmful and healthy views at different times. The beliefs and perspectives parents hold can impact how they make sense of, deal with, and adapt to the diagnosis (Rogers-Adkinson, Ochoa, & Delgado, 2003; Tarakeshwar & Pargament, 2001). When clinicians understand how parents interpret the causes and implications of their child's new diagnosis, they can better align their responses and treatments in ways that respect their starting point and help families find meaning in the midst of a new diagnosis.

Service Entry

Entry into early intervention or other school-based settings represents another major transition for both children with ASD and their families. The introduction of new routines, therapies, and educational settings can contribute to challenging behavior and anxiety for some children. Likewise, parents must learn to navigate a new system of professionals, policies, and jargon that can feel overwhelming and incapacitating. The emotional, spiritual, financial, and practical support (e.g., respite, camaraderie, prayer, pastoral counseling) from congregation members can be especially encouraging for families in the midst of this flurry of new experiences. At about the same time, families involved in faith communities may see shifts in where their child is served – from nursery programs to children's ministry programs. The inconsistency with which congregations are committed and prepared to support children with autism in existing religious education classes has left many families frustrated and excluded (Ault, Collins, & Carter, 2013; Speraw, 2006).

Marital Relationships

Although individual differences abound, parents of children with ASD tend to experience more stress, lower well-being, and higher divorce rates than other parents (Hartley et al., 2010; Meadan, Halle, & Ebata, 2010). Some parents report that their spirituality is a supportive factor that helps them navigate relational challenges and maintain their marriage (Ramisch, Onaga, & Oh, 2014). Others describe their faith community as a place of relationships and social networks that provides much-needed support. Helping these families connect to needed counseling, therapies, and support networks that honor or integrate their spirituality can be instrumental throughout one's marriage.

Transition to Adulthood

The transition from adolescence to adulthood presents another period of challenge for many families (Boehm et al., 2015). Graduation from high school marks the exit from the predictability and guarantee of educational services to an adult service system characterized by inconsistency and eligibility requirements. Families have described this transition as a time of heightened worry, stress, fear, change, and uncertainty. As access to formal services diminishes, parents may come to rely more heavily on internal familial, relational, and spiritual supports to cope with these challenges. They may also turn to their congregations for assistance during this transition. For example, a growing number of faith communities are involved in addressing the employment, housing, and relationship needs of young people with developmental disabilities (Carter, 2011; Carter, Bumble, Griffin, & Curcio, 2017). Helping families connect to or advocate for these supports can help them navigate this period of storm and stress more successfully.

Professional Roles

Although understanding and honoring the spiritual beliefs, commitments, connections, and resources of people with disabilities and their families is advocated as best practice across diverse fields, this area of work can be a place of hesitation and uncertainty for some clinicians. Concerns about the invasion of privacy, the perception of proselytizing, or the imposing of one's own orientations on others are sometimes cited by professionals as reasons for omission. In other cases, this aspect of the family experience is overlooked because clinicians are unsure how to address it well within their practice or because they presume it is being addressed adequately elsewhere. A number of national organizations have issued strong policy statements affirming the importance of carefully considering and thoughtfully supporting this dimension of the lives of individuals with disabilities and their families. For example, the American Association on Intellectual and Developmental Disabilities and The Arc (2010) crafted a joint position statement affirming the salience of spirituality to the people with disabilities and their families and advocating for the provision of needed supports and services in this domain. They note in this statement that, "Spiritual resources and faith communities are an underused resource in the community for people to exercise choice, develop relationships and social networks, demonstrate respect for cultural and family backgrounds, and serve others." TASH – an organization advocating for individuals with the most significant disabilities and their families – issued a similar resolution supporting "the right of individuals with disabilities to participate in spiritual expression or organized religion as they so choose and promot[ing] the provision of any and all supports needed by people with disabilities to so participate" (2003). Finally, the Joint Commission (2010) emphasized the importance of knowing how someone's cultural, religions, and spiritual beliefs and practices might influence the care professionals provide.

Postures and Practices

Clinicians have a ubiquitous role in the lives of families with members who have ASD. Because clinicians assume varied roles in the lives of these families, their interactions around issues of spirituality may also look different. For some clinicians, understanding the spiritual beliefs, strengths, and resources held by families can inform or enhance the delivery of services in ways that make them more relevant, valued, or effective. In other cases, clinicians may be directly involved in supporting families to express, explore, or enhance their spirituality. In other words, engagement depends on many factors, including the particular professional role, the context in which the clinician works (e.g., faith-based organization), the quality of the clinician's relationship with the family, the interests the family may have expressed in the past, and the type of services the clinician provides. Recognizing this range of possibilities, I offer the following broad recommendations for consideration.

Assume Relevance

Historically, the spirituality of children and adults with autism and other developmental disabilities has been overlooked, ignored, or poorly supported; so too have the needs of their families in this domain (Carter, 2007). A commitment to "universal aspirations" assumes that the experiences, relationships, and supports that are important to anyone in a community will also be important to people with ASD and their families. Indeed, studies affirm that the presence of a disability is not a predictor of the place and prominence of spirituality in people's lives (Boehm et al., 2015; Carter et al., 2016). Clinicians should anticipate that spirituality may be a relevant factor in the lives of any family they serve.

Avoid Presumptions

Although relevance should be assumed, presumptions should be avoided. First, not every family will consider spirituality to be an important aspect of their lives or an important consideration for service delivery. The same diversity of convictions and commitments that exist outside the disability community also exist within it. Although most Americans do identify as religious and/or spiritual, a growing number do not. Clinicians should avoid presuming that families – including those for whom spirituality is a prominent part of their lives – will see this area as applicable or appropriate to services. Second, the spiritual beliefs and priorities of families for whom spirituality is important are likely to be quite varied – both within and across religious denominations and spiritual traditions. Contemporary society is increasingly multicultural and multifaith. Clinicians should avoid presuming the families with whom they work will experience and express their spirituality in a particular way. Third, the spiritual stories of individuals with ASD and their families are rarely tepid; some have experienced extravagant welcome with a faith community, others speak of deep wounding (Ault et al., 2013; Tarakeshwar & Pargament, 2001). Clinicians should not presume that a family's faith community will necessarily be aware or supportive of the family's needs. Fourth, individual members of a family (e.g., mothers, fathers, siblings, other relatives) may not always hold the same perspectives and priorities when it comes to spirituality. Clinicians should not presume a uniform response from within families.

Ask Good Questions

The prior two points accentuate the importance of asking good questions and listening carefully to their responses – about the salience of spirituality to the family and about its relevance to service delivery. Understanding these issues is an important aspect of providing culturally competent services and helps ensure the care clinicians provide is congruent with the spiritual beliefs and practices of families. Sometimes this involves simply listening to families as they share their stories and circumstances, noticing references to spiritual interests and connections, and following up with relevant questions. Other times, clinicians take a more structured approach in which they directly ask questions about one's spiritual beliefs and support systems. In all cases, it is critical to create an atmosphere in which people are comfortable talking about issues that matter most to them.

Several spiritual assessment approaches can help clinicians navigate these topics in thoughtful and reflective ways (Carter, 2007). For example, the acronym HOPE (Anandarajah & Hight, 2001) provides a helpful structure to guide these conversations:

- H (Sources of Hope): What are your basic spiritual resources? What gives you support? What sustains you in difficult times?
- O (Organized Religion): What role does organized religion play in your life? What aspects are most and least important to you?
- P (Personal Spirituality and Practices): What spiritual practices are important to you? How would you describe your relationship with God?
- E (Effects on Care): How should your spiritual needs, strengths, and resources impact the supports and opportunities we provide?

The FICA (Puchalski & Romer, 2000) acronym provides another approach to framing these conversations:

- F (Faith and Belief): What brings you meaning? Do you consider yourself to be spiritual or religious?
- I (Importance and Influence): How important are these beliefs in your life? What influence do they have on the decisions you make?
- C (Community): Do you belong to a congregation or other spiritual community? How important is this community to you?
- A (Address or Application): How (if at all) would you like us to address these issues through our supports and services?

Although contemporary discourse sometimes equates assessment with evaluation, the root word of assessment means, "to sit alongside." This reminds clinicians that the primary goal of these conversations is *not* to appraise their spirituality, but rather to understand its place in the lives of families. When clinicians understand the beliefs and relationships families draw on for strength and sustenance, they are much better positioned to design treatments, supports, and opportunities that incorporate these values and priorities.

Revisit the Answers

The spiritual lives of individuals and families – whether or not ASD is part of the experience – are rarely static. The things that bring meaning to people's lives can deepen or change over time, as can the ways in which they participate in a faith community. For example, one ethnographic study found that parents of children with autism tended to cope early on by relying more heavily on service providers and family support; up to a decade later, these same parents tended to invoke their religious faith and other coping strategies as they adapted to unchanged circumstances (Gray, 2006). For clinicians working with families over time, periodically revisiting these questions can provide insight into whether the beliefs, commitments, and resources of families – as well as the ways in which they draw upon each – are different in the present from the past.

Connect to Supports

One way in which clinicians can support families is by helping them identify and connect to available social, instrumental, and other practical supports in their community. For example, some faith communities offer respite care, host parent support groups, provide spiritual counseling, arrange social events, or offer other supports that could be desirable to and beneficial for families raising children with ASD (Carter et al., 2016). Unfortunately, many families report considerable difficulty learning about these offerings or advocating for their creation. Furthermore, clinicians are usually part of a much larger team working in concert to support families. Tapping into the expertise and connections of these other team members can help clinicians identify faith-based community resources and supports they might not otherwise have known about.

Advocate Elsewhere

Faith communities often express uncertainty about how to invite, include, and support individuals with ASD and their families. Clinicians familiar with the needs of these families in their communities can be a resource to local congregations interested in becoming more accessible to and welcoming of these families. Any efforts a clinician already makes to promote greater awareness and knowledge of ASD in his or her community could also extend to faith communities.

Consider Commitments

It can be instructive for clinicians to reflect on their own beliefs, values, and biases related to the domain of spirituality. *What is it that brings meaning and* purpose to your own life? What is the place of spirituality in your own life – personally and professionally? What preconceived ideas do you hold about the role spirituality should play in the lives of the families you serve? Why do you react to this issue in the ways that you do? Such reflection can help ensure a clinician is supporting the individual preferences and commitments of families, rather than projecting his or her own expectations.

Strengthen Policies

Many organizations and agencies have developed policies that address the ways in which spirituality should be addressed within practice; others are silent or leave this issue to the discretion of individual clinicians. Clarifying the roles and responsibilities of clinicians can give them greater confidence in navigating this topic in their work. Do staff know whether, when, and how to inquire about the spirituality and support needs of the people they serve? Do they know when to provide direct support and when to make connections to others? Do they know where they can turn when they have questions or need guidance? As an organization, ask: What can we point to as an organization that indicates we view spirituality as a relevant dimension of the lives of the people we serve?

Conclusion

The spirituality of families can influence the ways in which they seek help, the persons from whom they seek help, the services they use, the resources available to them, and the relationships they have with professionals (Ravindran & Myers, 2012). Understanding the priorities and practices of families in this domain of life can be an essential element of providing culturally competent services and supports, as well as helping families to flourish.

References

American Association on Intellectual and Developmental Disabilities and The Arc (2010). Life in the Community: Spirituality. Retrieved from www.thearc.org/who-we-are/position-statements/life-in-the-community/spirituality

Anandarajah, G., & Hight, E. (2001). Spirituality and medical practice: Using the HOPE questions as a practical tool for spiritual assessment. American Family Physician, 63, 81–89.

Ault, M. (2010). Inclusion of religion and spirituality in the special education literature. The Journal of Special Education, 44, 176–189.

Ault, M. J., Collins, B. C., & Carter, E. W. (2013). Congregational participation and supports for children and adults with disabilities: Parent perceptions. Intellectual and Developmental Disabilities, 51, 48–61.

Boehm, T. L., Carter, E. W., & Taylor, J. L. (2015). Factors associated with family quality of life during the transition to adulthood for youth and young adults with developmental disabilities. American Journal on Intellectual and Developmental Disabilities, 120, 395–411.

Carter, E. W. (2007). Including people with disabilities in faith communities: A guide for service providers, families, and congregations. Baltimore, MD: Paul H. Brookes.

Carter, E. W. (2011). After the benediction: Walking alongside people with significant disabilities and their families in faith and life. *Journal of Religion, Disability, and Health, 15*, 395–413.

Carter, E. W., Boehm, T. L., Annandale, N. H., & Taylor, C. (2016). Supporting congregational inclusion for children and youth with disabilities and their families. *Exceptional Children, 82*, 372–389.

Carter, E. W., Bumble, J. L., Griffin, B., & Curcio, M. P. (2017). Community conversations on faith and disability: Identifying new practices, postures, and partners for congregations. *Pastoral Psychology, 66*, 575–594.

Ekas, N. V., Whitman, T. L., & Shivers, C. (2009). Religiosity, spirituality, and socioemotional functioning in mothers of children with autism spectrum disorder. *Journal of Autism and Developmental Disorders, 39*, 706–719.

Gray, D. E. (2006). Coping over time: The parents of children with autism. *Journal of Intellectual Disability Research, 50*, 970–976.

Hartley, S. L., Barker, E. T, Seltzer, M. M., Floyd, F., Greenberg, J., & Orsmond, G. (2010). The relative risk and timing of divorce in families of children with an autism spectrum disorder. *Journal of Family Psychology, 24*, 449–457.

The Joint Commission. (2010). *Advancing effective communication, cultural competence, and patient- and family-centered care: A roadmap for hospitals.* Oakbrook Terrace, IL: Author.

Koenig, H., King, D., & Carson, V. B. (2012). *Handbook of religion and health* (2nd ed.). New York, NY: Oxford University Press.

Luther, E. H., Canham, D. L., & Cureton, V. (2005). Coping and social support for parents of children with autism. *The Journal of School Nursing, 21*, 40–47.

Meadan, H., Halle, J. W., & Ebata, A. T. (2010). Families with children who have autism spectrum disorders: Stress and support. *Exceptional Children, 77*, 7–36.

Poston, D. J., & Turnbull, A. P. (2004). Role of spirituality and religion in family quality of life for families of children with disabilities. *Education and Training in Developmental Disabilities, 39*, 95–108.

Puchalski, C., & Romer, A. L. (2000). Taking a spiritual history allows clinicians to understand patients more fully. *Journal of Palliative Medicine, 3*, 129–137.

Ramisch, J. L., Onaga, E., & Oh, S. M. (2014). Keeping a sound marriage: How couples with children with autism spectrum disorders maintain their marriages. *Journal of Child and Family Studies, 23*, 975–988.

Ravindran, N., & Myers, B. J. (2012). Cultural influences on perceptions of health, illness, and disability: A review and focus on autism. *Journal of Child and Family Studies, 21*, 311–319.

Rogers-Adkinson, Ochoa, T., & Delgado, B. (2003). Developing cross-cultural competence: Serving families of children with significant developmental needs. *Focus on Autism and Other Developmental Disabilities, 18*, 4–8.

Salkas, K., Magaña, S., Marques, I., & Mirza, M. (2016). Spirituality in Latino families of children with autism spectrum disorder. *Journal of Family Social Work, 19*, 38–55.

Speraw, S. (2006). Spiritual experiences of parents and caregivers who have children with disabilities or special needs. *Issues in Mental Health Nursing, 27*, 213–230.

Tarakeshwar, N., & Pargament, K. I. (2001). Religious coping in families of children with autism. *Focus on Autism and Other Developmental Disabilities, 16*, 247–260.

Twoy, R., Connolly, P. M., & Novak, J. M. (2007). Coping strategies used by parents of children with autism. *Journal of the American Academy of Nurse Practitioners, 19*(5), 251–260.

22 Caregiver and Professional Perspectives

From Financial Planning Obstacles to Optimizing the Future

Nicole Piland Springer and Mitzi Lauderdale

The role of financial planning for families raising children with ASD is critical, but often goes unaddressed because of the other more pressing demands related to caregiving that absorb the majority of their time and energy (e.g., early-intervention services, occupational, sensory integration and speech therapy; Bekins, 2018; Center for Disease Control and Prevention [CDC], 2018; Cooper, Heron, & Heward, 2007). Although these are important steps for parents to make and sustain an optimal future for their child, financial planning is not a natural initial step families usually consider. There are many facets to financial planning and a comprehensive review is beyond the scope of this chapter, but this chapter will include financial planning guidance and information, along with perspectives shared directly by parents. It is important for families and professionals to know that there is not a "one-size-fits-all" approach to financial planning and planning happens across the lifespan, as opposed to at a single point in time.

This chapter will begin with an overview of a focus group study, which investigated the financial planning needs of special needs parents and caregivers in the hope of designing a more effective format and delivery of planning information for families (Lauderdale, Durband, Scott, & Springer, 2010; Lauderdale & Springer, 2011). The researchers met with caregivers to learn about their perceived barriers and challenges of financial planning for their loved ones. The goal was for parents and caregivers to share their struggles, successes, and perceptions related to financial planning. Participants in this project were caring for loved ones with a variety of special needs diagnoses, and some were dually-diagnosed, but over half of participants indicated that their child had ASD. Given the focus of this book, only quotes shared by caregivers of loved ones with ASD are included; however, the categories and themes described were identified during the analysis process using responses from all focus group participants.

Caregiver Perspectives

Financial Planning Obstacles

Participants were first asked, "What, if any, financial planning have you completed for your loved one? And, if you don't have a plan, what has kept you from planning or made it difficult for you to plan?" Four themes emerged under the category of financial planning obstacles (1) not knowing; (2) the time-consuming nature of the paperwork process; (3) not qualifying for or losing benefits; (4) existing out of pocket expenses. The participants repeatedly made references to "not knowing" in regards to what resources were available to them. One mother of a 14-year-old shared, "There is a lot of help out there that I didn't know was there. I think parents with little ones need to know that stuff (i.e., Medicaid waivers) to make their lives easier."

The sub-themes for the theme of "not knowing" included references made by participants about where to start the planning process or where to go, as well as the unknown regarding the future needs of their loved ones. One parent shared, "The whole process just seems so complicated … where do you start? … there is nothing out there that clearly states those steps for you" (mother, 14 y/o). Similarly, another parent expressed, "I think picking where to start is the biggest financial frustration." One mother expressed the desire to have one place to obtain information: "I would just like the resources and things to be easier to find. I mean they're out there, but unless you know the right person who knows the right thing to tell you, you're not going to find them" (mother, 16 y/o).

Another participant shared:

> I guess the unknown factor still. We just don't know where he is going to be at. He progresses all the time, he matures all the time. And I don't think I'm ready for that yet. So that keeps us from getting some of the planning done.
>
> (Mother, 10 y/o)

Theme two within this category contains key reflections by participants regarding the time-consuming nature of completing the forms and paperwork associated with planning. In particular, the following quote captures this obstacle quite well: "It's a lot of work, it's not like it is not worth it for your kids, but it's so time consuming when you have so much time being taken up …" (mother, ten y/o).

In response to a follow-up question, "what has been your biggest frustration thus far in planning for your loved one's financial future?" participants shared about not qualifying for or losing benefits they once had, due to changes in their family's financial status.

> My ex-husband made too much money before (to qualify) … and I've told lots of families before you're better off getting a divorce on paper … so that you can pay for your child's medical, because it is, it's next to impossible.
>
> (Mother, 17 y/o w/ASD & Cerebral Palsy)

The final theme identified within the financial planning obstacles category was related to existing out of pocket expenses. Participants reported concerns related to reaching coverage maximums, absorbing prescription costs, and the expense of co-payments for supplemental therapies. Ultimately, financial demands and challenges related to the caregiving cost for these families was described repeatedly by the participants.

Given that many families are higher utilizers of the medical system due to services needed in relation to their child's diagnoses, parents are often faced with challenges associated with health insurance authorization and reimbursement. Several participants made references to losing benefits in addition to fighting insurance claims. When children have extensive medical needs, it is not uncommon for them to reach coverage maximums.

The Guardianship Dilemma

The second category emerged in response to the question, "What is your biggest obstacle in creating an ideal future?" The themes identified from the focus group data were related to challenges with establishing guardianship and included (1) who will do it?; (2) the burden of caregiving; (3) it's a mother's job. Participants consistently shared and reflected about the struggle to identify someone who they would deem as an adequate guardian and caregiver for their loved ones in their absence. The following quote is an example of the struggle with this element of planning:

> What will happen to him when I'm gone? Where will he live? ... Take him places he needs to go? All that, and there's just not a lot of people who will step up and take on a disabled child.
>
> (Grandmother, 16 y/o w ASD, Bi-Polar Disorder)

A few sub-themes emerged from the data regarding the process of identifying *who* to establish as a guardian. Participants were also asked the follow-up question, "what is your greatest fear for your loved one's future?" and the sub-themes of (1) trust; (2) safety; (3) training someone emerged. Participants spoke about having great difficulty in identifying who would be a trustworthy guardian and who could manage the needs of their loved one. Some participant reflections included references about not trusting their own family members and staff at group homes or other residential entities. Others highlighted concerns about their loved one's safety and wanting their loved one to not be taken advantage of in their absence. Moreover, caregivers identified the desire to train someone to take on the caregiving role in the future; which was specifically in response to a question related to creating an ideal future. One participant shared about the lack of preparation if something unexpected happened to her.

> Immediately, if something happened to me, my husband would have nothing set up. So I don't have any idea where the kids would end up right now. I have absolutely no idea, and I think that's why we haven't put it in place yet because we just don't know who he would go live with.
>
> (Mother, ten y/o son)

An additional theme within this category included statements related to the perceived burden of caregiving. There was repeated evidence of the participants' recognition and awareness of the demands of caregiving. One mother of two children with ASD expressed, "I wouldn't want it to be a burden on anybody." Another mother stated, "I also wonder would it be a burden upon them, so I don't want it to be a burden on them, but financially there has to be something out there." Interestingly, many participants expressed the wish to prevent their loved one's siblings from being burdened by future caregiving needs. This was evident in the following participant reflection, "That is not her responsibility and it's not her cross to carry. It's not her burden." This was further echoed by a mother of a teenager who was dually-diagnosed, "I don't want it to fall on my other children because I want them to have a life. I want them to be there, you know, to see him, to love him, but not to take care of him."

Along with references by parents that siblings should not be expected to take on the caregiving responsibility for the child with ASD, a final theme emerged; specifically, that caregiving is "a mother's job." Many participants, the majority being mothers, highlighted that they "do all the work," "make all the decisions," and "do everything." The two father participants even made references that their level of involvement was not typical; with one father being the primary caregiver for the entire family because his wife also had a chronic health condition.

Related to this theme, two sub-themes were identified (1) nobody does it better and (2) hope that the loved one dies first. Two of the more profound quotes associated with the first sub-theme was, "nobody is going to protect him the way you are," or "treat them as kindly as the way I would," both expressed by mothers of teens. And yet, the final sub-theme included references that were particularly impactful – wishing the loved one would pass on before the caregivers and statements about all going (i.e., dying) together.

While it may be true that no one can do it better than the parents can, with a proper plan in place, which is well communicated with the future caretakers, continuity and excellent care can continue to support individuals with ASD. Based on the needs of the individual, plans will look different, but having a plan in place can ease the stress and provide some peace of mind for parents who are so invested in the lives of their loved ones.

Clinical Recommendations

Because families do experience unique emotional, relational, and financial stressors, there can be times when they could benefit from mental health treatment either individually as caregivers managing stress, relationally as couples in navigating planning decisions, and/or as a family in terms of protecting the relationships impacted by stressors. Thus, it is important to recognize the role that clinicians can serve in the lives of these families even if families present to therapy for matters beyond financial needs.

In particular, mental health professionals can make a huge impact on the financial and legal plans whether they realize it or not. According to Lauderdale and Huston (2012), families with a special needs child were 23 times more likely to have at least a special needs trust (i.e., a legal centerpiece to the plan) in place if they worked with a financial planner, and were three times more likely if they were encouraged by a mental health professional. This research was conducted to explore whether there was any sort of plan at all rather than assessing the quality of the plan. When working with professionals, it is important to identify appropriate financial planners, lawyers, trustees and mental health professionals who frequently work with families with a loved one with ASD (Nadworny & Haddad, 2007; Sharpe & Baker, 2007). A team approach utilizing financial, legal, and mental health professionals is ideal because there are so many facets to be considered and the complex emotional, social, legal and financial aspects can be overwhelming (Lauderdale & Huston, 2013).

In terms of hope for the future, it's also important for mental health clinicians to recognize that caregivers want the best for their loved ones, that is, to achieve independent living, when possible, and acquire a source of income doing something meaningful. There will be a significant range of possibilities for loved ones in terms of their meaningful contributions and abilities to achieve supportive or independent employment, but clinicians are encouraged to operate from a position of exploring possibilities and inviting conversations with caregivers about how to create what is possible, as opposed to focusing on what cannot be achieved.

Conclusion

Although it is difficult for families to imagine someone else caring for their loved ones as effectively as they do, caregivers are strongly encouraged to at least identify a safe and good enough option as a guardian, as opposed to leaving the designation unaddressed until a crisis emerges. Additionally, if families want to avoid placing the siblings of the special needs loved one in a decision-making dilemma or wish to remove the 'burden' of responsibility from their other dependents, then identifying a viable guardian is even more important.

References

Bekins, J. (2018). Allied Health Professionals: Enhancing potential through early childhood intervention and therapies. In B. S. Nelson Goff & N. Piland Springer (Eds.), *Intellectual and Developmental Disabilities: A roadmap for families and professionals* (pp. 148–157). New York, NY: Routledge.

Center for Disease Control and Prevention. (2018). Autism spectrum disorder: Treatment. Retrieved from www.cdc.gov/ncbddd/autism/treatment.html.

Cooper, J. O., Heron, T. E., & Heward, W. L. (2007). *Applied behavior analysis* (2nd ed.). Upper Saddle River, NJ: Pearson.

Lauderdale, M., Durband, D., Scott, J., & Springer, N. (2010). Special needs training: A focus group study. Paper presented at the Academy of Financial Services Conference, Denver, Colorado.

Lauderdale, M., & Huston, S. J. (2012). Financial therapy and planning for families with special needs children. *Journal of Financial Therapy, 3*(1), 62–81.

Lauderdale, M., & Huston, S. (2013). The team approach to planning for families with special needs dependents. *Journal of Financial Planning, 26*(3), 46–52.

Lauderdale, M., & Springer, N. (2011). *Financial planning education for families including children with special needs.* Unpublished grant report submitted to The CH Foundation.

Nadworny, J. W., & Haddad, C. R. (2007). *The special needs planning guide: How to prepare for every stage of your child's life.* Baltimore, Maryland: Paul H. Brookes Publishing Co.

Sharpe, D. L., & Baker, D. L. (2007). Financial issues associated with having a child with autism. *Journal of Family and Economic Issues, 28*(2), 247–264.

23 Evidence-Based Practices

Kevin Callahan and Susan M. Nichols

Summarizing and assessing the effectiveness of therapies and supports for parents, families, and practitioners within the ASD field is essential in helping to identify and obtain appropriate treatments. Parents and service providers today have access to a large variety of helpful resources and interventions that have been identified as evidence-based practices (EBPs) or promising "emerging" treatments to successfully address the diverse needs of individuals with ASD across both the spectrum of severity and the lifespan. Unfortunately, with so many available options, parents and mental health care clinicians often become overwhelmed during the selection and implementation of treatments. This chapter will provide information to help clinicians gain a basic understanding of the major therapeutic approaches in ASD, including comprehensive treatment models and individual intervention components, which have been demonstrated to be effective for children, adolescents, and adults with ASD. This chapter will also address ways to access potentially beneficial supports in the community and online.

Evidence-Based Practices in ASD Treatment

Clinicians and parents looking for effective therapies and supports for individuals with ASD should keep several fundamental considerations in mind while beginning their search. First, because of the large diversity of skills and deficits among individuals on the spectrum, it is important to understand that no single therapy or intervention can be said to be effective for *all* individuals with an ASD diagnosis. Thus, it is necessary to consider the severity of symptoms when assessing the type and intensity of potential interventions (National Autism Center [NAC], 2015; Thompson, 2011). Whether one is seeking treatment to address a wide range of functional skill deficits, such as communication, social interaction, and basic self-care or a focused intervention to improve or decrease a single target behavior, it is important to match therapies and supports to the needs of the individual. Before this can happen, parents and professionals must be aware of the available effective treatments from which they can select (NAC, 2015). Second, service providers should always evaluate the *evidence* of effectiveness for potential therapeutic approaches that may be appropriate for their unique situation. Fortunately, researchers have recently provided the empirical and social validity evidence needed to help consumers choose appropriate, effective treatments (NAC, 2015; Wong et al., 2015).

Within the past several years, research teams have conducted large-scale, systematic reviews of the autism intervention literature to determine which treatments have robust scientific support for their effectiveness (NAC, 2015; Wong et al., 2015). This research identified specific autism interventions considered to be "evidence-based." That is, the quantity, quality, and strength of the published research investigating the effectiveness of these practices support their use by therapists, parents, and other providers. The National Autism Center (NAC) and the National Professional Development Center on Autism Spectrum Disorder (NPDC) produced lists of established and confirmed EBPs in autism. Included among the EBPs on both lists are essential treatments such as behavioral and cognitive-behavioral interventions, naturalistic teaching strategies, parent training, and peer training (see Table 23.1).

Other related research has investigated which EBPs in autism intervention are *socially* valid. Social validity is another important piece of evidence to consider when choosing which types of therapies and supports to implement in one's clinic, school, or home. Generally defined as "customer satisfaction" with the goals, procedures, and outcomes of therapeutic programs and interventions (Wolf, 1978), social validity plays a significant role in the selection and effective implementation of EBPs in autism. Callahan and colleagues systematically analyzed more than 800 research articles cited within the NAC and NPDC reviews of autism EBPs to determine the level of social validation for each intervention. These researchers concluded that all of the strategies identified by the NAC and NPDC demonstrate at least *minimal* levels of social validity, although there is a wide range of evidence across EBPs (Callahan et al., 2017). In order to identify therapies which have the maximum potential to result in positive outcomes, parents and health care providers using and recommending autism treatments should be aware of those interventions having evidence of *both* empirical and social validity in support of their effectiveness. When considering the use of any of the EBPs listed in Table 1, consumers should feel confident that any of these strategies used alone or in combination with other EBPs may be effective for the individual.

Comprehensive Treatment Models

Comprehensive Treatment Models (CTMs) for young children with ASD provide well-described, intensive procedures within a clear conceptual or theoretical framework, which promote the development, functioning, and well-being of individuals with ASD and their families (Odom, Boyd, Hall, & Hume, 2010). Several theoretical orientations overlap the major CTMs in autism. To date, the most significant and best-documented treatment approaches are based on behavioral and developmental perspectives (NAC, 2015; National Research Council [NRC], 2001; Odom et al., 2010). The major theories guiding EBPs in

Table 23.1 Comparison of NPDC and NSP Practices

Comparison of NPDC and NSP Practices

Evidence-Based Practices Identified by the National Professional Development Center (NPDC) on ASD	Established Treatments Identified by the National Standards Project (NSP)													
	Behavioral Interventions	Cognitive Behavioral Interventions	Modeling	Natural Teaching Strategies	Parent Training	Peer Training Package	Pivotal Response Training	Schedules	Scripting	Self-management	Social Skills Package	Story-based Intervention	Language Training	Comprehensive Behavioral Treatment for Young Children
Antecedent-based Intervention	X													
Differential Reinforcement	X													
Discrete Trial Training	X													
Extinction	X													
Modeling			X											
Prompting	X													
Reinforcement	X													
Response Interruption/Redirection	X													
Scripting	X								X					
Task Analysis	X													
Video Modeling	X		X											
Time Delay	X													
Cognitive Behavioral Intervention		X												
Naturalistic Intervention				X										
Parent Implemented Intervention					X									
Peer-mediated Instruction & Intervention						X								
Pivotal Response Training							X							
Self-management										X				
Social Narratives												X		
Social Skills Training											X			
Visual Supports								X						

Language Training: Language training did not emerge as a focused intervention by the NPDC on ASD. Components of Language Training overlap with NPDC identified practices that may support language production, such as modeling, prompting, and reinforcement.

Comprehensive Behavioral Treatment for Young Children: The NPDC on ASD did not review comprehensive treatment models. Components of The Comprehensive Behavioral Treatment of Young Children overlap with many NPDC identified practices.

Exercise was identified as an emerging practice by the NSP.

Functional Behavior Assessment — The NSP did not consider Functional Behavior Assessment as a category of evidence-based practice.

Functional Communication Training — Functional Communication Training was identified as an emerging practice by the NSP.

Picture Exchange Communication System — Picture Exchange Communication System was identified as an emerging practice by the NSP.

Structured Play Groups — The NSP did not consider Structured Play Groups as a category of evidence-based practice.

Technology-aided Instruction & Intervention — Technology-aided instruction and intervention was identified as an emerging practice by the NSP.

NPDC 2017

ASD have several critically important common elements. For example, all CTMs specifically address the core deficits of the ASD diagnosis, including social-communication skills and restricted and repetitive behaviors (American Psychiatric Association [APA], 2013) and provide predictable routines within highly structured and supportive treatment environments. Further, because of the fundamental nature of communication deficits among individuals with ASD, all comprehensive therapies provide strategies for promoting improved functional communication. They also target related developmental domains such as social interaction and engagement, including play skills for younger children, and provide therapeutic/curriculum content that is delivered by staff who are highly trained and experienced in ASD (NAC, 2015). Comprehensive models that are behavior analytic in nature, such as early intensive behavioral intervention, should always be provided under the supervision of a Board Certified Behavior Analyst (BCBA) who has received specialized training and expert supervision while providing autism intervention (BACB, 2014). Certification and/or licensure by key members of the therapeutic team provides assurance of the minimal levels of training and experience needed to maximize treatment success.

In evaluating the essential components of treatment programs in ASD, Callahan and colleagues identified five major categories of functional activities that should always be present, including (a) Individualized programming; (b) Data-based decision making; (c) Use of empirically-based strategies; (d) Active collaboration; and (f) A focus on long-term outcomes (Callahan, Henson, & Cowan, 2008; Callahan, Shukla-Mehta, Magee, & Wie, 2010). Individualized programming requires the use of formal assessment tools to objectively measure all relevant domains of an individual's current levels of functioning (e.g., social competence, communication, physical functioning/motor skills, and academic/prevocational skills). The hallmark of data-based decision making is conducting ongoing assessment of these targeted goals in order to measure skill acquisition, assess client progress, and modify the delivery of therapy, if necessary.

According to Callahan et al. (2008) active collaboration seeks to ensure that autism services are delivered in a coordinated, collaborative, and multidisciplinary manner, which always includes parents as a fundamental member of the therapeutic team. A typical collaborative team providing coordinated care for persons with ASD will often include behavior analysts, speech and language pathologists, special education teachers, psychologists and/or therapists, developmental pediatricians, and other specialized professionals, in addition to parents and family members. Effective, ongoing communication is essential among the members of the active collaborative team. Communication about ASD services should always include planning and programming to ensure successful transitions and the generalization use of newly mastered skills within typical school, work, and community environments. It is important for service providers to discuss expected long-term outcomes and placements so that immediate steps can be taken within the individualized treatment plan to obtain these future goals.

Finally, intensity is a key consideration in the completion of effective autism interventions. Research indicates that the effectiveness of evidence-based treatments is highly correlated with the amount of time that intervention can be delivered by highly qualified and experienced professionals (APA, 2013; NRC, 2001). The National Research Council concluded that effective programs for school-aged children ideally provide a minimum of 25 hours per week of comprehensive programming, although fewer hours per week can also be appropriate for some individualized programs (NRC, 2001). Because of the tendency of children with more severe levels of autism to regress in their therapeutic progress if they do not receive consistent, continuous therapy, maximum intensity also generally requires year-round programming and a duration that spans several stages of childhood development (NRC, 2001). Regardless of whether treatment is delivered in-home or in clinical settings, parents and professionals should consider their ability to implement therapies at the highest levels of intensity appropriate for their situation and needs.

Extensive efforts have been taken to identify and assess CTMs in autism. In particular, a 2001 review by the National Research Council (NRC) examined CTMs and identified representative models. Recent studies have identified additional CTMs and systematically evaluated factors which could help providers and families select and implement treatment (Odom et al., 2010). Odom et al. concluded that there is a wide range of evidence about the overall quality and effectiveness of individual CTMs. However, the majority of models with strong evidence fall into an applied behavior analysis (ABA) theoretical framework, with services delivered in homes, schools, clinics, or within a combination of settings. Other models, some with equally strong evidence, are based largely on developmental or social learning theories emphasizing the importance of social relationships (e.g., the Denver Model) and/or organizing environments to be visually supportive for individuals with ASD (e.g., TEACCH). Because ABA is considered by many to be the most familiar and frequently used model in ASD intervention the sections below will describe this approach and discuss ABA's reported strengths and weaknesses.

The Applied Behavior Analysis Approach to Autism Treatment

Applied Behavior Analysis (commonly referred to as "ABA") stems from B. F. Skinner's psychological philosophy of behaviorism (Cooper, Heron, & Heward, 2007). ABA is best defined as "the science in which tactics derived from the principles of behavior are applied systematically to improve socially significant behavior and experimentation is used to identify the variables responsible for behavior change" (Cooper et al., 2007, p. 20). ABA uses specific methods that systematically change behavior in measurable ways. All treatments that are behavioral in nature are based on a set of shared assumptions about behavior and the most effective ways to change it. Specifically, ABA assumes that most social behaviors are learned and maintained by an individual's learning history.

By manipulating antecedents in the environment and systematically applying ABA's principles of reinforcement, new behaviors can be learned and undesired behaviors changed (Cooper et al., 2007). Behavioral interventions are designed to apply specific principles and related strategies, such as positive and negative reinforcement, punishment, extinction, modeling, and shaping, to improve socially significant behaviors. As seen in Table 1, many behavioral strategies are considered to be EBPs in autism intervention.

In ABA, instructional and therapeutic interactions are often considered within the context of an individually programmed three-term contingency – "ABC" – where an antecedent (usually a specific cue or instruction) occurs *before* the behavior and a pre-determined consequence happens *after* the occurrence of the targeted response. An example of a typical ABA interaction, or teaching trial, for a child with autism might include the delivery of a direction by a therapist (the antecedent, "Point to the red circle"), followed by the child making the correct behavior (points to the red circle from an array of three possible choices), followed by a praise statement (the consequence, "That's right! Good job pointing to the red circle!"). According to ABA, this kind of teaching interaction reinforces the target behavior and increases its likeliness to occur more frequently in the future.

Traditionally, ABA for persons with autism focuses on systematically teaching small, measurable behaviors, often in a one-on-one, highly structured setting. These "discrete" teaching trials are often repeated frequently in rapid succession to help the child acquire the new target skill quickly and to enable him or her to demonstrate the skill fluently and generalize the effective use of the new skill in different settings and situations (Schreibman, 2005). In ABA, behavioral responses are recorded and evaluated per objective definitions of the target behaviors and very specific criteria for their correct performance. Then these responses are graphed and analyzed so that therapists can assess progress continuously and make any necessary adjustments to the individualized program to ensure the target skills are learned and mastered.

Children with ASD who receive early, intensive ABA treatment which incorporates highly supportive teaching environments and also systematic programs for generalization of skills to occur within the natural environment are likely to make substantial gains impacting functional development that persists through the lifespan (Eldevik, Hastings, Jahr, & Hughes, 2012). According to the National Autism Center (NAC, 2015) and the National Research Council (NRC, 2001), an overwhelming amount of research indicates that strategies based in ABA are the most effective for skills-instruction involving children with autism.

The ABA model has many reported strengths, including robust research support for its effectiveness across individuals of all ages and severity levels (Schreibman, 2005). The inherent emphasis in ABA on objective, ongoing assessment of treatment outcomes – which, in effect, ensures positive outcomes – is another strength of this model. This focus on very specific descriptions of treatment procedures means that a client's program can be easily understood and replicated by virtually any therapist or caregiver with ABA training and experience. Finally, many current comprehensive treatment models incorporate teaching components derived directly from ABA, while they also integrate child developmental theories and approaches in both therapist-implemented models (e.g., Walden Toddler Program; Early Start Denver Model), and parent-implemented models (e.g., Early Social Intervention Project; Joint Attention Intervention) (NAC, 2015). Thus, ABA's impact is widespread across many current treatment models.

A variety of criticisms of ABA have been reported (Schreibman, 2005). Early critiques of the model focused on differences between the psychodynamic theory's internal emphasis and ABA's exclusive focus on modifying external environmental factors to bring about behavior change. Very early demonstrations of behavioral treatment included the use of aversive measures along with terminology, which was considered to be offensive by some observers. In addition, the highly structured nature of ABA treatment procedures can often appear "mechanical" to consumers, and subsequently, children's responses to ABA's Discrete Trial Training protocols have been called "robotic" and lacking in spontaneity. A criticism still reported frequently is the tendency for individuals receiving ABA treatment to become dependent on the prompts of therapists to elicit correct responses. While many of the criticisms of ABA have been addressed by practitioners and researchers, these issues may result in lower overall levels of social validity for the ABA approach (Callahan et al., 2017). As discussed above, if consumers of autism treatments do not fully support their goals, methods, and outcomes, they simply may not use the intervention, or deliver it less effectively.

Largely in response to the kinds of criticisms of ABA detailed above, the field of autism intervention, especially related to the treatment of young children, has moved toward the use of ABA strategies that are more naturalistic, and which allow individuals with ASD to learn new behaviors in their usual context and under more natural conditions. Although naturalistic behavior strategies are known by several different names, including Natural Environment Training, Pivotal Response Training, Incidental Teaching, and Milieu Teaching (NAC, 2015), they all share important therapeutic components. All naturalistic behavior strategies incorporate the use of behavior analytic principles. In fact, researchers have described naturalistic behavior strategies as a type of discrete trial teaching that is initiated by the child and results in the delivery of *natural* reinforcement (NAC, 2015), where instructional sessions occur within the context of the child's normal environments and routines, and follow the child's motivations and preferences for learning activities. To a casual observer, a naturalistic teaching interaction will often look like a child and adult playing together, with the therapist providing the child with enriched communication opportunities, and frequent choices for child-directed responses and activities. It is important to note that despite this appearance of spontaneous play, naturalistic instructional sessions are typically as structured as in traditional ABA, and the environment has been carefully arranged to encourage, promote, and maintain language, play, and other target skills in a way that is rewarding for the student, client, or child (Schreibman, 2005).

Similar to ABA's positive research results, naturalistic teaching methods have been reported to increase language and social skills, as well as other important target behaviors, for children with autism (NAC, 2015; NRC, 2001). Other important advantages of naturalistic behavior strategies include improved generalization of treatment effects (Schreibman, 2005) and increased acceptability of this intervention approach by parents and other practitioners (Schreibman, Kaneko, & Koegel, 1991). Schreibman and colleagues (1991) report that not only service providers, but also the children using naturalistic strategies, find this therapeutic approach to be more enjoyable and less aversive than discrete trial approaches. The main reported weakness of naturalistic approaches is the relatively lower level of scientific evidence to date supporting the superiority of this method over more structured therapeutic approaches. In summary, incorporating methods and techniques established in ABA and naturalistic teaching appear to be essential in the remediation of skill deficits for children with autism.

ABA and naturalistic therapies can be effectively delivered in any setting, including homes, schools, centers, and clinics. Board certified therapists in one's local area can be identified by visiting the Behavior Analysis Certification Board website. The NPDC website contains excellent supporting information about EBPs in autism, including user-friendly materials for parents, clinicians, and other service providers.

Public agencies and schools are required by law to provide Early Childhood Intervention (aged birth to two years) and educational programming support for students with autism, aged 3–22 (Individuals with Disabilities Education Act, 2004). The professional organization for special education, the Council for Exceptional Children, provides additional information about accessing specialized education and support services, as well as standards and evidence-based practices in public school settings for children with autism and other disabilities: www.cec.sped.org. Finally, an emerging delivery method for addressing the lack of trained therapists in some areas is telehealth, which uses remote viewing technologies to provide parents in remote areas with resources for training and supervising the implementation of ABA (Rogers & Vismara, 2014).

Conclusion

When looking for effective therapies and supports for individuals with ASD, clinicians and parents need to be aware of the available effective treatment and consider factors such as the severity of symptoms of the individual. It is also important for clinicians to be able to evaluate the evidence of effectiveness for potential therapeutic approaches. Being familiar with comprehensive treatment models such as ABA, the Denver Model, and TEACCH are also key.

References

American Psychiatric Association (2013). *Diagnostic and statistical manual of mental disorders* (5th Ed.). Arlington: VA: American Psychiatric Publishing.

Behavior Analyst Certification Board (2014). *Applied behavior analysis treatment of autism spectrum disorder: Practice guidelines for healthcare funders and managers* (2nd Ed.). Retrieved from www.bacb.com/wp-content/uploads/2017/09/ABA_Guidelines_for_ASD.pdf.

Callahan, K., Henson, R., & Cowan, A. (2008). Social validation of evidence-based practices in autism by parents, teachers, and administrators. *Journal of Autism and Developmental Disorders, 38,* 678–692.

Callahan, K., Hughes, H. L., Mehta, S., Toussaint, K. A., Nichols, S. M., Ma, P. S., ... Wang, H. (2017). Social validity of evidence-based practices and emerging interventions in autism. *Focus on Autism and Other Developmental Disabilities, 32,* 188–197.

Callahan, K., Shukla-Mehta, S., Magee, S., & Wie, M. (2010). ABA versus TEACCH: The case for defining and validating comprehensive treatment models in autism. *Journal of Autism and Developmental Disorders, 40,* 74–88.

Cooper, J. O., Heron, T. E., & Heward, W. L. (2007). *Applied Behavior Analysis.* Upper Saddle River, NJ: Pearson.

Eldevik, S., Hastings, R. P., Jahr, E., & Hughes, J. C. (2012). Outcomes of behavioral intervention for children with autism in mainstream pre-school settings. *Journal of Autism and Developmental Disorders, 42,* 210–220.

Individuals with Disabilities Education Act, 20 U.S.C. §1400 (2004).

National Autism Center. (2015). *National standards project, phase 2: Findings and conclusions: Addressing the need for evidence-based practice guidelines for autism spectrum disorder.* Randolph, MA: Author.

National Research Council. (2001). *Educating children with autism.* Committee on Educational Interventions for Children with ASD. Lord, C., & McGee, J. P. (Eds.), Division of Behavioral and Social Sciences and Education. Washington, DC: National Academy Press.

Odom, S. L., Boyd, B., Hall L. J., & Hume, K. (2010). Evaluation of comprehensive treatment models for individuals with autism spectrum disorders. *Journal of Autism and Developmental Disabilities, 40,* 425–437.

Rogers, S. J., & Vismara, L. (2014). Interventions for infants and toddlers at risk for autism spectrum disorder. In F. R. Volkmar, S. J. Rogers, R. Paul, & K. A. Pelphrey (Eds.), *Handbook of autism and pervasive developmental disorders* (4th Ed.), *Volume 2: Assessment, interventions, and policy.* Hoboken, NJ: John Wiley and Sons.

Schreibman, L. (2005). *The science and fiction of autism.* Cambridge, MA: Harvard University Press.

Schreibman, L., Kaneko, W. M., & Koegel, R. L. (1991). Positive affect of parents of autistic children: A comparison across two teaching techniques. *Behavior Therapy, 22,* 479–490.

Thompson, T. (2011). *Individualized autism interventions for young children: Blending discrete trial and naturalistic strategies.* Baltimore: Paul H. Brookes.

Wolf, M. M. (1978). Social validity: The case for subjective measurement or how applied behavior analysis is finding its heart. *Journal of Applied Behavior Analysis, 11,* 203–214.

Wong, C., Odom, S. L., Hume, K. A., Cox, A. W., Fettig, A., Kucharczyk, S. ... Schultz, T. R. (2015). Evidence-based practices for children, youth, and young adults with autism spectrum disorder: A comprehensive review. *Journal of Autism and Developmental Disorders, 45,* 1951–1966. doi:10.1007/s10803-014-2351-z.

24 It Takes a Village

Collaborating with Mental Health Professionals

Stephanie M. Peterson, Cody Morris, Denice Rios, Patricia Steinert-Otto, and Mandy Perl

There are several defining characteristics of individuals with ASD, including deficits in social-emotional reciprocity; deficits in nonverbal communication; deficits in developing, maintaining, and understanding relationships; stereotyped or repetitive motor movements; insistence on sameness, inflexible adherence to routines, or ritualized patterns; highly restricted, fixated interests that are abnormal in intensity or focus; hypersensitivity to input or unusual interests in sensory aspects of the environment; and disruptive behaviors (American Psychiatric Association, 2013). These characteristics may manifest themselves across a variety of contexts, such as the home, school, and community settings. Due to the interaction between the variety of characteristics an individual with ASD may display and the number of contexts in which this individual may interact, there tends to be several different service providers who may be involved with the individual with ASD. Examples of the types of service providers who may be involved in the treatment of an individual with ASD include (but certainly are not limited to) behavior analysts, family members, teachers, social workers, occupational therapists, physical therapists, speech/language pathologists, counselors, direct care staff, and physicians. Just as people with ASD contact a variety of contexts and environments in their lives, service providers and family members interact with individuals with ASD across a variety of contexts and settings. It is easy to see how this network can quickly become complex, confusing, and difficult to manage. Figure 24.1 attempts to summarize this complexity by illustrating the multiple contexts in which characteristics of ASD may manifest themselves and the care providers who may have primary responsibility for engaging in treatment across settings.

In order to best serve individuals with ASD, it is important for service providers and family members to work together in a coordinated fashion–sharing information, learning from one another, and ensuring that treatment goals and therapies are not at odds with each other or, better yet, are well coordinated.

The purpose of this chapter is to provide an overview of the different service providers who may interact with the individual with ASD. We provide a brief synopsis of the roles different service providers may play in treating the symptoms of ASD, the scope of practice for various service providers, as well as the types of training they have undertaken. We then describe some of the hurdles

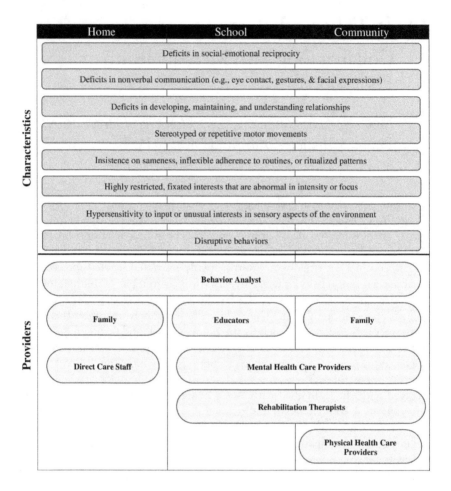

Figure 24.1 The top half of the figure shows the characteristics associated with ASD and that they manifest across many different environments. The bottom half of the figure illustrates the variety of individuals who might be part of the treatment of ASD and the environments in which those individuals typically interact with the individual with ASD.

service providers experience when attempting to collaborate together, as well as some strategies for effective collaboration.

The reader will notice that there is a heavy emphasis on behavior analysts as treatment providers for individuals with ASD throughout this chapter. This is because the psychoeducational treatment for ASD that has the most empirical support is applied behavior analysis (ABA) (Eldevik et al., 2009; National Autism Center, 2009; Rogers & Vismara, 2008; US Department of Health and Human Services, 1999), and behavior analysts are often the most qualified to provide this form of treatment. ABA is the application of behavioral principles to help solve meaningful human problems. It typically involves intervention strategies making changes to the environment (including how others interact with a person with ASD) to improve the skill deficits and decrease behavioral excesses characteristic in individuals with autism. There are several characteristics of ABA, but some of the most crucial with respect to autism treatment are (a) its reliance on behavioral theory and research, (b) frequent and direct measurement of targeted skills to measure progress toward skill mastery, and (c) changing antecedents and consequences (the events that occur just before or after a targeted behavior, respectively) to produce changes in behaviors (both skill development and behavioral reduction). ABA is applied in a variety of ways, depending on the age and needs of the individual with autism. (A full description of ABA as treatment is beyond the scope of this chapter. The reader is referred to a selected list of resources provided in the appendix to this chapter for more information on behavioral treatment.) While behavior analysts may be most qualified to deliver ABA interventions, other treatment providers also play a very important role in the lives of individuals with ASD. It is important for all service providers, including behavior analysts, to collaborate well in order to produce the best outcomes for the individual with ASD. Thus, throughout the chapter, we provide boxes describing case examples to demonstrate effective collaboration in the treatment of symptoms related to ASD. Because of the central role ABA plays in treatment of ASD, our case examples often have the behavior analyst playing a central role in the collaboration process. "Behavior analyst" is a relatively new and rapidly growing profession (Burning Glass Technologies, 2015). In our experience, many service providers do not know what a behavior analyst is, what a behavior analyst does, or what role the behavior analyst may play in the treatment of autism. Thus, we provide slightly more detail on the role, scope of practice, and training of behavior analysts than other treatment providers, many of whom people are already familiar with. Our case examples attempt to illustrate ways in which behavior analysts and other service providers have collaborated to provide the most efficacious and evidence-based treatment for individuals with autism. Most often, these examples deal with issues surrounding problem behavior in individuals with autism, given that our expertise lies in this area and this is a common area of difficulty for individuals with autism. However, the reader is encouraged to consider how the strategies described in the examples could be applied across a variety of problems.

Service Providers: Roles, Scope of Practice, and Training

Board Certified Behavior Analyst

Individuals most qualified to oversee the implementation of ABA treatments are behavior analysts who have been specifically trained to work with individuals with ASD. There is more than one credentialing body that certifies behavior analysts, the most common being the Behavior Analyst Certification Board® (BACB®).

Like with many other professions, training of behavior analysts is multifaceted and generally requires a specific set of rigorous courses designed to teach specific skills laid out by the BACB; at least a master's degree in either behavior analysis, psychology, or special education; and supervised fieldwork–or "internship"–in clinical settings. After an individual has completed all of these requirements, he or she is qualified to take the certification exam. If the individual passes the exam, he or she can become a Board Certified Behavior Analyst (BCBA). There is also a certification one can receive at bachelor's level called the Board Certified Assistant Behavior Analyst [BCaBA] and a certification one can receive with a high school diploma called a Registered Behavior Technician [RBT]. It is common for ABA to be delivered using a "tiered service-delivery model," where an RBT provides the bulk of the direct service to the individual with autism while being supervised by a BCaBA or BCBA. The BCaBA and, more likely, the BCBA provides the clinical direction, case management, and supervision for the case. (For a more thorough description of this model, the reader is referred to the BACB's *Guidelines for Health Plan Coverage of Applied Behavior Analysis Treatment of Autism Spectrum Disorder*.) A BCBA's job is to utilize strategies documented to be effective in the peer-reviewed behavioral research literature and other well-established treatment protocols to treat autism, while continually relying on direct observation to assess and evaluate the client's progress. Another important role the behavior analyst plays is to "solicit and integrate information from the client and family members and coordinate care with other professionals" (BACB, *Guidelines for Health Plan Coverage of Applied Behavior Analysis Treatment of Autism Spectrum Disorder*, p. 6).

Physical Health Providers

Physicians. Physicians are medical practitioners who receive graduate training in medical school and postgraduate supervised clinical experience called "residency." They provide a number of services to individuals with ASD including pediatrics, psychiatry, neurology, and general medicine. Physicians typically interact with individuals with ASD and families in clinical settings like primary care visits and medical screenings. While physicians' primary responsibility is to provide medical services, a physician (and especially a pediatrician) is often the first professional to interact with family and potentially begin to identify signs of ASD. In addition to providing standard healthcare services to individuals with ASD, many physicians prescribe psychiatric medications in an attempt to address behaviors related to ASD or other reported concerns. However, physicians' disposition to prescribe psychiatric medications is not without controversy. Over eight million children (0–17 years) are currently prescribed psychiatric medications, despite considerable risks of side effects and limited research substantiating their use (see Corrigan [2015] for more on this topic). In some cases, physicians may refer families and individuals to other professionals for specialized assessment and treatment for ASD.

To learn more about physicians, please research the American Medical Association (AMA).

Box 24.1 Tara (BCBA, Physician, and Nurse Collaboration)

Tara was a 12-year-old girl who lived with her adopted mother at home. The behavior analyst presently treating Tara and her mother was concerned with Tara's increased head hitting. Tara had detached the retina on her right eye due to head hitting and was in danger of detaching her left retina. Tara was referred to a team of behavior analysts who specialized in the assessment and treatment of severe behavior problems. An assessment of problem behavior would require exposing Tara to various conditions that might occasion problem behavior, however. The behavior analysts were reluctant to do this out of concern for Tara's safety. The behavior analysts consulted with Tara's physician on the matter. They explained the assessment to him and expressed their concern for Tara's safety. The physician concurred that it was risky to conduct the assessment and discussed alternatives with the behavior analysts. As a result, the behavior analysts decided to conduct an alternative assessment that would significantly decrease the likelihood that Tara would engage in head hitting. Additionally, the team worked closely with a nurse at the local clinic where Tara received services to identify specific termination criteria to determine if it was necessary to stop the assessment sessions. In addition, the nurse was present for all assessment sessions to observe and make the determination if the assessment should end. Fortunately, there was no need to end the assessment, and the behavior analysts were able to use the assessment information to design an effective and individualized treatment plan that her home behavior analyst and mother successfully implemented. In this case, collaboration between the parent, behavior analysts, nurse, and physician led to a positive outcome for the individual with ASD.

Nutritionists. Nutritionists assess and provide recommendations for addressing an individual's nutritional needs. Their training is typically at the bachelor's level, and they have usually completed supervised clinical experience in the field. Many medical settings like primary care offices may offer services by nutritionists, but nutritionists may also have their own offices. Families seeking services by a nutritionist do not typically need a referral and can simply contact a nutritionist in their area. Because individuals with ASD may have food aversions or sensitivities, consultation with nutritionists may be necessary to address nutritional deficits. Nutritionists may also recommend diets that attempt to treat ASD; the gluten-free, casein-free (GFCF) diet being the most commonly recommended diet for children with ASD. While there is some support for the GFCF diet, most research on GFCF has found it ineffective. In addition to questionable effectiveness, diets can be financially costly and have negative health side effects (see Foxx & Mulick [2015] for more on this topic). To learn more about nutritionists, please research the National Association of Nutrition Professionals (NANP).

Nurses. Nurses are healthcare professionals who provide a wide range of medical services including patient care, patient education, and preventive health care. There are many types of nurses including Licensed Practical Nurses which often requires an associate's degree and Registered Nurses which requires a bachelor's degree and completion of a nursing program. Nurses often specialize in a specific area of care like pediatrics or holistic health. Families and individuals with ASD will most commonly interact with nurses in settings where nurses are assisting physicians in providing medical services. To learn more about nurses, research the American Nurses Association.

Box 24.2 Thomas (BCBA, Nurse, and Direct Care Staff Collaboration)

Thomas was a 39-year-old man who lived in a group home with other individuals with developmental and physical disabilities. He had very limited vocal communication skills, relying on a few verbal utterances like saying "a-moo" to gain access to movies or television and "a-boo" to gain access to books/magazines. He displayed stereotyped and repetitive motor movements as well as restricted interests. Additionally, Thomas had physical disabilities that required him to use a wheelchair for mobility and a colostomy bag to manage digestive issues. Thomas engaged high levels of screaming and repeatedly put his hands down his pants. Thus, he was referred to a team of behavior analysts for assessment and treatment. The team conducted an assessment to determine why he was engaging in these problem behaviors. The assessment results suggested Thomas was screaming because his appropriate attempts to make requests tended to be ignored by in-home staff. For this, the behavior analysts worked with the group home staff to ensure they attended to and honored his requests for movies and books/magazines. Thomas appeared to be putting his hands in his pants in an attempt to remove his colostomy bag. Further assessment indicated that often, the colostomy bag had not been appropriately cared for by staff and needed attention. Upon making this observation, the behavior analysts questioned the direct care staff about the colostomy bag care routine. It became apparent that early-shift direct care staff assumed colostomy bag care was the responsibility of the later-shift direct care staff, who in turn assumed it was the responsibility of early-shift direct care staff. The behavior analyst, thus, sought to provide the direct care staff with clear expectations for colostomy bag care. However, the behavior analyst was not skilled in this area, so he consulted with the group home's nursing staff. The nursing staff reviewed the colostomy care instructions currently in place and realized they were not appropriate for the type of bag Thomas had. The nurse helped write appropriate, detailed instructions for the staff and told the behavior analyst it would be nice to develop a method of tracking whether the staff actually followed the steps. Given that creating data sheets to track human behavior is an area of expertise for behavior analysts, he happily agreed to create the data sheet. The nurse reviewed the data sheet when it was complete, noting it was a very helpful way to ensure staff followed the steps. The behavior analyst and nurse then jointly trained direct care staff on the new instructions and data sheet. As a result of this intervention, the direct care staff appropriately cared for Thomas' colostomy bag, and Thomas stopped putting his hands in his pants.

Rehabilitation Therapists

Occupational therapists. The American Occupational Therapy Association defines an occupational therapist as someone who "helps people across the life-span participate in the things they want and need to do through the therapeutic use of everyday activities" (About Occupational Therapy, 2017). Occupational therapists may receive training and specialize in different areas, but all occupational therapists are typically required to obtain a master's degree from an accredited program and pass a national certification exam. If the individual with ASD is school age and depending on the needs of the individual with ASD, occupational therapy may be a related service provided at school under the Individuals with Disabilities Education Act (IDEA) (1997). Common occupational therapy interventions include helping children with disabilities to participate fully in school and social situations, helping people recover from injury to regain skills, and providing supports for older adults experiencing physical and cognitive changes. In schools, occupational therapists most generally provide services in the area of fine motor functioning and more recently have become more involved in sensory motor processing. To address sensory motor processing disorders, occupational therapists often recommend Sensory Integrative Therapy (SIT). While SIT is commonly recommended for children with ASD, it is important to note that a preponderance of research indicates that SIT is ineffective and should be studied more before it is widely adopted as a treatment (see Foxx & Mulick [2015] for more on this topic). Despite issues with SIT, occupational therapists are valuable

---

Box 24.3 BCBA and Occupational Therapist Collaboration

Charity was an occupational therapist at a local school that was partnering with BCBAs to implement ABA in their special education classroom. The teachers, support staff (occupational therapist, speech/language pathologist, school psychologist), and BCBAs had monthly meetings to discuss the children's progress and make plans for future instruction. One day in the meeting, Charity stated she wanted to implement sensory integration therapy with some of the children with ASD in the classroom. The BCBAs balked a bit, stating that this was not evidence-based practice, and they had a concern about doing so. Charity acknowledged that the research was limited; however, she stated some new research was coming out on the issue. The school psychologist suggested that the team form a reading group and all parties could identify some research articles on the topic that the group could read and discuss. The team members agreed to this, each identified a few articles for the team to read, and scheduled regular meetings over the next couple of months to discuss the research findings, strengths, and limitations. All parties benefited from reading literature from related fields, and the team decided the research was still not convincing enough to implement sensory integration therapy at this time. Additionally, all team members had newfound respect for one another for being willing to come to the table and discuss a controversial topic in a professional manner.

in the treatment for individuals with ASD, so alternatives to SIT should be discussed with them and the treatment team. To learn more about occupational therapists, please research the American Occupational Therapy Association (AOTA).

Physical therapists. Physical therapists remediate gross motor impairments and promote mobility, function, and quality of life through examination, diagnosis, prognosis, and physical intervention. Educational criteria for physical therapy providers vary from state to state and from country to country, and among various levels of professional responsibility. Curricula in the United States are accredited by the Commission on Accreditation in Physical Therapy Education (CAPTE). Again, if the individual with ASD is school age, physical therapy may be a related service in the treatment of students with disabilities under IDEA at school. To learn more about physical therapists, please research the CAPTE or the American Board of Physical Therapy Specialties (ABPTS).

   Speech/language pathologists. Speech-language pathologists (speech therapists), considered related health care professionals along with occupational and physical therapists, specialize in the evaluation, diagnosis, and treatment of communication disorders. A common misconception is that speech-language pathology is restricted to adjusting a speaker's speech sound articulation. Speech therapy also concerns language and voice issues involved in communication. Speech therapists, certified by the state in which they are employed, must earn a Certificate of Clinical Competence in Speech-Language Pathology (CCC-SLP) from the American Speech-Language-Hearing Association (ASHA). Speech therapists working in the schools are critical team members in the diagnosis and treatment of ASD, given that a major deficit area for individuals with ASD is communication. To learn more about speech-language pathologists, please research the American Speech-Language-Hearing Association (ASHA).

Educators

Teachers. Broadly speaking, teachers are educational professionals, generally with graduate training, who are responsible for educating children and young adults. Teachers are licensed or certified in accordance with the state in which they are employed. Contrary to popular belief, teaching is a highly complex activity and there are many areas of specialization. Historically, general education teachers have provided instruction in basic subjects such as reading, writing, arithmetic, science, and social studies, to larger groups of "general education" students. Beginning around 1975, special education teachers began work with students eligible under federal and state law (IDEA) for specialized instructional intervention, typically described in the child's Individualized Education Plan (IEP). Differences in responsibilities for regular and special education teachers have blurred over the years such that in today's educational system all teachers work with a very diverse population of students having a variety of mental and physical health needs, as well as the full continuum of academic skill levels, including students with ASD. Effective teachers require an extensive set of skills, such as in-depth knowledge of learning, excellence in communication and engagement, classroom management, and individualized behavior programming. To learn more about teachers, please research the National Education Association (NEA).

Box 24.4 Jake (BCBA and Teacher Collaboration)

Jake was an eight-year-old boy diagnosed with ASD. He was referred to a team of behavior analysts specializing in severe problem behavior by his clinical psychologist because he was getting removed from his special education classroom and placed in a special school for children with disabilities due to his severe property destruction, physical aggression, and verbal outbursts. Additionally, Jake was hypersensitive to stimuli in the environment, had highly restricted interests, and was highly inflexible to change. Given that Jake was in danger of being removed from his school, the behavior analysts observed Jake in his classroom and spoke with school staff, which consisted of a behavior specialist, speech therapist, an occupational therapist, and a special education teacher. Given the severity of Jake's problem behaviors, it was recommended that Jake first receive treatment full-time in a treatment center to get the behaviors under better control in an environment where the intensity of treatment necessary could be implemented. After six months of intensive treatment at the BCBA's center, Jake's problem behaviors significantly decreased. The teacher came to the center to observe the treatment being implemented and worked with the behavior analyst to modify the treatment plan to fit the school environment. The behavior analyst then went to the school with Jake to train the teachers and ensure the treatment was effective at school. Following this close work between the special education teacher and behavior analyst, Jake had a smooth transition back to school and was able to continue participating in his school placement successfully.

School psychologists. School psychologists are professional psychologists based in schools who have obtained graduate degrees in psychology focused on educational applications. School psychologists are licensed or certified in accordance with the state in which they are employed. These professionals are often the first contact for families with children having difficulties in school. School psychologists are uniquely qualified members of school teams that support students' abilities to learn and teachers' abilities to teach. They apply expertise in mental health, learning, and behavior, to help children and youth succeed academically, socially, behaviorally, and emotionally. School psychologists lead the team of professionals responsible for assessment of students to determine eligibility under federal laws for special education (IDEA) including the educational diagnosis of ASD. To learn more about school psychologists, please research the National Association of School Psychologists (NASP).

Mental Health Care Provider

Clinical psychologists. Clinical psychologists are mental health practitioners who receive specialized graduate training, typically obtaining a PhD or PsyD from APA accredited programs. Clinical psychologists provide a number of services to families and individuals with ASD including therapy, psychoeducation, and parent training. Most importantly, clinical psychologists can administer assessments to screen for ASD and help families find appropriate services. Like many professionals described in this section, clinical psychologists specialize in specific areas, so not every clinical psychologist can provide assessment services for ASD. To learn more about clinical psychologists, research the American Psychological Association.

Box 24.5 Alicia (BCBA, Psychologist, and Teacher Collaboration)

Alicia was a six-year-old girl who attended Mrs. Washington's general education kindergarten class. Alicia engaged in high levels of noncompliance, physical aggression, and property destruction in her classroom and throughout the school. She also displayed lack of social-emotional reciprocity with teachers and peers. Because Alicia's behaviors were so disruptive and put herself and others at risk of harm, Alicia was continually removed from class, sent home, and not allowed to engage in certain activities like field trips. Alicia's mother grew concerned with the amount of class instruction that Alicia was missing and reached out to a team of behavior analysts to conduct an assessment and come up with strategies to help Alicia. One thing the behavior analysts learned during the assessment was that Alicia was one of the highest performers in her class for every academic subject. At the same time, the behavior analysts noted that Alicia was more likely to engage in problem behaviors when she was given non-challenging work. For instance, Mrs. Washington reported that Alicia was more likely to engage in disruptive behaviors if asked to trace numbers than if she were asked to independently work on a basic math worksheet. The behavior analysts hypothesized that Alicia may have been bored, and this may have contributed to her problem behaviors. They determined that it would be helpful to understand her academic skills better. Thus, they referred Alicia to a psychologist for cognitive ability and achievement testing. Based on the results of the assessment, the psychologist stated that Alicia was advanced for her age, but not enough to make her current kindergarten placement inappropriate. The psychologist was able to identify skill areas where Alicia was especially advanced. The behavior analyst worked together with Mrs. Washington to modify Alicia's instruction so she could independently work on more advanced material for skills she was ahead of her peers on, while still engaging in group lessons and activities for skills she was less advanced with. This decreased Alicia's problem behaviors, allowing her to successfully stay in her general education classroom, engage in more academic activities, and participate in field trips.

Counselors. Counselors are mental health care practitioners who are trained to work with individuals, families, and groups. There are a variety of specialties within the field of counseling, including but not limited to school counselors, marriage and family counselors, and vocational rehabilitation counselors. Counselors are required to have at least a master's degree from a counseling program and will have specialized training in their area of expertise. Individuals with ASD or families may seek support from a counselor for a number of reasons, such as peer relationship issues at school (school counselor), marital issues among parents (marriage and family counselor), or school-to-work preparation (vocational rehabilitation counselor). The type of counseling and the therapeutic model can vary based on the needs of the family members seeking such support. Many families benefit from participating in support groups where they can share with others who can relate to their experiences. To learn more about counselors, please research the American Psychological Association.

Social Workers

Social work services can play an important role in the success and progress of the treatment of individuals with ASD. Collaboration and communication with team members is an efficient way to break down social, emotional, and environmental barriers to treatment. Social workers can address these issues by identifying the emotional state of families when the child has received a recent diagnosis of ASD and are possibly entering intense ABA treatment. Many families experience feelings of denial and a sense of loss when their child is diagnosed with ASD, meaning the expectations of the "bright" future they had hoped for are gone. Working with families by providing psychoeducation, support, advocacy, and empowerment is the therapeutic process to help families work through identifying effective treatment options for their child.

The National Association Social Workers (NASW) states that the role of social workers is to focus on improving individual well-being in the context of family and other social structures, such as work and community. There are three distinct fields in which social workers practice: Mental Health/Substance Abuse, Child/Family/School Social Work, and Medical/Public Health. A family may encounter a social worker in any one of these areas across the lifespan. Social workers provide a large scope of services such as counseling–both individual and group, behavioral interventions, case management services, and referral assistance. Licensure can vary by level of education, with some social workers having a bachelor's degree and others having master's or doctoral degrees. Licensure requirements vary by state. To learn more about social workers, research the NASW.

Family

Family members play an important role in the lives of individuals with ASD. They often are the individual's first teachers and can be a "constant" among a variety of often-changing service professionals interacting with the individual with autism. As such, family members serve multiple roles, such as service coordinator, advocate, "taxi driver," emotional and physical support provider, direct care staff (and person responsible for implementing ABA therapy), financial provider, etc. Family members most directly impact the individual with ASD in the home and community settings. While they play an integral role in school settings, as required in individualized education or accommodation planning, parents and other family members rarely enter school settings to provide formal services for the individual with ASD.

Direct Care Staff

Direct care staff can consist of natural or paid supports. Natural supports are often family members, friends, and other identified community supports. Paid supports can consist of providers such as community living supports (CLS), respite providers, and behavioral technicians. Paid supports are often funded through community mental health organizations to assist families in implementing treatment plans in the home setting. If direct care staff are available to a family, they can provide the additional support to the family to help implement treatment strategies. This may help the family achieve their treatment goals more readily. In addition, some individuals may also have behavior plans that

---

Box 24.6 Dustin (BCBA and Parent Collaboration)

Dustin was an eight-year-old boy who engaged in severe aggression, property destruction, and self-injurious behavior at home and in the community. He displayed functional skills in verbal and nonverbal communication, but required ongoing support in this area. Dustin's mother could not often leave the house to run errands because he would tantrum so severely, and taking him on shopping trips with her was difficult because he tantrumed in the store. A social worker who served the family referred Dustin to behavior analysts for an assessment and treatment recommendations. The results of the assessment indicated that Dustin's problem behaviors occurred to get his mother's attention. Interviews and direct observations revealed that Dustin was very competitive. The behavior analyst taught Dustin and his mother how to play the Good Behavior Game (i.e., a strategy used to gamify a situation where the client can compete with an adult and "win the game" by behaving appropriately). The behavior analyst first came to the home to implement the treatment package with Dustin's mother. The behavior analyst stayed at the house while the mother left to run errands for increasingly longer periods of time (starting with ten seconds and progressing to 30 minutes), implementing the Good Behavior Game treatment. When that was successful, the behavior analyst accompanied the mother to the grocery store and helped the mother implement the Good Behavior Game in the store. Eventually, the mother was able to use the game to leave Dustin with a babysitter, as well as taking Dustin on shopping trips lasting up to 45 minutes without problem behavior.

are implemented to address specific behavioral problems in the home and community settings. Direct care staff can be very beneficial to the family in implementing these plans, because sometimes treatment and/or behavior plans may require more "hands" than the family has available. Often, there are few, if any, training requirements for an individual to serve as direct care staff. Typically, individuals are required to have a high school diploma, but rarely is further training or education required.

Hurdles to and Strategies for Effective Collaboration

Many times, the different service providers who interact with an individual with ASD find they are all targeting similar skills but may be using different approaches to treatment. Research shows that coordinated care and treatment of the same skills across multiple areas and with multiple professionals increases the probability of progress and success (Armstrong, DeLoatche, Preece, & Agazzi, 2015). Therefore, although professionals may approach treatment differently for various skills, it is important for them to communicate with each other to ensure long-term success and maintenance. While care providers affirm that coordination of care is best practice, professionals often do not coordinate with the other team members that interact with their client (Armstrong et al., 2015). Coordination and collaboration can be difficult to attain.

There are many reasons for the discrepancy between best practice and what care providers actually do when it comes to successful collaboration. First, most care providers make assumptions about intervention methods by other professionals (Donaldson & Stahmer, 2014). That is, care providers may have misunderstandings about each other's methods and overall philosophy (Donaldson & Stahmer, 2014). These misunderstandings may impact the likelihood of effective communication across disciplines. As a result, care providers may miss out on opportunities to collaborate for maximum treatment effects. Worse, clients may suffer when two or more care providers target a skill but approach treatment in a completely different way.

Another reason professionals may not always collaborate with each other is that they may not even know other professionals are involved with the client. Further, consent forms are needed for communication among an individual's team of professionals. If these forms are not completed, professionals may not be able to share information with one another. Here, parents play a key role in making sure professionals are aware of all the other treatment providers on the team and facilitating communication by ensuring consent to share information is provided proactively. One strategy that can be helpful is for parents to provide release of information before treatment starts so that care providers can easily share information.

The most common reason why care providers do not collaborate with other team members is that it is time consuming (Moh & Magiati, 2012). Care providers often must fill their day with billable hours, which typically involves direct work with clients. Very little time is left for indirect activities, such as meetings and phone calls with other care providers. Contacting other professionals that interact with a client and reviewing other professionals' treatment strategies typically falls under "indirect activities" that are not billable. One way to overcome this hurdle is to incorporate other care providers into the day-to-day activities of treatment. Additionally, care providers can rotate coordination of services week to week so that one party is responsible for updating the others on progress of treatment. Often, these activities again fall on parents, who are the constant in the individual's life across settings and care providers.

Various other issues such as who has the authority to treat specific aspects of the disability or to work in specific contexts can also lead to ineffective collaboration within teams. Sometimes cross-training, where care providers have the opportunity to train each other on the various strategies they use in their treatment (Donaldson & Stahmer, 2014), can be helpful in this area.

Summary

Individuals with ASD and their families interact with many different professionals throughout the lifespan for various different aspects of their treatment. In this chapter, we have outlined who these professionals are and the role they play in treatment. While this list is not exhaustive by any means, it does highlight the importance of a multidisciplinary approach to treatment for individuals with ASD. Moreover, a multidisciplinary team is needed to ensure the most successful treatment outcomes (Devlin & Harber, 2004). While it can be challenging for multiple professionals across multiple contexts to effectively collaborate, each professional plays an important role in supporting effective treatment and increasing the quality of life for individuals with ASD and their families. Family members often serve as key players in coordinating services for individuals with ASD. However, the behavior analyst, who also works across multiple environments with the individual with ASD, can serve a case coordination role as well. Furthermore, they have an ethical responsibility to do so, according to their ethical code and standards. The case examples presented here are an attempt to demonstrate how behavior analysts can help to facilitate effective collaboration among various disciplines to achieve positive outcomes for individuals with ASD.

References

About Occupational Therapy. (2017, December 20). Retrieved from www.aota.org/About-Occupational-Therapy.aspx.
American Psychiatric Association. (2013). *Diagnostic and statistical manual of mental disorders: DSM-5* (5th ed.). Arlington, VA: American Psychiatric Association.
Armstrong, K., DeLoatche, K. J., Preece, K. K., & Agazzi, H. (2015). Combining parent–child interaction therapy and visual supports for the treatment of challenging behavior in a child with autism and intellectual disabilities and comorbid epilepsy. *Clinical Case Studies, 14*(1), 3–14.

Burning Glass Technologies. (2015). US Behavior Analyst Workforce: Understanding the national demand for behavior analysts. Retrieved from: www.bacb.com/wp-content/uploads/2017/09/151009-burning-glass-report.pdf

Corrigan, M. W. (2015, March). Mind-bottling malarkey, medicine, or malpractice? *Psychology Today*. Retrieved from www.psychologytoday.com/blog/kids-being-kids/201503/mind-bottling-malarkey-medicine-or-malpractice.

Devlin, S. D., & Harber, M. M. (2004). Collaboration among parents and professionals with discrete trial training in the treatment for autism. *Education and Training in Developmental Disabilities*, 291–300.

Donaldson, A. L., & Stahmer, A. C. (2014). Team Collaboration: The use of behavior principles for serving students with ASD. *Language Speech and Hearing Services in Schools*, 45(4), 261. https://doi.org/10.1044/2014_LSHSS-14-0038.

Eldevik, S., Hastings, R. P., Hughes, J. C., Jahr, E., Eikeseth, S., & Cross, S. (2009). Meta-analysis of early intensive behavioral intervention for children with autism. *Journal of Clinical Child & Adolescent Psychology*, 38(3), 439–450. https://doi.org/10.1080/15374410902851739.

Foxx, R. M., & Mulick, J. A. (Eds.). (2015). *Controversial therapies for autism and intellectual disabilities: Fad, fashion, and science in professional practice*. Retrieved from https://ebookcentral-proquest-com.libproxy.library.wmich.edu.

Individuals with Disabilities Education Act of 1997, 105–117, 20 USC para. 1400 *et seq*. Retrieved from www.congress.gov/105/plaws/publ17/PLAW-105publ17.pdf.

Moh, T. A., & Magiati, I. (2012). Factors associated with parental stress and satisfaction during the process of diagnosis of children with autism spectrum disorders. *Research in Autism Spectrum Disorders*, 6(1), 293–303. https://doi.org/10.1016/j.rasd.2011.05.011.

National Autism Center. (2009). *The National Standards Project Phase 1: Addressing the need for evidence-based practice guidelines for autism spectrum disorders*. Randolph, MA; Author.

Rogers, S. J., & Vismara, L. A. (2008). Evidence-based comprehensive treatments for early autism. *Journal of Clinical Child & Adolescent Psychology*, 37(1), 8–38. https://doi.org/10.1080/15374410701817808.

US Department of Health and Human Services (1999). *Mental health: A report of the surgeon general*. Rockville, MD; Author.

25 Helping the Family Communicate with Technology

Stephanie Shire and Alyssa Tan

In families where a child struggles to effectively communicate with others, daily activities can become difficult and frustrating not only for the child, but also for those who are trying to support the child. Daily tasks and interactions are more complicated when the child is unable to tell others about his needs, or ideas. For example, a six-year-old boy named Jake has minimal clear spoken communication. Jake can approximate a few words, such as "more" and "all done," but has trouble communicating his specific needs and thoughts to his parents. When Jake's message is not understood by his parents, sometimes Jake cries and screams. Likewise, he rarely communicates with his younger brother, Mark, which has been discouraging to the family. Given Jake's limited ability to communicate, this poses significant challenges for Jake's family who are determined to help Jake engage in their family activities and learn to play with his brother. This chapter will address how Augmentative and Alternative Communication (AAC) methods can provide avenues for children to communicate in addition to spoken words. AAC can be used in a variety of contexts to help an individual engage with the people around them.

The terms "speech" and "language" are sometimes used interchangeably when discussing communicative abilities. However, speech is the mode of output for communication, while language is a cognitive skill that allows the individual to communicate via a code of symbols (Romski & Sevcik, 2005). For some children with ASD who have complex communication needs, the child may not use speech, but he or she may communicate in other ways, such as through emotions, body language, sign language, text messaging, emails, and even emoticons.

This chapter will focus on an introduction to AAC for children with ASD. AAC provides additional *modes* or methods for children to communicate in addition to or sometimes in place of spoken words. A person who uses American Sign Language is using AAC. A person who uses electronic technology where touch-activated buttons speak aloud the word or phrase when selected is using AAC. Similarly, a person who hands you a paper picture icon or points to a symbol from an array on a laminated page of paper is also using AAC. AAC can come in many forms that are individualized to meet the age and stage of the person using it to communicate. Clinicians who work with families with

ASD-related communication struggles should become familiar with the many modes of AAC that people can use to communicate. These methods may include sophisticated language systems or simple use of a single symbol to communicate a need. This chapter will address common myths regarding the use of AAC, a brief overview of recent research examining AAC with children with ASD and other developmental disabilities, as well as some basic strategies and considerations for clinicians who support families with children with ASD who communicate using AAC. We will illustrate these ideas through a case study of "Jake."

Box 25.1 What is AAC?

"Any system of communication that supplements (augments) or replaces (alternative) conventional speech in providing support for an individual that has a complex communication need" (Romski & Sevcik, 1997) and "that enables individuals to efficiently and effectively engage in a variety of interactions and participate in activities of their choice."

(Beukelman & Mirenda, 2005, p. 8)

Communication and Autism

Challenges in the development of spoken and nonverbal communication skills are central to receiving a diagnosis of ASD (see Chapter 2). In young children, limited nonverbal communication, delays in the development of spoken language, limited eye contact, and limited initiations of sustained social engagement/interaction are all indicators noted in autism risk and diagnostic assessments (Luyster et al., 2009; Wetherby, Watt, Morgan, & Shumway, 2007). As children grow and receive educational services, the range of communicative abilities may begin to flourish for some, and remain more delayed for others. For example, some children with ASD develop functional and even age-appropriate speech, although challenges may emerge when that language is used in dynamic social settings such as with interacting with peers. In contrast, for about 30–50 percent of children with ASD, the delays in the development of spoken communication are so great that by school age, they may have fewer than 20 spontaneous functional words to either request or to share with others and may be described as *minimally verbal* (Tager-Flusberg & Kasari, 2013). Across the spectrum of children with ASD, there are endless varieties of abilities and levels of comfort with spoken language. For some children, their use of spoken language differs across contexts and communication partners. For children who are *minimally verbal* in one context or another, one consideration in communication intervention is to provide access to AAC, which includes modes other than speaking to communicate. The research examining the use of AAC suggests that children with complex communication needs (including those with ASD, and other developmental disorders) can make gains with AAC, as well as show acceleration of gains in spoken language, when they have access to both spoken words and AAC within communication intervention sessions (Blischak, 2003; Kasari et al., 2014; Romski et al., 2010).

Improved communication can help enhance children's ability to engage in social interactions, as well as manage behavior more effectively (see reviews of AAC intervention literature: Iacono, Trembath, & Erickson, 2016; Schlosser & Wendt, 2008). AAC technology can be the bridge that allows the individual to get their needs met (e.g., making requests that others can understand), share thoughts and ideas (comment to share with others), and have positive social exchanges (e.g., greeting others and asking social questions such as, "What's your name?"). Improvements have also been noted in peer interactions when children have access to AAC (see review by Chung, Carter, & Sisco, 2013). Further, a body of research demonstrates that the development of functional communication skills (spoken and augmented) can lead to decreases in challenging behaviors (Mirenda, 1997). Challenging behaviors can be a form of communication where the child may cry, throw objects, scream, etc. in order to send a message that they may or may not have the words to deliver.

Research evidence is growing for the potential positive effects of AAC on children's communication, regulation, and social behavior. However, myths regarding the use of AAC are still relatively common including: (1) children will not learn to use spoken language if they can use AAC, and (2) AAC is only for older kids who have average cognitive skills.

Myth 1: Children Will NOT Speak if They Use AAC

A common concern for both clinicians and families is whether providing access to AAC will further delay or even stop the development of spoken communication. It is important to help those in the community understand that access to AAC will **NOT** hinder the child's spoken language (Millar, Light, & Schlosser, 2006). In fact, research is demonstrating that the opposite is true. Rather, access to AAC tends to accelerate children's spoken language (Kasari et al., 2014). Further, access to AAC may provide a method for communication while the child's spoken language grows in efficiency and clarity. The mechanism around why speech generating devices in particular may lead to these gains is still under study, but access to the additional consistent input from the device (the word is said the same way, with the same tone each time) plus spoken models together have been hypothesized to aid in learning. Another reason may be related to motivation, where the AAC provides additional novelty and motivation to kick start communication.

Myth 2: The Child is Too Young or is Too Far Behind to Use AAC

Another common misconception relates to the AAC user's age or cognitive ability. Some believe that children can be too young to use AAC or that the child has not acquired the foundational skills necessary to use and understand a device. Successful demonstrations of the use of AAC with infants and toddlers (see Drager, Light, & McNaughton, 2010) have debunked the myth that only older children can benefit from AAC. Early interactions can provide the groundwork for not only the development of language but also other key skills including play, cognitive, and social skills (Beukelman & Mirenda, 2013). As such, early access to AAC may provide a mechanism for children to communicate and engage with others more successfully in these critical interactions.

Children who are chronologically older, but developmentally young, can benefit from AAC in many ways. For example, AAC has been found to have positive impacts on speech production for young children who are not imitating speech (Cress & Marvin, 2003). Further, Snell and colleagues (2010) found gains in communication with AAC for children with significant cognitive delays, and Kasari et al. (2014) found gains in spontaneous communication in school-age children with ASD with developmental levels as low as 18 months (Kasari et al., 2014). Cognition is not a prerequisite to communication. Rather, improved language skills tend to promote cognitive growth (Goossens, 1989). There are many AAC systems that can be used, depending on the child's needs. Here are a few of the many modes of AAC.

Types of AAC

There is a wide array of both "low tech" and "high tech" types of AAC. Low tech modes might be as simple as paper and pencil, while "high tech" includes electronic technology like keyboards, tablets, laptops, or other specialized systems. It is important for clinicians to familiarize themselves with some of these options so that they can notice if a child is using another mode to communicate and begin to understand how they can engage with that child using their mode of AAC as well as spoken communication.

Box 25.2 Did You Know?

Using a device to communicate through typing (e.g., texting, typing out notes on a tablet, or using a specific AAC application to type out a message) is also considered AAC use. This is more common among older children or adolescents. If they are using a tablet, you can ask if they use it to communicate and find a way to incorporate it into your sessions.

Common low-tech systems include manual sign (e.g., American Sign Language), and the picture exchange communication system (PECS; Bondy & Frost, 1994) which uses paper symbols. Not every paper communication symbol is a "PEC." PECS refers to a programmatic system used to teach specified levels of communication through a hierarchy. Proper implementation of PECS is typically guided by a Speech-Language Pathologist (SLP) who has engaged in

222 Stephanie Shire and Alyssa Tan

certified PECS training. Fundamental to PECS is the exchange where the child hands a symbol to their interaction partner typically to make a request. Further communication skills (e.g., finding symbols in an array or book, longer utterances, commenting, etc.) are built upon this initial skill of exchange. PECS has been examined in two randomized trials. In one trial, school-age children with ASD who were randomized to PECS training versus delayed or no PECS training showed gains in the use of PECS to communicate, but their spoken language skills remained stable (Howlin, Gordon, Pasco, Wade, & Charman, 2007). In the second trial, preschoolers with ASD who were randomized to PECS showed more requests than those who received Prelinguistic Milieu Teaching (Yoder & Stone, 2006).

High-tech devices include speech generating devices (SGDs), which are also referred to as Voice Output Communication Aids (VOCAs). These can be as simple as a button that is programmed with one word or message (e.g., Big Mac), through interactive touch screen displays that require navigation through many folders, pages, and symbols. High-tech SGDs include devices dedicated solely for communication (e.g., Dynavox, GoTalk) as well as common devices (e.g., tablets or smart phones) that can be programmed with communication applications. It is important to consider the physical properties of the device such as screen size and weight, as well as customization options. Advances in technology have lessened some of the barriers to access AAC but have also led to a large market of platforms with varied research support. In a systematic review of tablets and portable media players, Lorah and colleagues (2015) found gains across 17 single case studies, while two randomized trials demonstrated effects on both the rate and amount of spoken and augmented communication (Romski et al., 2010; Kasari et al., 2014). SGD applications will vary in the degree to which you can customize the symbols and how those symbols are presented for use. It is important to gain a working understanding of what symbols the child is currently using, and the capabilities of the device. You may think about words that the child will need to be able to communicate in your activities together. Do you need to create new symbols? If so, how many, what will they look like, and how will you help the child to learn to use them? We will take a brief look at each of these important considerations and how you can begin to match these with the child's needs.

Key Considerations for Selecting AAC Type

Our goal is to help the child spontaneously, efficiently, and effectively communicate in sessions with the help of AAC. Some children are already avid, efficient, and fluent AAC users, while others are just beginning. First, let us look at two big picture considerations when it comes to interactions that include AAC: (1) communication efficiency, and (2) system transparency for communication partners.

One key consideration is *efficiency*, or the time and effort it takes for the person using AAC to construct and deliver their message (Mirenda, 2003).

When it takes a long time to construct a response or an initiation, the moment in the conversation may have passed or the interaction partner may have moved on to something else. This may be especially true for young children in dynamic peer interactions. Therefore, it is important to think about how best to organize the symbols the child will use to allow for the most efficient method to deliver their message. The faster the child can navigate the system and build the message, the better. It is also important to think about who the child's interaction partners will be. Interaction partners can be taught what type of communication to expect and to wait for it.

A second key consideration is the *transparency* of the symbols. How easy is it for all interaction partners to both understand the meaning of the symbol and use it to communicate with the child? Symbols with higher transparency are often concrete and the likeness to the item/action/event it represents is clear (e.g., photo, drawing). Research examining the development of effective communication partners reinforces that partners must be able to both send and receive messages successfully in order to be able to effectively communicate with the person using AAC (Kent-Walsh & McNaughton, 2005). Everyone must understand what the symbols mean for communication to occur. Sharing the intended meaning of new symbols added to the child's interaction partners will make the system accessible for partners across contexts.

In addition to these big picture considerations, we also look at the individual needs of the child, and their developmental level. For example, some children with ASD have visual or motor challenges that influence their ability to access a symbol system. Children's needs will vary regarding the types of symbols that are used (e.g., digital photos, cartoon/drawings, letters, words, phrases/sentences), their number, and how they are organized (e.g., single symbols, pages, folders, or books). The manner in which the symbols are presented and set up should be individualized to meet the child's specific needs, so each system may look a little different.

The following questions may help to guide AAC selection and development:
What symbols/words can the child use appropriately and consistently? The observer should pay attention to the type of language that the child already uses – what is the *function* of the communication – is it to make a request or get a need met (e.g., to go to the car, to get a snack, to get a favorite item)? Or perhaps it is to share ideas, comment, or even converse socially (e.g., share an exciting event or a novel toy). Language can be used for many purposes, including gaining or clarifying information, to request, to protest, and to comment. This is important to remember since the person using AAC is restricted to the vocabulary present in the system. It is good to use words or phrases that will be used most frequently during natural communication. These can be a combination of verbs, adjectives, nouns, pronouns, adverbs, and/or prepositions. Focus on vocabulary that is meaningful and important to the specific individual. This means creating a match between the child's cognitive level and vocabulary and it could also mean incorporating culturally or contextually relevant words.

How long and complex is the child's communication? Early communicators may only be using one symbol at a time (one-word utterance) and only a small range of symbols, while others may be generating sentences and long conversations. Notice the length and level of the child's spontaneous utterances – this means the words the child can generate without prompting. Try to match the child's length and level of communication. For example, if the child is using two words at a time, notice how the child is connecting the two words and sending their message. For example, activating one icon with both words, connecting two icons (e.g., pushing two buttons, two signs, two icons on a sentence strip), or typing words.

What types of symbols are being used? Not all symbols are created equal! Some are easier to understand (more transparent) and some more abstract. A transparent symbol is very close to the thing it represents, and thus, often easier to understand (this relationship may also be referred to as "iconicity"). For example, a photo of a red gala apple is a direct transparent match to the exact red gala apple it represents. We can also learn to understand that an artistic representation such as a red glass ball with a green top due to its color and general shape also represents an apple. However, the latter requires greater abstraction and likely a more thorough understanding of what an apple is to make that connection. As symbols become further away from the thing they represent, they become increasingly more challenging to understand. For many young or early communicators, photos of the object, action, event, or person will be the easiest to understand and the best place to start. Other symbol systems that require specialized knowledge of what the symbol represents (e.g., manual sign, Blissymbols) mean that more training and supports are required to help partners (potentially including young siblings or peers) learn to communicate using these means too.

Monitoring communication: Are the child's needs changing? We all learn and grow, and hopefully children's communication skills also advance over time. Continue to evaluate the needs of the child and adjust accordingly. For example, new vocabulary may need to be introduced to expand the child's conversational repertoire. Consultation with the child's SLP may support additional changes.

Organizing the symbols: How many and where do they go? A smaller number of symbols will be easier for a new communicator to get started. Although fewer symbols will be easier to navigate, this also restricts the child's available vocabulary. One key consideration is whether the child is able to scan a few symbols and pick the one that represents the word they want to say (this is called *discrimination*). It is essential that the child understands what the symbols stand for in order for them to communicate effectively. Therefore, when the child is not discriminating, (e.g., seems to press symbols randomly or not at all, seems to be working on trial and error) the family can seek additional support from their SLP who can work with the child to develop these skills.

For children who are navigating their way through a large number of symbols, the system should be arranged consistently in order to maximize efficiency in the search for symbols and construction of the message. One way is to group symbols for one activity together (e.g., all words for a trip to the zoo). Another way is to categorize the symbols by word type (e.g., nouns, verbs, prepositions, etc.). The goal is to find an organizational method that is meaningful to the child and within their ability to independently navigate.

Strategies to Interact and Communicate Using the AAC: Jake and Mark

At first, AAC may feel awkward, but it will become more natural as individuals practice pairing spoken words with AAC. This means, when an individual says "hello!" to greet the child, he or she will also say hello with the child's AAC (e.g., press the button to speak hello, exchange the icon, or demonstrate the sign). Let us walk through an example of an interaction with a child named Jake who has ASD. First, we must understand the context in which Jake will be asked to communicate. In this example, a clinician is working with Jake and his sibling, Mark. The goal is to foster more positive social interactions during play activities and help Jake communicate his needs and ideas. Jake is brand new to using AAC. His parents are working with a SLP to begin using an application on a tablet (high tech). Jake and Mark both like to play with Lego blocks, but they often fight when they play, so the clinician sets up the device for this activity. Jake can say a few words verbally, so for this activity they will begin with a three by three screen (a total of nine symbols) that includes symbols for words he knows and a few new words. The clinician sees that Jake's other pages use photos of objects and events to represent the words, so she follows this format. The clinician selects words that best reflect the play activity they will engage in (i.e., block, build, more, want, green, red).

Set up the Environment

Now the clinician's goal is to set up the physical space so it is easy for everyone to access both the activity and the AAC. The clinician gives Jake the easiest and most direct access to the device by keeping it in sight and easily within his reach. She will do the same with the materials for the activity. She sets up a chair for Jake facing a chair for Mark. In between them is a small table with blocks and the AAC placed closest to Jake. Both Jake and Mark can easily see each other, reach the blocks, and reach the AAC. The clinician sits next to the table, so she can face both boys and reach the materials, and the AAC. She makes sure the page with the blocks' vocabulary is open and available.

Notice and Respond with the AAC

Now that the boys are at the table, the clinician is ready to use the AAC (tablet) in conjunction with her spoken language to help Mark respond to Jake with both AAC and spoken words. Jake reaches toward a red block and says, "reh." Given the context, Mark can assume that his brother wants the red block. The clinician encourages Mark to respond by giving Jake the block, while saying "red," and then pressing the "red" icon on the tablet. By saying both the word and pushing the button, Mark is learning to model communication for his brother and rewarding Jake's initiation.

Model with the AAC

The clinician can also show Jake how to use new words to talk about the blocks. She takes a turn with the boys and puts a block on the tower they are building together. As she places the block, she says "build," and reaches to press "build" on the tablet. Such models expand the child's vocabulary by demonstrating how to use relevant words that are paired with significant actions and objects in the activity.

Conclusion

AAC can provide children with complex communication needs additional modalities to express their thoughts, needs, and ideas. Learning about different communication modalities can give professionals more flexibility in the ways they interact with and support children who use AAC. Each child communicates in different ways, and clinicians can help with using AAC for different forms of communication needs.

References

Beukelman, D., Mirenda, P., & Ebooks Corporation. (2013). *Augmentative and alternative communication: Supporting children and adults with complex communication needs* (4th ed.). Baltimore: Paul H. Brookes Pub.

Beukelman, D., & Mirenda, P. (2005). *Augmentative and alternative communication: Supporting children and adults with complex communication needs.* (3rd ed.). Baltimore, MD: Paul H. Brookes Pub.

Blischak, D. M. (2003). Use of speech-generating devices: In support of natural speech. *Augmentative and Alternative Communication, 19,* 29–35.

Bondy, A. S., & Frost, L. A. (1994). The picture exchange communication system. *Focus on Autistic Behavior, 9*(3), 1–19.

Chung, Y. C., Carter, E. W., & Sisco, L. G. (2013). A systematic review of interventions to increase peer interactions for students with complex communication challenges. *Research and Practice for Persons with Severe Disabilities, 37*(4), 271–287.

Cress, C., & Marvin, C. (2003). Common questions about AAC services in early intervention. *Augmentative and Alternative Communication, 19*(4), 254–272.

Drager, K., Light, J., & McNaughton, D. (2010). Effects of AAC interventions on communication and language for young children with complex communication needs. *Journal of Pediatric Rehabilitation Medicine, 3*(4), 303–310.

Goossens, C. (1989). Aided communication intervention before assessment: A case study of a child with cerebral palsy. *Augmentative and Alternative Communication, 5,* 14–26.

Howlin, P., Gordon, R. K., Pasco, G., Wade, A., & Charman, T. (2007). The effectiveness of Picture Exchange Communication System (PECS) training for teachers of children with autism: A pragmatic, group randomised controlled trial. *Journal of Child Psychology and Psychiatry*, 48(5), 473–481.

Iacono, T., Trembath, D., & Erickson, S. (2016). The role of augmentative and alternative communication for children with autism: current status and future trends. *Neuropsychiatric disease and treatment*, 12, 2349.

Kasari, C., Kaiser, A., Goods, K., Nietfeld, J., Mathy, P., Landa, R., ... & Almirall, D. (2014). Communication interventions for minimally verbal children with autism: A sequential multiple assignment randomized trial. *Journal of the American Academy of Child & Adolescent Psychiatry*, 53(6), 635–646.

Kent-Walsh, J., & McNaughton, D. (2005). Communication partner instruction in AAC: Present practices and future directions. *Augmentative and Alternative Communication*, 21(3), 195–204.

Lorah, E. R., Parnell, A., Whitby, P. S., & Hantula, D. (2015). A systematic review of tablet computers and portable media players as speech generating devices for individuals with autism spectrum disorder. *Journal of Autism and Developmental Disorders*, 45(12), 3792–3804.

Luyster, R., Gotham, K., Guthrie, W., Coffing, M., Petrak, R., Pierce, K., ... & Richler, J. (2009). The Autism Diagnostic Observation Schedule – Toddler Module: A new module of a standardized diagnostic measure for autism spectrum disorders. *Journal of Autism and Developmental Disorders*, 39(9), 1305–1320.

Millar D., Light J., Schlosser R. (2006). The impact of augmentative and alternative communication intervention on the speech production of individuals with developmental disabilities: A research review. *Journal of Speech Language Hearing Research*, 49, 248–264.

Mirenda, P. (1997). Supporting individuals with challenging behavior through functional communication training and AAC: Research review. *Augmentative and Alternative Communication*, 13(4), 207–225.

Mirenda, P. (2003). Toward functional augmentative and alternative communication for students with autism: Manual signs, graphic symbols, and voice output communication aids. *Language, speech, and hearing services in schools*, 34(3), 203–216.

Romski, M. A., & Sevcik, R. A. (1997). Augmentative and alternative communication for children with developmental disabilities. *Mental Retardation and Developmental Disabilities Research Reviews*, 3(4), 363–368.

Romski, M., & Sevcik, R. A. (2005). Augmentative communication and early intervention: Myths and realities. *Infants & Young Children*, 18(3), 174–185.

Romski, M., Sevcik, R. A., Adamson, L. B., Cheslock, M., Smith, A., Barker, R. M., & Bakeman, R. (2010). Randomized comparison of augmented and nonaugmented language interventions for toddlers with developmental delays and their parents. *Journal of Speech, Language, and Hearing Research*, 53(2), 350–364.

Schlosser, R. W., & Wendt, O. (2008). Effects of augmentative and alternative communication intervention on speech production in children with autism: A systematic review. *American Journal of Speech-Language Pathology*, 17(3), 212–230.

Snell, M. E., Brady, N., McLean, L., Ogletree, B. T., Siegel, E., Sylvester, L., ... & Sevcik, R. (2010). Twenty years of communication intervention research with individuals who have severe intellectual and developmental disabilities. *American Journal on Intellectual and Developmental Disabilities*, 115(5), 364–380.

Tager-Flusberg, H., & Kasari, C. (2013). Minimally verbal school-aged children with autism spectrum disorder: The neglected end of the spectrum. *Autism Research*, 6(6), 468–478.

Wetherby, A. M., Watt, N., Morgan, L., & Shumway, S. (2007). Social communication profiles of children with autism spectrum disorders late in the second year of life. *Journal of Autism and Developmental Disorders*, *37*(5), 960–975.

Yoder, P., & Stone, W. L. (2006). Randomized comparison of two communication interventions for preschoolers with autism spectrum disorders. *Journal of Consulting and Clinical Psychology*, *74*(3), 426.

26 Self-Compassion and Raising a Child with ASD

Sigan L. Hartley and Geovanna Rodriguez

Introduction

Children with ASD vary widely in functioning and severity of symptoms, but all exhibit difficulty with social-communication and display restricted/repetitive behaviors and sensory sensitivities (APA, 2013). Moreover, about one-third to one-half of children with ASD have an intellectual disability (CDC, 2015) and nearly two-thirds evidence emotional and behavior problems such as hyperactivity, inattention, and anxiety (McStay, Dissanayake, Scheeren, Koot, & Begeer, 2014). These symptoms, impairments, and emotional and behavioral problems can create unique parenting challenges and contribute to the heightened level of parenting stress reported by parents of children with ASD (Estes et al., 2013). Parents of children with ASD also experience stress and stigma related to being in a society that was not designed for neurodiversity (Kinnear, Link, Ballan, & Fischbach, 2016). On average, parents of children with ASD, when compared to parents of typically developing children, have an increased risk of poor psychological well-being, including lower ratings of global psychological well-being, depressive symptoms, and anxiety (Ekas & Whitman, 2010; Kuusikko-Gauffun et al., 2013).

While these parents may be at increased risk for such issues, there is tremendous within-group variability in these outcomes, and despite these unique parenting challenges and stressors, parents of children with ASD report great enjoyment and joy from parenting (Potter, 2016). This chapter reviews scholarship from our own research group, as well as that of others, on four aspects of self-care – sleep, social support, partner relationship quality, and positive emotion and self-kindness – found to be related to positive psychological well-being in parents of children with ASD. Each section ends with recommendations for clinicians.

Sleep

The Importance of Sleep

Not getting enough sleep can make it difficult to cope with child-related challenges. Studies have found that, as a group, parents who have a child with ASD report poorer sleep quality (e.g., wake up earlier and sleep less) than do parents of children without disabilities (Lopez-Wagner, Hoffman, & Sweeney, 2008; Meltzer, 2008). In part, the poor sleep quality of parents may be due to the sleep problems of their child with ASD. Studies indicate that 44–83 percent of children with ASD experience sleep problems (Meltzer & Mindell, 2008); if children aren't sleeping well, this often means parents aren't sleeping well either. The heightened risk for poor sleep quality in parents of children with ASD may also be due to the elevated level of parenting stress typically reported in this group (Estes et al., 2013). Stress can interfere with the body's ability to relax (Meltzer & Mindell, 2008), such that parents of children with ASD may be trapped in a sleep-stress cycle: they experience a night with poor sleep, which makes them prone to experiencing more stress the next-day, which then contributes to poor sleep the following night, and so on (Doane & Thurston, 2014).

There is evidence that not getting enough sleep may shape parenting experiences. In our research, we found that mothers of children with ASD who had a higher average quality of sleep across a two-week period reported that their son or daughter with ASD had less severe emotional and behavioral problems relative to mothers who had a lower average quality of sleep (Mihaila & Hartley, 2018). Thus, mothers who regularly get good sleep may perceive child emotional and behavioral problems differently (as less severe) than mothers who are not getting good sleep, and/or may have had more emotional resources for managing and preventing child emotional and behavior problems. For both mothers and fathers of children with ASD, sleep quality had a strong effect on parents' daily positive and negative mood, much more so than did any child variables (e.g., severity of child's emotional or behavioral problems) that day.

Clinician Recommendations

Routinely getting high quality sleep appears to be a critical, but often overlooked, self-care strategy for fostering positive psychological well-being in parents of children with ASD. Clinicians should consider the following: first, parents of children with ASD should be screened for sleep problems. Second, when assessing parent sleep problems, clinicians should consider the potential role of sleep problems in the child with ASD as a contributing factor. Third, low-cost efforts (e.g., brochures and brief psychoeducation sessions) to teach parents of children with ASD about tips for good sleep habits may be helpful. Examples include creating a sleep schedule and sticking with it (e.g., regular bed time and wake time), using relaxation methods, limiting caffeine consumption in the evening, limiting technology at least one hour prior to sleep, and trying to get at least 30–45 minutes of physical activity each day. In addition, parents with severe sleep problems may consider discussing pharmaceutical treatment options with a specialist.

Social Support

Cultivating Effective Social Support

Parents of children with ASD often turn to partners, family, and friends when faced with a difficult challenge or when feeling run-down. There is substantial evidence from studies on the general population (August, Rook, & Newsom, 2007) and on parents of children with ASD (Ekas, Timmons, Pruitt, Ghilain, & Alessandri, 2015) that social support is critical for optimal parent psychological well-being. Broadly, these studies find that more social support is related to better parent psychological well-being. However, research suggests that different types of social support, and support from different sources, are not equally effective. In some cases, social support can be *positive*, and experienced as helpful and as an expression of love and care. In other cases, social support can be *negative*, and experienced as intrusive, insensitive, and unwanted (Newsom et al., 2005).

In our research on families of children with ASD, one's partner was typically their primary source of both *positive* and *negative* social support. Moreover, social support from one's partner (both *positive* and *negative*) had stronger ties to parent depressive symptoms than did social support from other sources (Hickey, Dubois, & Hartley, 2018). The most frequent type of *negative* social support experienced by parents of children with ASD was found to be informational social support (e.g., intrusive advice or unhelpful information). Overall, emotional support (e.g., listening to concerns) and instrumental support (e.g., providing assistance) from one's partner, family, and friends was more likely to be experienced as *positive* and helpful than informational social support (e.g., providing advice or information). In other words, although often well-intended, when others attempt to provide advice to parents of children with ASD, this is often not experienced as helpful. Of all the types of social support, *negative* emotional support (e.g., critical comments, or lack of comfort or expression of care), and especially from one's partner, had the strongest association with parent depressive symptoms. Thus, support from one's partner has powerful consequences for psychological well-being, and the presence of *negative* emotional support appears to take the greatest toll.

Clinician Recommendations

Efforts to increase social support is an important self-care strategy associated with positive psychological well-being in parents of children with ASD. Clinicians should consider the following recommendations: first, efforts should focus on both increasing *positive* social support, as well as decreasing *negative* social support. Indeed, evidence suggests *negative* social support – intrusive, critical, and unwanted attempts at support – has a stronger association with parent psychological well-being than *positive* social support. Second, efforts should target social support from one's partner, for those in a partner relationship, as this is often the most common source of both *positive* and *negative* social support.

Efforts aimed at one's partner should pay particular attention to finding ways to decrease *negative* emotional support (i.e., insensitive or critical comments or lack of expression of care in time of need). One strategy for achieving this may be to get couples to clearly communicate with each other about the helpful and unhelpful ways in which their partner can support him/her. Couple therapy or enrichment groups may also serve an important role in helping partners stay emotionally connected. In the context of couples therapy, parents can discuss their emotions in a safe space that fosters empathy and understanding with one another. Third, it may be helpful to encourage parents of children with ASD to provide similar directions to their family and friends about how they would like to be supported. In particular, family and friends may need direction on how to provide informational support (e.g., advice and information) in ways that are experienced as helpful.

Partner Relationship Quality

Attending to the Partner Relationship

Parents who have a child with ASD typically share the ups and downs of parenting with each other. Growing evidence suggests that in two-parent households with a child diagnosed with ASD, a healthy couple relationship is a key self-care strategy for positive psychological well-being. As a group, parents of children with ASD report lower couple relationship satisfaction (Brobst, Clopton, & Hendrick, 2009), more frequent, intense, and severe couple conflicts (Hartley et al., 2017b), and have an increased risk of separation/divorce (Baeza-Velasco, Michelon, Rattaz, Pernon, & Baghdadli, 2013; Hartley et al., 2010) relative to parents of children without disabilities. Yet, despite this group-level risk, there is a wide range of couple relationship experiences among parents of children with ASD. Many parents are in longstanding and highly satisfying relationships (Hartley et al., 2017b, 2010). Unfortunately, these positive outcomes are often overshadowed in media coverage of ASD, misleading parents of children with ASD to fear that their couple relationship is fated for failure (Doherty, 2008; Solomon & Thierry, 2006).

A growing body of research has examined the behaviors that may be influenced by child ASD status and factors that differentiate couples who are thriving from those who are not. In our studies, we have used a daily diary method to examine the everyday couple relationship experiences of parents who had a child with ASD, relative to parents of children without disabilities, as they naturally and spontaneously occur in everyday life. We found that parents who had a child with ASD reported spending an average of 21 minutes less per day with their partner than did the comparison parents who had children without disabilities (Hartley, DaWalt, & Schultz, 2017a). Although this difference may not sound like much, those 21 minutes add up to mean that parents of children with ASD spend nearly 2.5 hours less per week with their partner than their peers who have typically developing children. This reduced time could account for why fathers of children with ASD reported experiencing less daily emotional closeness with their partner than did comparison group fathers. Moreover, reduced couple time could, in part, explain why both mothers and fathers of children with ASD reported engaging in fewer positive couple interactions such as sharing jokes, having a meaningful conversation, or being intimate than the comparison group. The reduced couple time of parents of children with ASD may be due to increased parenting demands (e.g., taking the child to therapy sessions, meeting with the special education team, and assisting the child with daily life activities). With limited couple time, what appears to fall by the wayside is time for emotional closeness – sharing thoughts and feelings about one's day – and time for fun and enjoyable couple activities.

We also found that everyday stress from parenting experiences can spill into couple interactions and vice versa (Hartley, Papp, & Bolt, 2016). In one direction, mothers of children with ASD were found to experience fewer positive couple interactions (e.g., joking with partner, fun activity with partner, etc.) following a day with high parenting stress. This suggests that highly stressful parenting drains mothers' resources so they have less energy for positive interactions with their partner. In other words, following a day with high parenting stress, mothers of children with ASD may feel too tired to take the time to say something nice to their partner or make a joke. In the other direction, mothers of children with ASD experienced higher parenting stress following a day with more negative couple interactions (e.g., critical comments to partner, ignored partner, etc.). Thus, the negative tension that came from within the couple relationship carried into parenting experiences, resulting in more stressful parenting.

Overall, studies indicate that global couple relationship quality has strong ties to the psychological well-being of parents of children with ASD (Ekas et al., 2015; Harper, Taylor Dyches, Harper, Olsen Roper, & South 2013). In other words, if a parent is unhappy in their couple relationship they are often unhappy overall. There is also reason to believe that the couple relationship may be particularly critical to psychological well-being in the context of high stress – such as that associated with having a child ASD – than in the context of low stress. In a high stress context, there may be a stronger need for having a positive partner relationship. In part, this may be due to the important role of partner social support (Hickey et al., 2018). Indeed, in our studies, the association between daily couple relationship behaviors and parent daily positive and negative mood was stronger for parents of children with ASD than for parents of typically developing children (Hartley et al., 2017a).

Clinician Recommendations

In summary, for parents of children with ASD in a couple relationship, attention to the quality of the relationship is an important self-care strategy. Clinicians may want to consider the following for fostering adaptive couple experiences. First, efforts should be made to debunk myths that the relationships of parents of children with ASD are destined to fail. Yet, clinicians should also acknowledge the difficulty of extraordinary parenting demands and how this may limit the amount of time couples have to engage in positive couple inter- actions. Second, educating parents about helpful behaviors that often go to the wayside – emotionally connecting and participating in fun activities – may help prevent this pattern. Parents of children with ASD could be encouraged to try to find time (even five minutes a day) to emotionally connect with their partner and share stories. Parents of children with ASD should also be guided in identi- fying ways to increase positive couple interactions, such as giving their partner a compliment over their lunch hour. Third, teaching parents about the possible carryover of emotions from the parenting domain to the couple relationship domain, and vice versa, may help them recognize and limit the spill over of neg- ative emotions.

Positive Emotion and Self-Kindness

Fostering Positive Emotion and Self-Kindness in Daily Life

Recent research has focused on the importance of positive emotion and self- kindness in daily life. Mindfulness, self-compassion, and benefit-finding are increasingly receiving attention as means of achieving positive psychological well-being in everyday life for parents of children with ASD. Mindfulness broadly refers to efforts to foster greater attention to and awareness of experi- ences in the present moment, while maintaining a stance of openness and curi- osity (Bishop et al. 2004). Emerging evidence suggests that mindfulness-based interventions can lead to reduced stress and increased positive psychological well-being in parents of children with ASD (Singh et al., 2014). Benefit-finding is a term that refers to efforts to find the positives in a negative or stressful event (Helgeson, Reynolds, & Tomich, 2006). For parents of children with ASD, types of benefit-finding in the face of child-related challenges could include: considering new possibilities, focusing on growth of character, appreciation of what is going well, spiritual growth, identifying the positive effects of the child, and increased understanding (Samios, Pakenham, & Sofronoff, 2009). The use of benefit-finding has been found to be associated with better couple relation- ship outcomes in parents of children with ASD (Ekas et al., 2015).

Finally, for parents of children with ASD, self-compassion includes inten- tional efforts to foster self-kindness (e.g., being gentle, supportive, and caring toward oneself), a sense of common humanity (e.g., recognizing that mistakes and hardship are universal experiences), and being mindful (e.g., recognizing distressing thoughts and emotions but not ruminating on them; Neff & Faso, 2015). Research suggests that engaging in self-compassion is associated with more positive psychological well-being, including higher life satisfaction, hope, and goal reengagement and lower depression and parenting stress in parents of children with ASD (Neff & Faso, 2015).

Clinician Recommendations

Evidence suggests that efforts to acknowledge but let go of negative emotions, while fostering positive emotions and self-kindness, is associated with positive psychological well-being in parents of children with ASD. Clinicians should consider the following recommendations. First, it may be important to encourage parents of children with ASD to consider mindfulness, benefit-finding, or self-compassion strategies, both formally and informally. Second, parents of children with ASD can be guided in applying these strategies in their everyday life. Some examples include: mindful breathing (taking a few moments to purposefully pay attention to and become aware of air coming into and out of body), taking a moment to write down a list of all the positive things that you have going on (e.g., gratitude journal), and writing a compassionate letter to yourself as if you were a friend who you were supporting through a bad day. Third, acknowledge the importance of your self-care for others. When parents have their individual needs met, they are better able to focus on the needs of their partner, child, and family, and appreciate positive parenting experiences that reduce stress and elicit positive emotions.

Conclusion

Parents of children with ASD are at increased risk of poor psychological well-being because of the unique parenting challenges and cultural stigma they are often faced with. Self-care strategies that may be of benefit to parents of children with ASD include focusing on good sleep quality, cultivating effective social support, attending to the partner relationship quality, and fostering positive emotion and self-kindness. Each of these self-care strategies has been linked to better psychological well-being in parents of children with ASD.

References

American Psychiatric Association (APA) (2013). *Diagnostic and statistical manual of mental disorders*. 5th ed. Arlington, VA: APA.

August, K. J., Rook, K. S., & Newsom, J. T. (2007). The joint effects of life stress and negative social exchanges on emotional distress. *The Journals of Gerontology, Series B: Psychological Sciences and Social Sciences, 62*, S305–S314.

Baeza-Velasco, C., Michelon, C., Rattaz, C., Pernon, E., & Baghdadli, A. (2013). Separation of parents raising children with autism spectrum disorders. *Journal of Developmental and Physical Disabilities, 25*, 613–624.

Bishop, S. R., Lau, M., Shapiro, S., Carlson, L., Anderson, N. D., Carmody, J., & … Devins, G. (2004). Mindfulness: A proposed operational definition. *Clinical Psychology: Science and Practice, 11*(3), 230–241.

Brobst, J. B., Clopton, J. R., & Hendrick, S. S. (2009). Parenting children with autism spectrum disorders: The couple's relationship. *Focus on Autism And Other Developmental Disabilities, 24*(1), 38–49.

Center for Disease Control and Prevention (CDC). (2015, December 9). *Autism Spectrum Disorder*. Retrieved January 25, 2016, from www.cdc.gov/ncbddd/autism/index. html.

Doane, L. D., & Thurston, E. C. (2014). Associations among sleep, daily experiences, and loneliness in adolescence: Evidence of moderating and bidirectional pathways. *Journal of Adolescence, 37,* 145–154.

Doherty, S. (2008). Arrested development: The day-to-day struggles of autistic children affect entire family. *The Capital Times.* July 2:25.

Ekas, N. V., Timmons, L., Pruitt, M., Ghilain, C., & Alessandri, M. (2015). The power of positivity: Predictors of relationship satisfaction for parents of children with autism spectrum disorder. *Journal of Autism and Developmental Disorders, 45,* 1997–2007. https://doi.org/10.1007/s10803-015-2362-4.

Ekas, N. V., & Whitman, T. L. (2010). Autism symptom topography and maternal socio-emotional functioning. *American Journal of Intellectual and Developmental Disabilities, 115,* 234–249. doi:10.1352/1944-7558-115.3.234.

Estes, A., Olson, E., Sullivan, K., Greenson, J., Winter, J. Dawson, G., & Munson, J. (2013). Parenting-related stress and psychological distress in mothers of toddlers with autism specgrum disorders. *Brain Development, 35,* 133–138.

Harper, A., Taylor Dyches, T., Harper, J. Olsen Roper, S., & South, M. (2013). Respite care, marital quality, and stress in parents of children with autism spectrum disorders. *Journal of Autism and Developmental Disorders, 43,* 2604–2614. doi:10.1007/s1080-013-1812-0.

Hartley, S. L., Barker, E. T., Seltzer, M. M., Floyd, F., Greenberg, J., Orsmond, G., & Bolt, D. (2010). The relative risk and timing of divorce in families of children with an autism spectrum disorder. *Journal of Family Psychology, 24,* 449–457.

Hartley, S. L., Papp, L. M., & Bolt, D. (2016). Spillover of marital interactions and parenting. Stress in families of children with autism spectrum disorder. *Journal of Clinical Child & Adolescent Psychology,* 1–12. doi:10.1080/15374416.2016.1152552.

Hartley, S. L., DaWalt, L. S., & Schultz, H. M. (2017a). Daily couple experiences and parent affect in families of children with versus without autism. *Journal of Autism and Developmental Disorders, 47*(6), 1645–1658. doi:10.1007/s10803-017-3088-2.

Hartley, S. L., Papp, L. M., Mihaila, I., Bussanich, P. M., Goetz, G., & Hickey, E. J. (2017b). Couple conflict in parents of children with versus without autism: Self-reported and observed findings. *Journal of Child and Family Studies, 26*(8), 2152–2165. doi:10.1007/s10826-017-0737-1.

Helgeson, V. S., Reynolds, K. A., & Tomich, P. L. (2006). A meta-analytic review of benefit finding and growth. *Journal of Consulting and Clinical Psychology, 74*(5), 797–816.

Hickey, E. J., Dubois, L., & Hartley, S. L. (2018). Positive and negative social exchanges experienced by fathers and mothers of children with autism. *Autism, 22*(4), 469–478.

Kinnear, S. H., Link, B. G., Ballan, M. S., & Fischbach, R. L. (2016). Understanding the experience of stigma for parents of children with autism spectrum disorder and the role stigma plays in families' lives. *Journal of Autism and Developmental Disorders, 46,* 942–953. https://doi.org/10.1007/s10803-015-2637-9.

Kuusikko-Gauffun, S., Pollock-Wurman, R., Mattila, M.-L., Jussila, K., Ebeling, H., & Pauls, D., et al. (2013). Social anxiety in parents of high-functioning children with autism and Asperger Syndrome. *Journal of Autism and Development Disorders, 43,* 521–552.

Lopez-Wagner, M. C., Hoffman, C. D., Sweeney, D. P., et al. (2008). Sleep problems of parents of typically developing children and parents of children with autism. *The Journal of Genetic Psychology, 169*(3), 269–279.

McStay, R. L., Dissanayake, C., Scheeren, A., Koot, H. M., & Begeer, S. (2014). Parenting stress and autism: The role of age, autism severity, quality of life and problem behaviour of children and adolescents with autism. *Autism, 18,* 502–510.

Meltzer, L. J., & Mindell, J. A. (2008). Behavioral sleep disorders in children and adolescents. *Sleep Medicine Clinics*, 3(2), 269–279.

Meltzer, L. J. (2008). Brief report: Sleep in parents of children with autism spectrum disorders. *Journal of Pediatric Psychology*, 33, 380–386.

Mihaila, I., & Hartley, S. L. (2018). Parental sleep quality and behavior problems of children with autism. *Autism*, 22(3), 236–244.

Neff, K. D., & Faso, D. J. (2015). Self-compassion and well-being in parents of children with autism. *Mindfulness*, 6(4), 938–947.

Newsom, J. T., Rook, K. S., Nishishiba, M., et al. (2005). Understanding the relative importance of positive and negative social exchanges: examining specific domains and appraisals. *The Journals of Gerontology, Series B: Psychological Sciences and Social Sciences* 60: 304–312.

Potter, C. A. (2016). "I accept my son for who he is – he has incredible character and personality;" fathers' positive experiences of parenting children with autism. *Disability & Society*, 7, 948–965.

Samios, C., Pakenham, K. I., & Sofronoff, K. (2009). The nature of benefit finding in parents of a child with Asperger syndrome. *Research in Autism Spectrum Disorders*, 3, 358–374. doi:10.1016/j.rasd.2008.08.003.

Singh, N. N., Lancioni, G. E., Winton, A. S., Karazsia, B. T., Myers, R. E., Latham, L. L., & Singh, J. (2014). Mindfulness-based Positive Behavior Support (MBPBS) for mothers of adolescents with autism spectrum disorder: Effects on adolescents' behavior and parental stress. *Mindfulness*, 5, 646–657.

Solomon, E., & Thierry, L. (Producer) and Thierry, L. (Director). (2006). Autism everyday [motion picture]. USA. Autism Speaks.

Index

Page numbers in **bold** denote tables, those in *italics* denote figures.

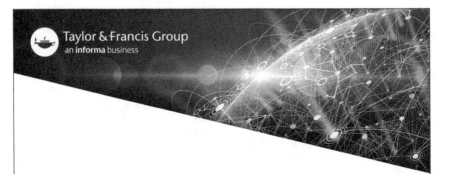